THE STORY OF
COLCHESTER ZOO

THE STORY OF
COLCHESTER ZOO

S.C. KERSHAW

The
History
Press

First published 2013

The History Press
The Mill, Brimscombe Port
Stroud, Gloucestershire, GL5 2QG
www.thehistorypress.co.uk

British Library Cataloguing in Publication Data.
A catalogue record for this book is available from the British Library.

ISBN 978 0 7524 9346 6

Typesetting and origination by The History Press
Printed in Great Britain

CONTENTS

LIST OF ABBREVIATIONS

AFTW	Action for the Wild
ALF	Animal Liberation Front
BIAZA	British and Irish Association of Zoos and Aquariums
CERCOPAN	Centre for Education, Research and Conservation of Primates and Nature
CITES	Convention on International Trade in Endangered Species of Wild Fauna and Flora
EAZA	European Association of Zoos and Aquaria (Formerly 'European Community of Zoos and Aquaria')
EEP	European Endangered Species Programme
RVC	Royal Veterinary College
RSPCA	Royal Society for the Prevention of Cruelty to Animals
UFAW	Universities Federation for Animal Welfare
ZLA	Zoo Licensing Act 1981

ACKNOWLEDGEMENTS

THIS BOOK IS an independent work. Colchester Zoo does not necessarily share all the ideas expressed in it. This book is also imperfect and despite all best efforts there are bound to be inaccuracies. Frequently, for example, it has been impossible to precisely identify particular species or sub-species of animals from Colchester Zoo's past. Nevertheless, I do believe that this book presents as good a likeness of Colchester Zoo as has been possible under the circumstances – indeed, accurate to a degree which would have been quite unattainable without the help offered to me by many people.

My sincerest thanks go to the Tropeano family – Dr Dominique Tropeano, Anthony Tropeano and Sarah Knuckey (*née* Tropeano) – who have been gracious and accommodating throughout.

I am indebted to Clive Witcomb, Colchester Zoo's Volunteer Team Co-ordinator, who believed in this project from the moment I first suggested it to him, and to Nicola Guy, Declan Flynn, Lucy Simpkin and Jenny Briancourt at The History Press, whose invaluable assistance brought it to completion.

Special thanks go to the ladies of Stanway Hall: Charlotte Bradshaw, Alex Downing, Rebecca Moore and Sarah Waddington, without whose help this book could not have been produced.

Thanks go to BIAZA's Executive Director, Dr Miranda Stevenson, and to Dr Koen Brouwer, former Executive Director of EAZA, for their interest in this book and for the benefit of their wide experience. Thanks are also due to Nathalie Evans and Nicola Barlow at Twycross Zoo and to Jeremy Keeling at Monkey World.

I am immensely grateful to Peter Johnson for his time and observations, as well as for the use of his photographs, plans and designs. My work would also have been far harder without the assistance and enthusiasm of Joan and Fred Honisett.

Special thanks go to the staff of Colchester Library for the use of their archive of microfilm prints of the *Colchester Gazette*, the *Colchester Express* and the *Essex County Standard*, which proved invaluable in the reconstruction of Colchester Zoo's story. Thanks go also to the various staff bodies at Colchester Borough Council, Colchester Crematorium, Stanwell House, Colchester Visitor Information Centre, and Colchester Resource Centre – especially Jerry Bowdrey, Catherine Newley and Sophie Stevens, whose interest in this book extended beyond expectations.

Thanks are due to the staff at RAF Cranwell, Sefton Council, the UK Home Office Border Agency, and the V&A Blythe House Reading Room. Particular thanks go to Chrissie Kirby at BALPPA, to Elizabeth Carter at UFAW, to Michael Palmer, Archivist and Deputy Librarian at ZSL, to Erica Donaghy, Assistant Archivist at the ROH at Covent Garden and to Izzy Ghafori-Kanno at Kraft Foods. Thanks are due also to Dawn Avery, RSPCA Chief Inspector (Essex Group), as well as to former Colchester RSPCA inspectors Peter Scott and Colin Strong.

Special thanks are reserved for Andrew Brown at the *Southport Visiter* and for Robert King, Shirley Brown and all the staff at Newsquest for helping me in my research. I shall be eternally grateful to all those people who took the time to respond to my public appeals, including Southport's Sandra Ellis, Gabrielle Hutchinson, Denise Roney and June Trees, and Colchester's Lynne Horner, Brenda Kirk, Richard Martin and Susan Wilson.

Thanks go to Russell Tofts of the Bartlett Society and also to Colchester historian Christina Edwards for freely sharing so much information with me and for lending me a great deal of material. Thanks go also to John Jennings, Sheila May, Mrs V. Gray, Glyn Cheeseman, and Anne and David Barbour for the use of their various photographs and films.

They will deny it, but important assistance was given by Libby Armstrong, Deborah Povey and Valeria Paz at Essex University's Department of Philosophy and Art History. Thanks are due also to a great many more people inside and outside Colchester Zoo who have similarly oiled the wheels of this project in a variety of ways, including Martin Allen, Stephen

Blaxland, Gavin Duffy, Chris Grimmett, Kate Knight, Martine Lindley, Susy Long, Revd Gerard Moate, Paul Nash, Georgina Porazka, Robert Putt, Neil Ransom, Don Sturgess, Penny Stynes and many others.

Thanks also go to every person and organisation that permitted the use of their photographs in this book. In some cases, however, it has not been possible to contact the copyright holder, despite all attempts. My apologies go to those whom I have not been able to trace.

The warmest thanks of all must go to the staff and associates of Colchester Zoo and Southport Zoo, past and present, who gave up their time to assist me and to share their memories, skills and experiences. Among many already named, they include: Ben Abbott, Kate Broad, Rebecca Brown, Sarah Cooper, Gordon Dean, Cliff 'Stormy' Fairweather, Glen Fairweather, Samantha Greenhill, Heather and David Grist, Richard Hazelgrove, Matt Hunt, David and Christine Judge, Mark and Terry Larner, Vickie Ledbrook, Wendy Lehkyj, John Malseed, Sheelagh Marron, Heather McCabe, Mike and Jean Parish, Gordon Pennington, Carole Petrie, Jennie Roberts, Jez Smith, Amy Sutcliffe, Kate Taylor, Roland 'Peter' Touzell, Edmund Tuxford, Jo Wheatley, Laura Witheyman, Peter Zwitser and many more besides.

Apologies go to anyone who has been forgotten here, but the final thanks must now go to my enduring friends Peter Vergo, Nigel Norie and Dan Fawcett, as well as to my mother, Jennifer Bowen, whose joint encouragement and assistance, great and small, made this book possible.

This book is dedicated to all of Colchester Zoo's visitors, past, present and future.

PROLOGUE

COLCHESTER IS MOST famous for being attacked. First came Boudica, in around AD 60, who burned the town flat. It was later ruined by Fairfax in 1648 during the English Civil War, and in George Orwell's *Nineteen Eighty-Four* it became the site of Britain's entry into World War Three, when a nuclear bomb was dropped on the local garrison. Colchester has also long borne the brunt of cultural attacks, being maligned along with other Essex towns as a place of nothing more than vacuous women in white stiletto heels and of violent skinheads revving battered Ford Escorts. The time is now right, in this new century, to affirm that if ever such statements were true, this is no longer the case.

Before the 1990s, Colchester had struggled with itself. It had undergone a period of startlingly rapid modernisation in the 1960s, paying the price with economic problems in the 1970s and a lack of social unity in the 1980s. But despite the voices calling Colchester a swamp of mediocrity, the town was starting to emerge as markedly un-mediocre. Since 1990, Colchester garrison has become one of the finest military units in the world, and the University of Essex, on Colchester's eastern flank, has in the last two decades been ranked among the best universities in England.

Colchester Zoo, a third great establishment in the town, has likewise grown since the early 1990s into a national landmark and has become one of the foremost zoos in Europe. The quality of Colchester Zoo is today recognised by all those working in zoology – even world-leading zoos have been paying attention to its achievements.

Local pride in the zoo has been steadily growing for many years, and there are plenty of people who recognise its contributions to zoology at regional and international levels, understanding that it has become an institution of the very first rank. Yet this has not always been so and the shadow of Colchester Zoo's troubled past has long hung over the place.

There remain a great number of people who have not visited the zoo for a long time and who imagine it still to be an embarrassment to the town. Many of the zoo's present staff members recognise a common type of visitor – one who has not been to the park for thirty-odd years and who goes round the zoo in disbelief that it could be the same place they visited in the 1970s. Sometimes they are surprised to learn that it was not shut down for good, and are amazed to find it still here, stronger than ever.

Colchester Zoo's story spans an unbroken fifty years. It opened in 1963 and in 2013 celebrates its half century. Reaching this milestone has not been easy. The zoo has faced many traumas over the years and often it seemed that disaster was at hand. The greatest test came in the mid-1980s when the park almost collapsed amid public concern regarding declining standards and allegations of animal abuse.

Since that time, Colchester Zoo has made great efforts to put the past behind itself and succeeded in this admirably; perhaps too admirably, for its past was allowed to be almost completely forgotten. When I joined the zoo as a member of the volunteer staff in 2011, I was astonished to find that no one could tell me anything about its origins. People could not even agree on the year in which the zoo had opened, let alone the specific day. None of my colleagues could tell me with any clarity who had founded it, and no one seemed to know why a zoo had even been opened in Colchester at all.

There were some vague tales among staff and visitors of an eccentric old man who had long ago bought the zoo and run it into the ground. There were a few improbable stories of leopards being walked around on leashes; some insisted that the zoo had once had gorillas and giant pandas, while others denied this. In short, no one seemed to know anything for certain. There were few pictures and fewer documents and almost everything was lost in time.

In the spring of 2011 a simple but smart timeline poster exhibition was set up in one of the zoo's education centres. It was a big hit and many members of staff were taken aback that such a great proportion of their visitors were genuinely interested in the zoo's past. This timeline showed major recent events at the zoo, which the majority of visitors of course remembered. But as one walked along the timeline, further and further back in time, the story steadily became patchier, until, at last, the deep history of the zoo was marked simply as 'Pre-1983' and had hardly more to show than a couple of old tickets and a few black-and-white photographs.

These photographs were not, however, just any old snaps. One showed a balding, smiling man holding a friendly cheetah on a chain; another depicted a laughing woman apparently hugging a full-grown male lion. It was clear that these people, whoever they were, surely had some kind of story to tell.

When, in the autumn of 2011, I first suggested writing this book in order to discover and to tell their story, the zoo's directors expressed no objection but warned me that little would be found. A handful of records and photographs remained but the old days had been largely disremembered. Even those people who willingly recalled these years at the zoo had no more than the sketchiest, most threadbare memories, unfurnished with dates or names. Nonetheless, with some persistence and a little bloody-mindedness, the full story of Colchester Zoo has slowly passed into the light. Now, for the first time the tale is told of this singularly remarkable institution, as well as that of its predecessor, Southport Zoo, further north in Lancashire.

PART ONE

OUT OF AFRICA

Then something even odder happened: he accidentally grasped
a warm, thick mane of hair as a roar swelled
before him – a soft, slow, lion's roar.

– Friedrich Nietzsche (1844-1900)

1

THE KINGS AND QUEENS
OF BIRKDALE

MOST ESTATE AGENTS worry about rats. Frank Norman Farrar was different. He had a young adult lioness living in the house which he also shared with his second wife at No. 36 Westbourne Road in Birkdale, one of the most desirable areas in the attractive and wealthy northern seaside resort of Southport in Lancashire.

Frank was no stranger to risk and excitement. Born in 1911 near Leeds, he had spent his teenage years working in the short-lived but substantial zoo his father had opened in 1924 near Scarisbrick New Road in Southport. Frank had later volunteered for the RAF in 1940, three days after Prime Minister Winston Churchill's declaration that the Battle of Britain was about to begin, when the British air force was the last remaining obstacle which blocked Hitler's dream of global demolition.

Thanks to the bravery of young men such as Frank in the summer of 1940, the RAF provided Hitler's first military defeat. As the Second World War moved on and began to develop into a truly inter-continental war, Sergeant Farrar found himself stationed variously all over Europe, Africa and Asia as part of the RAF's Air Sea Rescue Service, mainly picking up Allied pilots whose planes had ditched into the English Channel, the Mediterranean Sea or the Gulf of Aden. The end of the war found him stationed in India. He was demobbed on 22 December 1945.

Early in 1946, Frank returned home to his wife and his six-year-old daughter, Daphne. He soon found work helping to restore buildings that had been damaged by German bombs. This quickly led to more specialised work in restoring churches, and he even developed a nice little side-line in stained-glass artistry, replacing broken church windows in towns all over Lancashire.

Housing was a flourishing industry after the ravages of wartime. Many families were homeless and looking for somewhere to live, and other families, free at last to get on with their own lives once again, were selling up and moving around the country, creating much business for estate agents. Frank knew an opportunity when he saw one, and soon found a position as the manager of the Southport branch of an estate agency called Knights National, which had offices dotted all down Britain's north-west coastline.

By 1950, Frank was divorced from his first wife and was almost into his forties. He was doing excellent business at Knights and he personally owned a number of properties around Southport that brought him a steady income. The end of the war meant that, slowly, more fine foods had become available to the public than had been for years. Frank, as usual, dived right in, and opened several profitable little businesses in the town, including a tidy basement confectionery shop on Lord Street called The Biscuit Box, and a delicatessen on Eastbank Street, which sold items that had not been seen on British shelves for a decade.

Surely by this point his taste for adventure and enterprise had been sated? Southport was a pleasant town to live in; Frank had many friends and the paradisiacal life of a bachelor beckoned. He had not, however, counted on a woman called Helena who swept into his office at Knights National one morning in 1950.

Like Frank, Helena had recently divorced and urgently needed a place for herself, her son and her daughter to live. Frank took her to see a flat which he had available to let in the town. He liked her immediately and as they got talking he invited her to lunch at the Grand National, which was running later that day at Aintree, just down the road. Helena clearly liked Frank straightaway too, for she accepted.

Helena was a powerful woman in build, thought and speech. She was, perhaps, getting on a little in years, but still had the looks of a minor Hollywood starlet, with her high cheekbones and a pile of immaculately sculpted blonde hair. She intrigued Frank with her peculiar Dutch-Australian accent; she was well-travelled, knowledgeable and held firm opinions on all matters, and she appealed strongly to Frank, who had been deeply frustrated by the boredom of life with his ex-wife.

Helena had been born around the same time as Frank (though she always lied about her age) and, like Frank, had been through a few adventures in her time. She had been one of several children born to a family of Dutch immigrants living just outside Sydney in Australia. Sydney had then been a town of a mere quarter of a million people and very different to the huge metropolis of nearly five million souls that it is today. Growing up on an orange farm on the outskirts of this tiny centre in the early years of the twentieth century, Helena was exposed to just about as rural a life as any other Australian and spent much of her time playing in the outback.

Helena was a girl born completely without fear and she grew up a little wild. Spending much time in the Australian bush, she learned to befriend and tame wild animals. Although she was the youngest in the family, her older siblings would not go near the outhouse until Helena had gone in and removed the snakes, spiders and scorpions from behind the lavatory and under the seat.

But Helena soon left the bush behind. Her grandmother in the Netherlands had often complained to Helena's mother that she had never seen her grandchildren. All the family (but for the father) therefore decided to take a pleasant holiday to Europe, but the ship on which they travelled foundered and Helena, along with all the passengers and crew, had to be rescued from the ocean waves. Helena's grandmother read of the disaster in the newspapers and feared that her family had been lost at sea. When at last they turned up on her doorstep in the town of Nijmegen (on the German border with the Netherlands) her relief was such that she never let them return to Sydney. Helena's mother often wrote letters to her father, but the grandmother hid every single reply forthcoming from Australia and Helena never saw her father again.

Helena had effectively become a resident of the Netherlands and was having to adjust quickly to urban European life. She was now eleven years old and was being bullied mercilessly at school for she did not know the language. This, coupled with the perceived indifference of her father to the family, no doubt helped to turn Helena from a brave little girl into a tough young woman.

The Olympics in the 1920s were very different to the Games today with their police escorts and surface-to-air anti-terror missiles. They were open affairs in which people were much freer to mix with competitors and officials at the events, and when the Games came to Amsterdam in 1928, young Helena was among those who attended. While mingling in the crowds, she made a good friend of one of the British athletes. So good, in fact, that they married not long afterwards and Helena moved to England with him.

By 1950, Helena had been with this man for over twenty years and had borne him two children. Unfortunately the marriage had turned sour and she and the children were subjected to physical violence. She left her husband and his home without any clear idea of where she might go. Her options were somewhat limited for there were not many people to whom she could immediately turn: her father was lost to her; one of her brothers had died in a concentration camp during the war; and her mother had also met an untimely end – during the Nazi occupation of the Netherlands she had refused to step out of the way of a group of German soldiers, had been butted with the end of a rifle for her insolence, and had died of abdominal injuries.

However, after the many losses and struggles of Helena's early life, things seemed to be looking up as she unexpectedly found herself sitting opposite this affluent and charmingly flamboyant estate agent named Frank over luncheon at Aintree. The Grand National of 1950 was as sensational a day out as any Britain then had to offer. It was the first Royal National since before the Second World War, with King George VI and his Queen in attendance along with their young princess, Elizabeth, and Marina, Duchess of Kent. Though the Grand National comes in the cruellest month of April, in that year it was a glorious summery day for which almost half a million people turned out.

Helena was a life-long gambler but unrepentant: problem gamblers are only those who lose and she never lost. She won on Freebooter, the favourite at 10/1 (the first favourite to win at the National for twenty-three years), launched home by jockey Jimmy Power with fifteen lengths to spare. All the horses were safely returned, unlike the bookies, who were rinsed for everything they were worth by the crowds. In short, it was a good day all round, especially for Frank and Helena whose future fate together was sealed by this happy day. Helena's insistence on paying for the meal would probably have embarrassed other men of the time, but those who knew Frank would have said it probably endeared her to him all the more.

They were married within weeks and complemented each other brilliantly. Helena was a determined and practical woman, but tended to rub people's fur the wrong way, which often caused what might otherwise have been perfectly avoidable problems. Frank, on the other hand, was a silver-tongued joker who could never take anything seriously and whom everyone absolutely loved. He had grand ambitions and a good head for finance but often lacked focus in his work. Helena brought to the marriage a no-nonsense sense of purpose that countered Frank's dreaminess, and

Frank, for his part, became Helena's public relations counsel, always able to smooth the waters which she habitually stirred up.

If either of these two middle-aged newly-weds had thought that they were due a quietly contented life, having travelled the globe and found the right partners at last, this was thrown out of the window in early 1952, when they were driving one day through Manchester. They saw a large group of people clustered around a shop window, shouting and banging on the glass. Helena noticed it was a pet shop and ordered Frank to pull over to see what the commotion was about. Inside the shop window was a trapped and terrified young lion from which the jeering crowd was trying to elicit a response. Helena took pity on the creature: she marched straight into the shop and bought him on the spot. On their way home to Southport in the car she christened him Samson.

The Farrars were quite used to living with animals. Helena had, for instance, tamed a wild koala back in her orange farm days. Frank had grown up with his father's elephants at the little zoo on Scarisbrick New Road and had kept a great number of his own rabbits, bantam chickens, dogs and cats. Neither of them appear to have had animals when they met, but shortly after they were married they set up a small riding school together, and it was not long before a retired racehorse came to live with them – the first of countless animals that came to live with the pair over the years.

Starting with the racehorse, the Farrars slowly began to acquire a reputation for taking in unwanted creatures, and their animal family at Westbourne Road grew. To begin with, the animals were small and comparatively easy for the Farrars to keep; a few parrots arrived, then they took in an armadillo rescued from cruel treatment, and before long they had a dexter bull in the garden and a cobra in the greenhouse.

But a lion was another matter. It would be almost a decade before Joy Adamson would amaze readers with her book *Born Free*, about domestic life with a lioness on a game reserve in Kenya. Yet here was an estate agent and his wife raising a cub in exactly the same way, in the fashionable part of a densely populated British coastal tourist resort.

Samson was still small, however. So small, in fact, that it was some time before Frank and Helena realised that Samson lacked the necessary equipment to qualify for such a name and renamed her Sammy (though 'Samson' remained in use as well). For the moment, Sammy was simply a playful smudge of golden fur. However, lions have a tendency to grow and her appetite seemed to be growing in accordance. Sammy was, however,

Frank Farrar in later life. (Fred and Joan Honisett)

perfectly tame and Helena was often seen walking her around Birkdale on a leash as this lioness began to grow up. Many stories are told of the horror expressed by Southport locals when they saw these two ladies coming. People who did not know about Helena would laugh when they saw her at the end of the street with a 'dog' so large they said it looked almost like a lion, only to scatter, wild-eyed, when she approached closer. There is no doubt that Helena enjoyed giving people a fright and watching the streets empty at her advance. A story is told of the surprise the local vicar had when he dropped in for tea one afternoon and casually ran his hand over what he too thought was a big dog lying against the end of the sofa.

It was not long before Sammy was really starting to fill out into a fine huntress and it became clear that things could not continue in this way. One afternoon, while sitting in his office at Knights National, Frank Farrar asked himself, 'What the hell am I going to do about this damned lion in the house?' He was having trouble getting his mail delivered after the postman had been terrified almost out of his mind at coming face-to-face with Sammy in the garden one day. Many tradesmen would no longer come near the house, and the various members of the Farrar household, including Helena's son and daughter from her first marriage, were also struggling with Sammy – they found, for instance, that they were often being made late for work and school; she would make it impossible for them to go out until they had played with her for a while. Sammy had also recently jumped the garden fence and wandered Birkdale on her own, terrifying the local children. The police had not been terribly impressed by that at all. The neighbours had been patient but had grown more anxious as the months had passed and Sammy had grown up, and they eventually set up a petition to have poor Sammy removed. What was Frank to do? He could not sell Sammy or give her away: Helena would divorce him on the spot. Helena and Sammy now came as a package, and the choice was either to return to his bachelor life, which seemed extremely dull in contrast to life with Helena, or keep Sammy in the house until he ended up before the magistrate. What if Sammy should wander off alone again and get hold of a child? What would then happen to Sammy once the authorities got hold of her?

Gabrielle Hutchinson (known to everyone as Gaye) was Frank's secretary at Knights National. She recalls as if it were yesterday that unusually quiet afternoon at the office when Frank was thinking these things over. Frank was also reminiscing that day about his childhood, and ended up talking about his father's zoo, back in the years before the war. It had been a lot of fun and he missed it: the hustle and bustle; the excitement; the gangs of local children skipping behind him and old keeper Winrow as they walked the elephants down to Southport beach to bathe the animals in the Irish Sea.

There was one other desk-worker in the room with Gaye that day and she distinctly remembers catching this man's eye. They looked at each other and then back at Frank and then at each other again, as their boss started to hatch the idea of starting up his own zoo. Within mere minutes Frank had built an entire animal park in his head and was imagining all the possibilities and enjoyment there might be had from such a project. Frank had his solution and it appealed to him in every way – Helena could keep Sammy and the neighbours would be satisfied. A zoo would probably do very good business too, since there was no serious, direct competition for that sort of thing in Southport at the time. It even solved the problem of the huge appetite Sammy had for meat (which was still rationed in the early 1950s and horribly expensive on the black market). One of the reasons people went to a zoo was to feed the animals, and Frank saw straightaway that this had a great financial angle: not only would he save the money on 10lb of meat a day, but people would actually pay him to bring their scraps to Sammy!

And so started a remarkable thirty-year career in zoology for Frank and Helena Farrar. All the pieces of the puzzle had been there, waiting to be put in the right places. The two of them were natural animal handlers; Frank had considerable experience in starting and maintaining small businesses; and his work in estates allowed him to work smoothly through the process of acquiring land and planning permission. His life in the RAF had won him many contacts around the world and even a smattering of knowledge of a number of local dialects from far-off places – ideal for a person intending to collect exotic creatures.

The scheme required a great deal of paperwork and many meetings with the aldermen of Southport Borough Council. Even so, in next to no time the Farrars had everything in place to begin building their new zoo on a couple of acres of vacant land near Southport beach, next to the town's famous Pleasureland resort which had recently reopened after the war. A cage for Sammy duly went up as soon as the perimeter fence was completed, followed quickly by several other enclosures.

Southport Model Zoo, as it was officially named, was ready by 1953. According to one person, the guest of honour who opened the zoo was George Cansdale, the Superintendent for the Zoological Society of London

Frank and Helena Farrar's lioness, Samson (Sammy), at about five years of age in Southport, spring 1957. (Fred and Joan Honisett)

(of which Frank was now a member), who would become better known in later years as a regular guest on children's television shows such as *Blue Peter*.

Now that Southport Zoo was up and running, and Sammy was safely locked away on the beach, the Farrars' neighbours were no doubt thrilled that they could at last feel safe in their homes. Little did they realise that in helping Frank and Helena to decide to open a zoo they had in fact made a rod for their own backs. Within a short time Helena had bought another cat, a one-year-old Asian lion cub, from a department store in Liverpool. This time there was no mistake about the gender and it was soon clear that he was going to grow up into a large beast indeed. He was given the name Rajah, deriving from the Hindi word for 'king', but acquired the nickname 'Big Boy', for even by the age of two-and-a-half he had fleshed out to a weight of 350lb and was still growing fast.

When Sammy had been living at home, the neighbours had at least known that she was always around. Rajah, on the other hand, lived at the zoo with Sammy but Helena would forever be bringing him home out of the blue. Now the long-suffering residents of Westbourne Road didn't know what to expect from one day to the next. Only notionally was Rajah a resident of the zoo really, for he spent many days with Helena at Westbourne Road. Whenever he went back to the zoo after a long spell at Westbourne Road, Helena had to sleep with him for a couple of nights to make sure he was settled with Sammy again.

Endless stories emerge from the 1950s about the luckless grocery boys, engineers, gasmen and travelling salesmen who chanced upon the house of Rajah. One of Helena's closest friends recounts the story of a washing machine repairman who was busy at work in Helena's kitchen when he felt a large, rough tongue at his cheek, which he thought was their dog asking for attention. When he turned to look straight into the large green eyes of Rajah he passed out instantly. Rajah continued to lick his face, which woke the man up again, whereupon he took another look at the lion and fainted a second time.

Helena was no more in the habit of remembering to warn people about Rajah than she had been about Sammy. She took pleasure in shaking the locals out of their suburban complacency, especially when she and Frank were raising young exotic animals by hand. A local boy, one David Kennedy Eveson, then working for Dewhurst's butcher shop in Chapel Street, recalled making a delivery of two legs of mutton to Westbourne Road. He was greeted at the door by Helena and Rajah, whose sniffing nose suddenly caused David to become conscious that his apron was covered

Helena and two-year-old Rajah at home in 1956. (Fred and Joan Honisett)

in blood and meat. He meekly assented to Helena's invitation to step inside for a moment, whereupon he found himself confronted by a leopard cub and a young orangutan called Porky who came and put his arm round his shoulders.

One might think that the bother surrounding Helena's tame lions would eventually have died down as Southport Zoo became firmly established. It was not so: there was more interest than ever. Rajah, an exceptionally beautiful lion with a luxurious and delicately groomed mane, won many admirers and soon became something of a local celebrity, even simply as an animal to visit and feed in the zoo. Unwitting visitors would be captivated when Helena, dressed in her housewife's twinset and pearls, would step into Sammy and Rajah's cage to feed them great hunks of bloody horseflesh by hand, play games with them, or pour water from a watering can over them on hot summer days.

Both Sammy and Rajah had been housetrained like any other pet cats and had learned to leave their business in the garden at Westbourne Road. Once they were installed at the zoo, it transpired that they preferred not to mess their cage and sometimes had to be taken out on leads into Princes Park nearby, which caused an even bigger commotion than before.

It is possible that the clamour surrounding the Farrars' lions might eventually have petered out somewhat had Southport been an out-of-the-way place with little passing traffic. However, the town was a prime holiday destination in Britain in the 1950s, which meant that there was a steady stream of people constantly moving through who had probably never seen a live lion before – certainly never one on a leash – and who raised a fresh din about the whole thing with each new week.

Helena and her lions fascinated the local press, and there were subsequent hurrahs sent out about it in the national press, which eventually resulted in Pathé News coming down to film Helena and Rajah at Westbourne Road in about 1956. The Pathé clip shows Helena being dragged down the front steps of No. 36 Westbourne Road by Rajah. She plays with him in the garden with a tennis racket and some coloured balloons. A close-up shows him gently gnawing on her arm as she pushes him away with a chuckle, before she hand-feeds him milk from a large washing-up bowl. This clip would have been shown repeatedly in movie theatres all over the country between main feature films, along with news items and other clips of general interest. At a time when a trip to the cinema was still a genuine national pastime, Rajah could quite comfortably have claimed to be the most famous lion in Britain.

2

DAYS AT THE BEACH

B Y THE MID-1950S Rajah had been discovered by the movie world
and it was at this time that Helena and Frank began to prepare him to
appear in a new film with Gordon Scott, the Arnold Schwarzenegger
of his day. Scott made five *Tarzan* movies between 1955 and 1960, with
Rajah appearing in three. This was new territory for Frank and Helena,
most of whose time had lately been spent building up Southport Zoo and
drawing people in.

It seems that the Farrars, with their vivid personalities, fitted in well with
the colourful and creative people who once inhabited the mainstream movie
world. Given that their animals were also expertly trained and well behaved,
and that handsome payments were forthcoming for such appearances by
Rajah, it is hardly surprising that this venture into the world of film-making
was to be merely the beginning of a long association between the Farrars'
animals and the world of show business.

Jackie Granger, who lived a few streets over from the Farrars, became
Rajah's chauffeur for his film and television appearances when Rajah was
selected to appear in a picture called *The Jungle Princess*, possibly a re-hash
of the hit 1936 film of the same name. Frank and Helena were driving a
Rolls-Royce Silver Cloud in the mid-1950s, a model that did not meet the
needs of transporting a rather large lion. The Farrars had, therefore, been
forced to ask van drivers in Southport to give them a lift to Elstree Studios,
way down south in Hertfordshire. No one had seemed much interested
in sharing a 400-mile round-trip with poor Rajah, and in desperation the
Farrars offered Jackie £20 for the job (equivalent to about £400 today).
Jackie accepted and enjoyed the day a great deal, commenting that Rajah
was 'a real Christian' all the way to London and back. He recalls pulling over

RAJAH, TARZAN'S FAMOUS LION, SOUTHPORT ZOO

Postcard of Frank (far right) and Helena with Rajah in Southport in the late 1950s. (Fred and Joan Honisett)

for fuel and watching the pump-station attendant walk over to the van only to see Rajah's great head staring through the window at him; naturally, he turned and ran, begging them to leave his forecourt. Jackie liked this sort of thing as much as Helena and Frank and he became a regular driver for them, taking all sorts of animals, from the very smallest creature right up to their first elephant, all over the country.

It was at about this time that Rajah appeared in Terence Young's film *Safari*, with Victor Mature and Janet Leigh (later of *Psycho* fame). When this film came to town, Ken Lloyd, the manager of Southport's Gaumont cinema theatre, had the idea of inviting Rajah down for a private screening. Frank eagerly agreed, seeing it as great publicity for the zoo. It was only a stunt, of course, and Rajah would 'watch' merely a portion of the film alone with the Farrars and Mr Lloyd in the auditorium, just long enough for the town's press photographers to get some good shots.

Mr Lloyd remembered that the local fire brigade chief happened to show up at the cinema that day, to make his routine safety checks on the building.

His suspicions were aroused when he found the doors of the auditorium locked and would not believe Mr Lloyd's protestations that there was a lion loose in the cinema. Eventually Mr Lloyd had to let him in. As soon as the fireman's eyes adjusted to the gloom he saw that the lion was not, after all, a lie. Mr Lloyd said he had never seen a man move so fast as when this fireman dived up one of the balcony support columns, then slid back down and dashed off to lock himself in the ladies' powder room.

Rajah is also said to have appeared in a television series called *White Hunter*, which aired in 1957, but there are many media appearances that have been forgotten, and it is impossible to make a list of them all. The same goes for another of Southport Zoo's inhabitants: Frank's tame leopard, Big Chief Horrible Noise or 'Chiefy'.

Chiefy had been born in India (possibly Bengal) in June 1954. He arrived at Southport Zoo just before April of the following year and soon appeared in many high-profile films and television programmes. Postcards of Chiefy that were on sale at Southport Zoo declared rather grandly that he was 'the world's most famous leopard', which was probably not far off the mark. Though a full list of Chiefy's celluloid appearances cannot be compiled, it is safe to say that any British or perhaps even American film made between 1955 and 1965 which features a male leopard stands a good chance of having been a Chiefy feature.

THE WORLD'S MOST FAMOUS LEOPARD "BIG CHIEF HORRIBLE NOISE," SOUTHPORT ZOO

Postcard of Big Chief Horrible Noise, 'Chiefy', the leopard at Southport Zoo, probably from the early 1960s. (Fred and Joan Honisett)

Gabrielle Hutchinson with a spider monkey at Southport Zoo, March 1955. (Gabrielle Hutchinson)

Without doubt, Frank had been making far more money than one could have expected from a small zoo charging a few pennies a head, no matter how busy it might have been. He had already given up his estate agency work by this time, along with some of his other business interests. Claims that individuals such as Chiefy were having careers spanning more than 130 major film and television appearances must therefore be regarded as being broadly accurate, for it seems that this was the Farrars' main money-making venture. The price put on one of the Farrars' film contracts, for instance, was in excess of £100 a day (equal to nearly £2,000 today).

By 1962, Frank was once again being offered the opportunity of settling down to a quiet life. Even ignoring the lucrative film work, Southport Zoo itself had become an enduring success and was now bringing in just about enough money for him and Helena to live a reasonably comfortable life together. Local people felt a strong attachment to this zoological attraction and it perfectly complemented any out-of-towner's holiday of ice creams and paddling in the sea.

The government's Holidays with Pay Act of 1938 had newly guaranteed paid leisure to the working class. Notwithstanding the Second World War, it meant that greater numbers of ordinary British people had time and money

Helena with Rajah at Southport Zoo, mid-1950s. (Fred and Joan Honisett)

to spend in places like Southport and its little zoo. Throughout the 1950s, Frank and Helena enjoyed big crowds coming to see their collection, for they offered the masses the kind of fun which had been so resolutely denied them throughout the first half of the twentieth century, what with all its swollen industrial squalor, military bloodbaths and economic disasters.

In British zoos of the post-war years, contact between visitors and animals was much more liberal than it is today. One could feed any creature through the bars of its cage, stroke its fur or hold its paw. Some people miss this old style of zoo life but it came with risks, not least to the visitors. A local visitor, Denise Roney, recalls as a young girl being pressed up against one of the ape cages at Southport Zoo and losing her brand-new pretty multi-coloured pinafore to the large, light-fingered primates within. It was as much as her father could do to stop Denise being dragged to the very top of the cage wall as the animals pulled at the fabric. The apes managed to get the pinafore and, though it was later retrieved, it was utterly ruined, much to the dismay of little Denise. Such calamities were, however, simply all part of a day at the zoo in the 1950s and no one really complained.

One regular visitor, Joan Honisett, had fallen in love with this quaint seaside zoo when she and her husband Fred had first visited in 1960. They were southerners, but Fred worked for Boots and had just been appointed manager of a chemist branch in the Southport area. Joan did not know anyone in the town but had always felt a kinship with animals and ended up visiting the zoo every single day for three months.

She got to know the animals of Southport beach very well indeed, and one day noticed that Sammy (who was about nine years old by this point) was staggering slightly. Joan happened to remark aloud to the blonde lady standing next to her that the lioness did not look at all well. Helena turned and replied that Sammy was indeed very ill; she had a tumour on the brain and was due to be put down by the vet before long. Joan was herself aghast and could see through Helena's stoicism that it was certain to be a grim day when it came. The two women talked for some time that day, and a friendship was formed that would last for thirty years.

Helena was fiercely loyal to those who shared her love for animals and upon whom she felt she could depend, and she would come to rely on Joan a great deal. Joan had happened to appear at just the right time for the Farrars, as Gaye Hutchinson, who had slowly evolved into the zoo's secretary, had got married and given up work, as women tended to do in those days. Gaye recalls that Helena was 'a tower of strength in every possible way' to Frank

Joan Honisett with ostriches, 1960s. (Fred and Joan Honisett)

as he pursued his projects, but behind Helena after 1960 was Joan Honisett. Helena could see right away that Joan had the innate talent for winning the confidence of animals and found in her a perfect ally. Joan threw herself into her work at Southport Zoo. She remembers them as happy days, for Frank and Helena had surrounded themselves with good people. Frank's sister Mabel, who lived next door to the Farrars at Westbourne Road, often used to help out at the zoo, and Mabel's young daughter Angela also frequently came down to the zoo to work there and to play with the animals.

One Southport local, a man named Norman Dean, proved, like Joan, to be a gift to Frank and Helena. Norman was about the same age as Frank, was equally competent and had a love for animals. He had been a shopkeeper but, like so many others, ended up spending all his spare time at Southport Zoo, absorbed with the animals and the antics of the ebullient Yorkshireman who ran the place. In time, Norman became an honorary staff member, helping to muck out the stables and small paddocks. At about the same time that Joan joined as the zoo's secretary, Norman, at the age of fifty-one, closed his business and became a regular keeper for Frank. Especially taken with the big cats, Frank and Helena would later say that Norman had possessed a special talent for the handling of large creatures and that these animals would always approach him with trust. Frank in particular recognised this and often asked Norman to accompany him in television appearances for the BBC and suchlike.

Any other zoo of its kind might have been quite content to remain a children's petting zoo, with mainly rabbits and goats along with a few spectacular animals to draw the crowds. That was not, however, Frank's style: in the narrow confines of Southport Zoo he was trying to build a serious animal collection. Within a short time the number of animals had ballooned to include a Highland cow, an elephant, a family of ostriches, a bear and thirty-five species of primate, along with a steadily increasing group of big cats.

Southport Zoo also appears to deserve credit for certain isolated achievements. A newspaper of the time declared that the Farrars' zoo had made history by being the first in the world to successfully breed a De Brazza's monkey. Although difficult to prove this, successful monkey breeding was rare in Britain even in the 1960s, and the act of producing a young De Brazza's monkey would have been noteworthy at the very least.

A place such as central Africa, where these monkeys had come from, was no longer the vast blankness seen on many nineteenth-century maps,

Right Helena grooming Rajah, 6 August 1959. (Fred and Joan Honisett)

Below Helena with Samson (centre) and Rajah, September 1957. (Fred and Joan Honisett)

Postcard of a lion-tailed macaque (species formerly known as Wanderoo monkey), possibly from the early 1960s. (Fred and Joan Honisett)

yet it remained a difficult place to travel freely into in the 1950s, never mind one from which to collect exotic animals. The principal method of international travel was still by sea, and zoo-bound creatures emerging from such places used to die by the score on the long return trip to northern Europe. Furthermore, once the survivors had arrived (often in very sorry states of health) it seems that few zoos were able to keep such types of animal alive for more than a few months, owing to improper diets, poor medicine, incorrect heating levels and bad enclosure design.

For a species such as the De Brazza's monkey to survive in a small British zoo and to breed successfully was of some interest, and appears to have been reflected in the value of the animals. Frank was, at this time, starting to find additional work as an international dealer in rare animals, and in the days when British zoo animals were still given a monetary value, the parent De Brazza's monkeys (named Miki and Griff, after a popular country music duo of the time) were said to be worth £500, equal to £10,000 today. Once baby had arrived, all bets were off as to what the trio might be worth.

Yet, breeding success aside, one cannot escape the fact that Southport Zoo was essentially what we would today call a 'menagerie' – a word within the zoo world which strictly refers to a much older type of zoo-keeping whereby animals would be kept permanently in rows of featureless, barred crates for close-range inspection by the public, rather in the manner of a picture gallery. Southport Zoo was above average by the standards of the day, but Frank wanted a real modern zoo, not a menagerie, and he was running out of room. What had started as a mere hobby based around a home for a pet lioness had become a full-blown tourist destination at which the British public demanded to see a constantly refreshed collection of weird and wonderful creatures. The Farrars started to think about providing more space for the many additions to their collection.

It was clear that public demand, as well as the Farrars' ambitions and abilities, had outgrown the existing limits of the site. If they were to give a better life to the animals they had collected and bred, as well as to continue to guarantee the commercial success of their business, they would have to expand.

For one reason and another they were not able to acquire more land at Southport to extend the existing zoo. Joan Honisett recalls that Frank considered buying another established zoo, but then again, he was much too adventurous to go round buying up other people's businesses. He was more the sort of person to start a business and then sell it on. And this is exactly what he did now with his remaining Southport businesses – the biscuit shop and the delicatessen were sold off and negotiations were opened with the Ravensden company for the sale of Southport Zoo. It was clear that Frank and Helena were aiming at a huge change in their lives and were casting their net wide.

3

RAJAH GOING SOUTH

FRANK HAD HIS mind set on something quite different from the zoo at Southport. He was now after a large country seat where he could build a proper animal park. One of the first places he looked at was a historic pile with the somewhat appropriate name of Birdingbury Hall in Warwickshire, a few miles south-west of Rugby. This plan unfortunately came to nothing and Rugby Zoo was not to be.

Shortly afterwards, Joan was sent a Colchester newspaper, which her mother had posted to her as a reminder of home, in which Helena happened to spot an advertisement for the sale of a place called Jacques Hall, near Manningtree in deepest East Anglia, more than 200 miles from Southport. A planning application was passed to the town authority in November 1962. The response among the Manningtree and Bradfield locals was one of incredulity and hilarity. Concerns were raised about safety and a protest ensued. The owner of the farmland surrounding Jacques Hall eventually declined to allow a right of way for Frank's proposed zoo and this plan was abandoned, like Rugby Zoo.

In retrospect, Manningtree Zoo had not been an ideal prospect. The town has often proudly claimed the distinction of being the smallest in the country and also, like the projected location of Rugby Zoo, Frank's animal park would have been quite some distance from the nearest major urban centre. Less than a third of British families owned a motorcar in 1962 and it would have been much harder to get people into such remote places than it was to entice holidaymakers straight off Southport beach.

It was to be third time lucky for the Farrars. Helena was on a promotional tour with Southport Zoo's bear, which had, by then, become an official mascot of the National Coal Board. While in Cambridgeshire, Helena popped over the county line to have a look around Essex. North Essex in particular remained exceptionally rural, and it appealed to Helena, who remained at heart a child of the Australian bush. She wanted some of the open space of her childhood back. She wanted trees and lakes and, at the centre of it all, a big and secluded old house for herself, Frank and her cats to live in together. She knew instantly that she had found what she was looking for when she came upon a place called Stanway Hall on the western edge of Colchester, which was then up for sale along with many acres of adjoining land. Frank shortly came down to take a look and was just as spellbound by the estate as Helena had been. They signed the contracts around New Year's Day 1963.

The estate of Stanway Hall had probably started life as the last watering place for horses on the Roman road ('stone way') out of Colchester before making the river crossing near what is now the village of Heckfordbridge. It seems to have belonged to the great Earl Byrhtnoth, who died at the Battle of Maldon in 991, after which his widow passed it to the King, Ethelred the Unready. Stanway remained for many years in the possession of the English crown, passing through the ownership of Canute and Edward the Confessor, down to Harold, the last Anglo-Saxon king of England. After Harold was slain at the Battle of Hastings and London was taken, Stanway was counted among the huge swathes of the island claimed by William the Conqueror.

By the twelfth century, Stanway had been given away by the monarchy, and the estate went on to be bought and sold by many rich and influential families through the centuries. The first substantial house on the site seems to have appeared in the first years of the reign of Henry VIII, after Thomas Bonham had acquired the majority of the estate. This original Stanway Hall must have quickly attained some considerable grandeur for it became, a century later, the family home of Sir John Swinnerton, Sheriff of London in 1602, Lord Mayor of London in 1612 and former supplier of the royal wine to the court of Elizabeth I.

After Swinnerton had lived there, Stanway Hall continued to pass through many hands until, in the late years of the nineteenth century, Thomas Moy, a fabulously wealthy local coal merchant, acquired the house. He demolished almost the entirety of the vast old Hall and replaced it with a rather smaller and neater Victorian house, which still stands on the land today. The Moys lived in this new Stanway Hall until, it seems, at least 1937. By 1962 it was owned by the family of Douglas Miller, who had made a very good living as clothing manufacturers.

A young girl called Heather Cardy lived opposite Stanway Hall on the other side of the old Roman road. Her mother cleaned for the Millers and Heather was always welcome in the Hall and its grounds all through her childhood. She remembers spending her early years playing in and around the house or wandering around the distant copses and boating on the lakes. Heather was dismayed when the Millers announced that they were to sell Stanway Hall and move away; their business was going through difficult times and they could no longer afford to keep such a large estate. At the time, everyone assumed that the Hall would be turned into a nice, quiet rest home for the elderly. It came as a surprise, then, when a comical northerner and a loud foreigner showed up, determined to build a zoo.

And determined they were. Helena had been mesmerised by the rural aspect of the place on sight and had made up her mind. It was a well-known beauty spot and people who used to pass by there up until 1963 remember it as a fine slice of Constable country. There were few bushes and trees by the roadside then and any walker or passenger in a car or bus would be treated to the sight of a lush green valley, furnished with fabulously overgrown Lebanon cedars, rolling down to a quaint old boathouse upon a string of small lakes which were always thick with birdlife.

Frank had readily seen what Helena saw in the park, but what probably clinched the deal for him was the ruined and picturesque church of All Saints, which stood a stone's throw to the east of the Hall and came as part of the estate. The church of All Saints, which still stands today, is perhaps the third such building on the foundations. An old Anglo-Saxon church apparently stood there originally, and it seems that this was replaced by the Belhus family in the late 1200s or early 1300s. This new church did not last terribly long, and most of the structure collapsed in 1381. The nave seen today was rebuilt in around 1400, at about the same time that the church's current west tower was added. By the late 1400s, All Saints was a thoroughgoing parish church for Stanway, with its own officer and alabaster altarpiece. After 1580, however, All Saints was stripped of the role of parish church in favour of St Albright's Church on the Copford Road to the north.

It was at this time that the ownership of the Stanway Hall estate split into several hands and it is probable that All Saints would have fallen into disrepair had John Swinnerton not gathered full ownership of the Hall and land for himself twenty years later and set about renovating the church for use as a private family chapel. Sir John made many alterations, including the addition of the north porch (bearing his coat of arms) and a number of new windows.

All Saints' Church in the grounds of Stanway Hall, Colchester, around 1950. (Miss Harrington)

The church Frank saw in 1962 had long since become a ruined and overgrown hulk; it had apparently been gutted by fire in 1685 and was then left disused. Frank's experience as a renovator of bombed-out buildings, including churches, in the late 1940s gave him big ideas about doing the church up. Certainly he recognised it as a good potential attraction for the zoo, adding a little romantic piquancy to what was already an area of outstanding natural charm.

Once the estate belonged to Frank and Helena, it seemed unlikely that they would fail. After all, they had many wonderful animals already and had ten years of experience running a successful zoo. Now, here they were in a magnificent wooded park, which was just about walking distance from a town of some considerable size. Colchester was theirs for the taking, and they had left themselves just enough time to construct a smart zoo before the Easter holidays (traditionally the most important date on the zoo calendar) and start to recoup some of the gigantic financial outlay of their new project. Then came the big freeze.

The weather had generally been clear in north Essex throughout December 1962, around the time that Helena had first visited Stanway Hall.

As Colcestrians ate their festive meals on Christmas Day, disappointed that it was not a white Christmas despite the recent couple of days of frost, not one of them could possibly have suspected that they were about to witness the death of the country's oldest recorded town.

The snow began at midday on Boxing Day and froze hard overnight on the ground as temperatures reached -13 degrees centigrade. Down at the coast nearby, at Mersea Island, ice was seen on the sea and gathering on the beaches. People of Mistley and Manningtree stood on the banks of the Stour estuary watching the waves of the tide pack up layer upon layer on a great wall of ice along the shore.

The wintry weather grew steadily worse into New Year 1963. At the very moment when Frank and Helena were signing their names for Stanway Hall, Colchester was quietly beginning to shut down. Local angling was off – every pond, lake and small river was frozen solid – and ice floes were seen drifting down the Colne through the borough. The Strood Channel between Mersea Island and the mainland began to look like an Antarctic ice shelf. The ancient oyster fisheries, dating back to Roman times, reported the loss of almost their entire layings, raising questions about the survival of the industry after 2,000 years. Colchester United missed one match, then another, followed by another. Diesel was gelling in bus and car engines everywhere, and local schools were closing. Grave diggers were having to use braziers and flame-guns to break the ground open, and firemen complained that their water hoses were useless, their tanks and pipes having frozen.

This was not merely a lot of snow falling gently everywhere. This winter was one of bitter gales which blew up huge drifts of snow, some more than 8ft deep. Train journeys to London were taking over four hours, and when the local railway lines started to become completely snowed under, the town's soldiers came to dig them out only to find that all the points had seized up anyway.

By the middle of January, the mighty Blackwater River was iced from bank to bank and all its vessels were trapped within. Outlying towns and villages in the area – Birch, Peldon, Stoke-by-Nayland – were lost behind thick curtains of snow: unreachable and un-contactable. At one point, no traffic was able to get in or out of Harwich for thirty-six hours. Clacton was likewise cut off from the rest of the country. A group of policemen taking bread out to the stranded people of Little Bromley were forced to abandon their car and continue their aid mission through the blizzard on foot. Power cuts were reported in Braiswick and Lexden, and the brand new power station at Bradwell would later fail – even the station's back-up generator would freeze solid and the town's nuclear engineers would be forced to work long and hard by torchlight to get things running again.

Things began to turn sour for Colchester when the local gasworks reached the point of shutting down, as its coal stock had almost run out and no barge could reach it to deliver more – the whole surface of the River Colne was frozen over. As a result, the threat of influenza and hypothermia across the borough became a very real one, forcing the authorities to call in sappers from the garrison to crack the river with explosives.

On the night of Tuesday 22 January 1963, this ancient town finally gave up its struggle as temperatures reached a staggering low of -35 degrees centigrade. Colchester's citizens awoke on Wednesday to a silent dawn: thousands of birds had died as they slept, and even the anti-freeze had frozen in the engines of Colchester's vehicles.

On that strangely silent morning the new Colchester was born. To be sure, the snow continued to fall, including a full fifteen days in February. It remained 2ft deep in most places and lingered into the following month, and by 4 March there had been seventy-two nights of below-freezing temperatures. People could scarcely remember what summer weather felt like. However, temperatures did not again fall down to the depths of that fatal night in January and, on 5 March, the temperature suddenly jumped to 16 degrees, warmer than some days in the previous August.

A perceptive person might have seen that a new Colchester had been emerging in this thaw. For one thing, there was a large zoological park now frantically trying to get built in the west of town. As spring came on fast, Frank and Helena found they had very little time to ready their zoo. Their construction work had been badly delayed by the exceptionally horrific winter conditions and if they were not ready in time for Easter it would be very difficult for them to get through the year; if they were not ready for the summer, they might lose everything. People who knew them at this time say that they were living a hand-to-mouth existence and skirting very close to financial trouble.

Things were, nevertheless, beginning to happen at Stanway Hall. The first employees were appointed and most of Heather Cardy's family ended up working for the Farrars: her mother was retained as a cleaner and her father, Alf, who had worked on Stanway Hall Farm next to the Hall, was taken on for Frank's new zoo. Even Heather's boyfriend, David Grist, was

Stanway Hall in spring 1963. (David Grist)

made Frank's gofer and soon became involved in the park's construction work. Also retained by Frank and Helena was the Millers' gardener, George Andrews, a grumpy but loveable old local man who looked on the youngsters' new zoo with some bemusement.

Two animal keepers were appointed early in 1963. Ronald Physick, a twenty-year-old 6ft white Jamaican, who had come to England at the age of seventeen, became Colchester's first official zookeeper. Ron had considerable experience of professional life with animals, having worked as a keeper at Paignton Zoo and later at an animal transportation firm in London, often travelling to the Americas. Ron's laid-back, loose Caribbean demeanour and specialism in primates led to the affectionate nickname of 'Monkey Boy'. The second keeper to be appointed was a chap by the name of Tony Hiller, who had no doubt intrigued Frank with his extra-curricular hobby of taxidermy.

A few more people were employed late in the spring: a young man called Douglas Rushworth; a sixteen-year-old bird keeper named Sheelagh Marron; and Patience Cole, who ran her own horse stable elsewhere in the borough. This, along with Ann Gales who was employed in the café, appears to have been the full staff in the earliest days of Frank's zoo at Colchester, and all of them worked like men and women possessed in order to build up the park in time for Easter. Easter Sunday was to fall on 14 April that year,

L-R: Keepers Ron Physick and Tony Hiller with David Grist outside the gift shop at Stanway Hall Zoo Park, 1963. (David Grist)

Keeper Douglas Rushworth with a young stump-tailed macaque named Peter at Stanway Hall Zoo Park, November 1963. (Sheelagh Marron)

and it was obvious that they would miss that important holiday and lose a great deal of money. If they missed the beginning of summer, the game would likely be up before it had even begun.

The papers had been making the most of Frank's extravagant claims back in February that Stanway Hall Zoo Park, as it was known, was going to rival the great Whipsnade animal park to the north-west of London. There was excited talk of his foreign trips to pick up exotic animals, many of which were now counting down their days in quarantine. Frank was painting a striking picture to the press of this new zoo, which would be a comprehensive collection of animals from every face of the globe. Some journalists were making credulous assertions to the effect that Stanway Zoo would soon be ranked among the top six European zoos. The veracity of such things aside, there now lay a great burden of expectation on the Farrars to ensure that their zoo, however it would turn out, should be of a high standard despite having lost valuable time and revenue to the snow.

The first job carried out at Stanway Zoo was the creation of a perimeter fence. Many animal enclosures followed quickly, but the first to be completed, just as at Southport a decade earlier, was the lion house, which was proudly placed at the very centre of the park. This was the beginning of the animals arriving at the zoo, as they would continue to do so for some time. It is presumed that some of the Southport collection remained at home in Lancashire, but even if every Southport animal had come to Colchester they would have occupied a mere corner of the new site. In order to fill Stanway Zoo, Frank hurriedly had to organise animals coming in from all over the world in a very short space of time. Fortunately, people such as David Grist were handy to have around, and for weeks they made many trips for Frank, picking up creatures from zoos and ports all over the country.

The big moment for Helena came late in May 1963, when it was time for her lions to be moved. Wherever her lions lived, she lived: this was the point of no return. She and Frank were selling up their whole life at Southport and whatever struggles they now faced, Stanway Zoo simply had to work. By this point Sammy had been dead for a while, but Rajah (now nearly ten years old) had a new mate: two-year-old Queen (or 'Puddy', as Helena called her) who appears to have been given as a cub to the Farrars by Hollywood star Kirk Douglas.

Norman Dean was chosen as the most trusted person to drive the cats the great distance from Southport to Colchester. A bed of straw was

Right Keeper Patience Cole with an Asian black bear cub, October 1963. (Sheelagh Marron)

Below David Grist installs a section of the first perimeter fencing at Stanway Hall Zoo Park, 1963. (David Grist)

Kirk Douglas gave a lion cub named Queen to the Farrars; it is believed that this is Queen as a cub. (Fred and Joan Honisett)

made in the van and Queen and Rajah were settled in. Rajah was an experienced traveller but everyone was less sure about Queen. However, the van had an open cab, so Helena, riding up front beside Norman, would readily be able to soothe any disturbance along the way. Prepared thus for the arduous journey to Essex, Helena and her cats left the zoo and the town of Southport behind them.

About twenty miles out of Southport, near Newton-le-Willows, Norman began to feel quite ill, complaining of stomach trouble, and was starting to faint away at the wheel. Helena made him pull over at a chemist's shop by the side of the road. Inside the shop he collapsed and was taken quickly to a hospital at St Helens.

Helena was forced to telephone for another driver to catch up with her and help her finish the journey. Nothing fazed old Rajah these days; he did not mind waiting half an hour in the van. Young Queen was, for her part, rather confused by the whole thing and Helena had to comfort her furry head in her lap as passers-by looked in through the van window with wonder. It seems that while she was sitting in the van, waiting with her cats, Helena began to reflect on the new life that she and Frank were headed for. They were not old but they were no longer young – they were both past fifty. Her husband was still full of life and ideas and she trusted him but he was starting to look a little aged. They had staked every penny they had on a new zoo in a town which they did not know and which was administrated by people who did not seem overly keen to take them in. They were leaving friends behind: in a few short years they had become excellent friends with Fred and Joan Honisett. Frank and Fred got on well but were each very much wrapped up in their own work – Joan, on the other hand, had become a second daughter to Helena and was trusted with everything she had, from her animals to the zoo's takings to her most private thoughts. She was also leaving behind her real family – her children having grown up and started their own lives in Southport – and she was worried how this would affect their relationship.

Helena's relief driver arrived before too long and the journey continued. Upon arrival at Stanway Hall, Helena was shocked to learn that Norman was dead. She and her cats had arrived safely in Colchester that day, but Helena was superstitious. (In later years she would describe May as her unlucky month.) Frank was doing an admirable job of dashing about, furiously trying to conjure his city of animals out of the Stanway soil overnight, but would it be enough? They had originally planned to open at

Keeper Norman Dean (centre) with Southport Zoo's baby elephant in the 1960s. (Fred and Joan Honisett)

Easter, which had now passed. They had then aimed at the last weekend in May; this had also now gone. Spring was ending, summer was approaching, the park was not open and there was still much work to be done.

Norman Dean had been their most trusted keeper and had been as devoted to the lions as Helena. He had, together with the Farrars, watched Southport Zoo grow from a purposeful accident into an international business and had been an important part of their success. The day her lions moved to Colchester was the day, for Helena, on which Stanway Zoo truly became a zoo. To have suddenly lost fifty-three-year-old Norman at the very same moment was a dismal omen indeed.

4

JACKETS OFF

FRANK AND HELENA walked down to the gates at ten o'clock on the morning of Sunday 2 June 1963 to open Stanway Hall Zoo Park to the public for the first time. Queues of cars stretched out of sight in both directions; as the gates opened they began to stream into the car park, and would do so for hours. The roads of Stanway were packed all day and every single vehicle supplied by Colchester's various bus companies was full to capacity. Scores of families were seen marching down Maldon Road pushing prams.

Even now, though, Stanway Zoo was not quite ready: visitors saw staff tearing around, frantically putting up signs, species labels and so forth, and there were still some building contractors putting the finishing touches on many of the new enclosures. This proved to be a blessing, for Frank suddenly realised he needed all the pairs of hands he could find. A young builder called Cliff Fairweather, who had been doing a little construction work for Frank at the zoo, was there that morning and suddenly found himself being dragged up to the front gate to help take entrance money.

Frank put a white coat with large pockets on him and pointed him in the direction of the incoming cars. Within a matter of minutes, Cliff's coat pockets were overflowing with notes and coins as the drivers, passengers and walkers flooding through the gates all but threw great handfuls of money at him. He was soon stuffing banknotes into his trouser pockets, which were likewise filled in short order. Laughing, he, like the other workers on the gate around him, started simply shoving the cash down his shirt front.

Frank then sent him to find Helena, who was upstairs in the Hall. Cliff waddled off up to Helena's office whereupon he turned out his wardrobe, dumping money all over the floor. Helena was not convinced of the

Stanway Hall Zoo Park seen from Maldon Road in around 1963. Stanway Hall can be seen in the centre distance. (John McCann Photography)

honesty of this man who had braved Colcestrian motorists that morning, and made him come back just as he was turning to leave for the zoo gate again, in order to make sure all his pockets were absolutely empty. Cliff was deeply offended, but this was the hardness of Helena who was generally contemptuous and suspicious of newcomers. Frank, on the other hand, was always there to play the good cop: when Cliff complained that Helena had not thanked him or even apologised when his pockets had been found empty, Frank simply laughed and said, 'Don't pay any attention to her, love.'

However, if facing Frank's wife had been a sobering experience that morning, the surprise that awaited Cliff when he later returned with more money to Stanway Hall was more sobering still. Steeling himself for another encounter with Helena, he opened the front door and put one hand on the stair banister, only to look up and see before him a large cheetah sitting alone on the staircase, staring hard at him in that dirty yellow fashion in which only a cheetah can stare. Cliff backed away as slowly as he could out through the door and quickly slammed it shut. He took to banging on

53

the door and calling out, at which Frank put his head out of a first-floor window to ask what he wanted. Cliff said he wanted to come up but that there was a cheetah loose in the house. Frank told him not to be silly, that it was only Kinna. Cliff was not at all sure but Frank would not come down to him, so he cautiously opened the front door again and crept gingerly up the stairs past Kinna, who sniffed at him and licked the back of his hand with a tongue like flint sandpaper.

Frank did, however, have to take careful note of the complaints of certain other people around the zoo that day. Traffic was now down as far as Shrub End and the police, who had arrived early in the day, warned Frank that if he did not start to get things moving quicker on the gate then cars would be queuing through Colchester town centre. All the shirt-stuffers, including Frank, began to work twice as hard to cope with the numbers coming in.

It was a blazing hot day and it was clear that Frank and Helena had underestimated the appeal of their zoo. The throng of people inside the park was enormous. The crowds made it difficult for many to see the animals; and the queues for lemonade, ice cream and the arresting modern novelty of a self-service espresso bar, extended far out of Stanway Hall all day. Despite this, everybody present was simply delighted by the Farrars' zoo. In particular, they were amazed at the animal collection they saw around them. Reports are vague but it seems there were striped hyena, gibbons, condors, golden lion tamarins, coatimundi, paca, a pair of Brazilian tapir, a brown pelican from Brazil, four eagle owls, peacocks, ocelots, two emus, a male grison, European red deer, fruit bats, a pair of lion-tailed macaques, wapiti, wallabies, a pair of fish eagles, an Indian python, marabou storks, Highland cattle, Ankole-Watusi cattle, sarus cranes, a mother and baby llama, and a family of spider monkeys. Near to the zoo's entrance was a walled pool for otters from the Himalayas. Stanway Hall's old coach house had been converted into various animal enclosures containing monkeys, rodents and birds, and just in front of this was a pen for a pair of raccoons. In the yard stood two scruffy Shetland ponies, which had not quite shed their winter coats. Also at the zoo were two Asian black bear cubs, both about six months old, who had been born at Whipsnade. One of the cubs was called Debbie, after a little local girl called Debbie Salmon, who had attended a private preview that Frank had conducted at the zoo during the previous week. The newspapers had gleefully lapped up this sort of detail, as had the public.

Then there was Joey the red kangaroo, who had come to Frank and Helena back in Southport. They had acquired him from a sailor who had

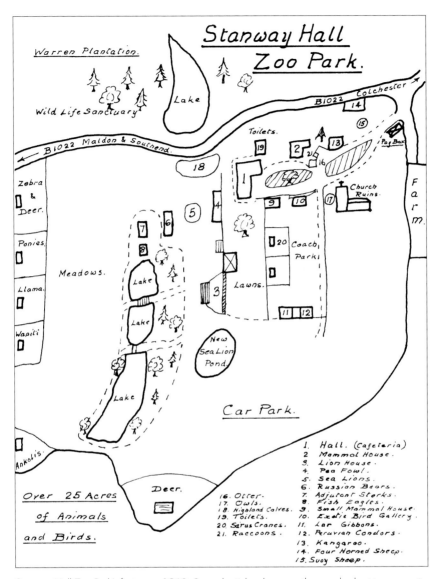

Stanway Hall Zoo Park's first map, 1963. Several articles shown on the map had yet to appear in the zoo due to delays. (Fred and Joan Honisett)

arrived in Liverpool with what he had originally thought was a wallaby but which had kept growing and growing throughout the long voyage back from Australia, and had started to become quite a powerful young buck. Joey is rumoured to have been the animal who famously knocked down world light-heavyweight boxing champion Freddie Mills during the 1962 Christmas season at Bertram Mills' Circus. That kangaroo's name was given as George but it is possible that it was the same creature, for Frank often took Joey for public appearances and had very close ties with Bertram Mills in those days.

A favourite among the crowds was a tame, one-year-old stump-tailed macaque called Peter. There was a friendly and talkative macaw called Mac, whom Frank had kept as a pet for fifteen years and who entertained people endlessly. (Like Joey, a number of the Farrars' talking birds came from sailors. Many of these birds became special favourites among the zoo's visitors over the years, on account of the disgusting insults they would trade with each other.) There had been several chimpanzees at Southport Zoo; Frank still had one, also called Mac, with whom some visitors were reported to have become quite besotted. It seems that there was probably also a tame orangutan on show, which had made the front page of the *Essex County Standard* back in February after the government of Borneo had presented him to Frank. But the great highlight for everyone, just as had been the case back at Southport Zoo, was the beautiful Rajah at the very heart of the park, who was stroked by adults and children alike through the bars of his cage.

Into the late afternoon things began to calm down a little. Children entertained themselves feeding the ducks and geese beside the lakes in the shade among the rhododendrons. A jazz band played dixie on the wide lawn outside the Hall as the sun drifted down through the hot late afternoon sky, while the picnicking crowds lazed on the grass, surrounded by George Andrews' immaculate roses. As the last people dropped away when evening began to fall and Frank closed the gates on the first day, the staff was amazed to see that the people of Colchester had left their new zoo exactly as they had found it, with no litter anywhere.

The next day, Whit Monday, they did it all over again, and by the end of the opening weekend some 14,000 people had visited the zoo. Frank said it seemed as if half the town had come down to Stanway Hall. This was not true, but the number did amount to perhaps one in five Colcestrians – an enormous proportion.

David Grist with Joey the red kangaroo at Stanway Hall Zoo Park, 1963. (David Grist)

OFFICIAL GUIDE

STANWAY HALL ZOO PARK

EAST ANGLIA'S OWN ZOO
Open daily from 10am to 8pm

Free car park for patrons
Admission prices: Adults 3/- Children under 14yrs 1/6
Reduced terms for parties
3 miles from Colchester on the B1022 to Maldon

FIRST OPENED IN MAY 1963

Stanway Hall Zoo Park's second guidebook from 1963 or 1964. The opening date is given incorrectly as 'May 1963', which was missed due to delays. Furthermore, the park's name had already begun its slow change to Colchester Zoo. (Fred and Joan Honisett)

To the east of the town, in grand symmetry with the zoo, the foundations of a new county university, which had been under discussion for a few years, were being laid. If anyone had imagined that Wivenhoe Park was about to be filled with sublime neo-Gothic college libraries, filled with dozing dons who were dreaming of Donne, they were due a surprise when a cluster of new International Style blocks started to appear around Wivenhoe House in black brick and bare concrete. New-fangled subjects like Sociology were reported to be on the university's syllabus, and the new team of professors was said to be the youngest ever assembled in a British university. Albert Sloman, the university's mastermind (and, like Frank, a Second World War RAF hero), was shortly to become the youngest person ever to deliver the Reith Lecture. Eyebrows were raised when a female was even found among the academic staff.

Along with the zoo and the university a major reshaping of the garrison was already well underway, helping to push Colchester in a new, contemporary direction. Since 1857 the town had been talking about building proper public baths and suddenly, from 1963 onward, a scheme started to be drawn up for the development of the old Mercer's Farm, just below Castle Park, into a swimming pool complex. The announcement had already been given that the largest of three new north Essex hospitals was to be built in Colchester, and planning for this 800-bed monster on Turner Road began in earnest from 1963.

The old heart of Colchester – once described as 'the very heart of very England' – was being ripped out, eventually replaced with thoroughly modern oddities such as a new concrete and glass public library and large pedestrianised consumer parades. Movements for a new inner ring road, eventually to comprise Cowdray Avenue, Southway and Balkerne Hill, seemed at the time as if a motorway was trying to throttle the town centre. By 1967 there would be serious proposals put forward that Colchester, Ipswich, Felixstowe and Harwich, and all the land in between, should be fully developed into one single urban unit: a miniature London which might economically rival the eastern half of the capital itself.

The railway line from London to Clacton had been electrified in 1962 and the travelling time to the capital from Colchester had been slashed to just fifty minutes. This resulted in a commuter boom in Colchester, similar to that seen all over the Home Counties and the South. In 1961 there had been a mere 350 commuters using Colchester's North Station. By the end of the decade that number would rise to 2,000; by 1972 the number would stand at 3,200. These people, though no doubt possessed of starry-eyed ideas of living among trees instead of pylons, had no genuine wish to live in an old-fashioned farming town. They and their families, whether moving in from London or otherwise becoming newly exposed to big city life, demanded new transport structures, new houses and new civic amenities.

But if there was one thing that these new Colcestrians and the old could both agree on, it was that they all wanted to enjoy themselves. Indeed, the whole of Britain wanted to start enjoying itself for the world had recently and consciously come within minutes of annihilation. Nuclear fright-films such as *On the Beach* and *The Day the Earth Caught Fire* had already been doing the rounds for a while when the Cuban Missile Crisis of October 1962 hit headlines around the world, after Britain's closest military ally, the USA, discovered that the Soviet Union had been building missile bases a mere 100 miles off the North American mainland. The possible consequences were discussed with considerable alarm in most news outlets. The big freeze followed and 20ft snow drifts were seen all over Britain for weeks, so it is hardly surprising that the country as a whole went a little hysterical when the sun came out again in the following year.

Lower end of Colchester Zoo, looking north along the far western edge in the mid-1960s. (Fred and Joan Honisett)

The big story for Britain in 1963, coinciding with the big thaw, was of course Beatlemania. The 'Fab Four' were bringing with them a new gospel of permanent fun and freedom for which the British nation, after the Cuban Missile Crisis and the exceptionally hard winter, was very much in the mood. Britons had each quietly resolved never to have to endure such misery again, and started to buy up cars, central-heating systems and new electric stoves by the thousand.

The Farrars' zoo, in a strange way, was Colchester's own little slice of Beatlemania, having been parachuted from Merseyside into a very grey world. A person today can scarcely imagine just how boring Colchester was in 1962. True, there was the Corn Exchange which held evening dances for ex-servicemen and which occasionally put on professional wrestling shows, and there were also lots of worthy clubs, such as the Beekeepers' Association, the Debating Society, the North Countrymen's Society and the Townswomen's Guild. Furthermore, there were a number of amateur dramatics companies, religious organisations and sporting associations, including Colchester United who had recently been promoted out of the fourth division. There was also a handful of cinemas in town (though one of these, the Cameo, catered mainly to a select part of society concerned with special-interest European 'art' films). This was all good and well but there

The llama paddock at Colchester Zoo, May 1964. (Sheelagh Marron)

was positively no place for a young modern family to spend a whole day out together cheaply, easily and on their own terms. The summer fêtes and the famous Colchester military tattoo offered just such good, wholesome family fun and were wildly popular, but these were fleeting events tied to specific dates on the calendar. If one wanted to enjoy a full day out on one's own time, it meant an uncomfortable and potentially expensive haul to Clacton beach. With the opening of Colchester Zoo, all that changed.

From 1963 onward, for 3*s*, or 1*s* 6*d* for a child (equivalent to about £1.80 and 90p today), one could get a full day's access to Stanway Hall's brand-new zoo, with its rapidly changing collection and various food outlets, as well as special events running from time to time. The zoo was just about walking distance from town, was provided with a good bus service, and was open all year round, from early morning each day until dusk. In other words, one could go to the zoo cheaply, regularly and at one's convenience with little planning. And this is exactly what people did, week after week, which resulted in Frank's zoo quickly becoming firmly established as a part of the town's landscape, both physically and mentally.

Even the conservatives in the town were won over. Perhaps the heady excitement of the first summer at Frank's zoo helped to allay fears about the nature of the emergent Colchester, and allowed many of the town's other new projects to proceed for a time with only slight resistance. If there did remain any objections, these no longer mattered: it was already too late. Things were subtly but surely beginning to change in the soul of north Essex: the place would steadily become more casual, more diverse, more cosmopolitan and more unpredictable.

A couple of weeks after the grand opening of Frank's zoo, an article in the *Essex County Standard* made the revelation that the Reverend Aubrey Moody, vicar of Feering, had taken off his jacket at a local summer fête. Before very long, newspapers would be filing reports of Colchester aldermen brazenly removing their jackets en masse at town council meetings. Clearly, there would be no turning back.

5

FROM CAROLINE TO CALLAS

THROUGHOUT THE FIRST summer at Colchester Zoo (as many people were already calling it), the collection expanded considerably, as did the crowds. From Whipsnade Zoo came hog deer and miniature sheep; a South African springhare had arrived by July; more waterfowl were brought in for the lakes; and various bird species, including king vultures, as well as many types of monkey (possibly even golden-headed lion tamarins), continued to swell the collection. A big hit with the public was Boris, a vast eleven-year-old Bactrian camel who arrived around August as part of an animal exchange with Moscow Zoo.

The first of Colchester Zoo's many generations of sea lions appeared towards the end of June. A trio of Californian sea lions were flown in from Los Angeles to London, where local animal transportation specialist, Mike Parish, picked them up. His wife, Jean, recalls that it was so hot that particular June that they had to stop the van at every petrol station between Heathrow and Colchester in order to hose the animals down with water, much to the amusement of other motorists. Upon arrival at the zoo, the sea lions garnered a great deal of attention in the press and among the people of Colchester.

Frank had signed off his large advertisement for the zoo's grand opening by saying that he hoped people would find his zoo 'a very novel outing' – something that they had done and were continuing to do. Frank knew the value of novelty for his zoo and now, in the grounds of Stanway Hall, he had the space to provide a great deal of novelty, with a lot more in the years to come. His first season had been a triumph. Even to the very end of the summer, late into September, visitor numbers were high, with 7,000 people reportedly visiting on Sunday 15 September when Colchester's Carnival

Queen, Marion Sheppard, met a pair of newly arrived Grant's zebras to christen them Stars and Stripes.

As the warm days ended and the winter nights drew in, Frank held a big party in Stanway Hall for everyone who had helped to make Colchester Zoo's first year a success. His staff were there, along with all the builders, suppliers and journalists whom he now counted as friends of the zoo. There was music and drinks and Frank entertained everyone enormously with his irrepressible silliness. He brought some of the animals into the Hall, including the zoo's huge python, for everyone to meet. The night was topped off with the showing of a film Frank had made for Canadian television, which documented his recent animal-collection travels in the Himalayas, Assam, Bengal and other parts of Asia, along with footage of Helena and himself riding elephants through the forests of Africa.

Colchester Zoo's first winter was quiet. It was hard to attract visitors in colder, wetter weather, since so much of the zoo was exposed to the elements, but Frank's publicity skills never let him down and the park continued to feature virtually every week in almost every local newspaper all the way through to the following season, which started in the biggest way possible.

The year 1964 was the year of Caroline or, rather, Carolines. Frank had been out some months earlier to inspect a herd of Asian elephants at a zoo in West or East Germany with an eye to buying a suitable calf. On Friday 10 April 1964, a largish four-year-old female became the first elephant to take up residence in Colchester for more than eighty years, since the materials for the construction of Colchester's gigantic municipal water tower (named Jumbo after London Zoo's famous elephant) had begun to arrive in town on river barges in 1882.

Elephant circuses had also frequently marched down Colchester High Street over the decades, but Caroline was the first elephant to become a true Colcestrian and there was great public excitement surrounding her arrival. It was, however, clear from the moment Caroline arrived at the zoo that she was a rather unwieldy animal. She showed contempt for all efforts to train her to work with the keepers during feeding and cleaning. In fact, she did not seem to like human company at all.

Cliff Fairweather recalls replacing some of the fence around the old Nissen hut in which Caroline was living by the early days of May. He and his workmates were almost finished and had only one section of fence left to go when Caroline dashed out, grabbed Cliff around his waist and tried to

Patience Cole with Bactrian camel Boris, October 1963. (Sheelagh Marron)

pick him up. A nearby keeper had to hit her trunk with the flat of his spade until she let Cliff go.

Caroline continued to prove intractable. Helena eventually allowed her courage to flower into stupidity when she resolved one day that she would succeed where the men had failed, and decided to take Caroline out for a walk. Disregarding the protestations of the keepers, she slung the elephant's trunk over her shoulder and led Caroline out towards one of the fields. The two of them had not walked more than twenty yards together when Caroline tossed Helena against a wall, breaking her arm and shattering her collarbone. Talking to the press afterwards, Helena declined to admit it was she who had been at fault, declaring that May was, after all, her unlucky month.

The Farrars gave up on Caroline. She was sold and replaced with a calf: a younger elephant that Frank and his staff intended to train from scratch. This second creature, an African elephant that arrived from Uganda on 22 June, was a sweet little soul whom Frank also named Caroline. Sadly, she died after just ten days at Colchester Zoo on 2 July. The pathology report concluded that she was already diseased before she arrived at Colchester.

Helena with a coatimundi at Colchester Zoo in the 1960s. (Joan and Fred Honisett)

Frank surmised that she had perhaps been weaned too quickly earlier in life and that her health had suffered as a result. This Caroline was replaced by a third elephant before the autumn of 1964, and on Sunday 13 September, Carnival Queen, Gilly Williams, christened her Caroline.

Why were they all named Caroline? The reason was a fourth, much more famous Caroline, who was bobbing in the North Sea just over three miles off Felixstowe. The good ship *MV Caroline*, home of Radio Caroline (Britain's first pirate radio station), had been beaming the Swinging Sixties into homes all over East Anglia since March that year. Radio Luxembourg had already been offering a similar audio diet to Radio Caroline for many years, but the signal had been weak and often subject to interference. When Caroline's signal – strong, clear and consistent – appeared, it caused a national convulsion as it confidently bypassed the whole establishment and filled housewives' kitchens and children's bedrooms everywhere with a continuous stream of the dangerous, lewd and generally irresponsible sounds of the Stones, James Brown, The Supremes and the like. The government was outraged and would put a stop to it in 1967, but in 1964 there was no law governing broadcasts from international waters and so Caroline was on everyone's radios and lips.

Radio Caroline and Colchester Zoo were, in fact, two versions of the same thing, and there was clear evidence of change in the town by now. Tastes were changing; desires were changing. The traditionalists and censors warned against all these new trends but the British public were no longer interested in sermons. They wanted *Carry On* films, ten-pin bowling alleys, bingo halls, pizzerias, and all the other evil manifestations of modernity which self-appointed moralists preached against, especially where the working classes were concerned.

For an old boy, Frank appears to have been surprisingly in touch with this movement in popular culture. Colchester Zoo's café, for example, was furnished with what was said to be the first-ever music video jukebox in a zoo, providing songs such as 'The House of the Rising Sun' alongside the animals. As soon as Radio Caroline appeared, Frank lost no time in striking a deal with the pirates, who became the official adopters of his elephant. A general adoption scheme for members of the public would not appear for another decade but this, Colchester Zoo's very first animal adoption, turned out to be excellent publicity for both the zoo and the station. Predictably, many cartoons and poems linking the two appeared in the press and, of course, each incoming elephant had to be named Caroline in order to maintain the link.

It would seem that Colchester, though one of the least likely of all towns to jump on the modernisation wagon, was among those places that most heartily and speedily adopted the new ways of living in Britain. A prescient editorial in the *Standard* had foreseen as early as February 1963 what Colchester Zoo portended for the town, remarking that new impositions such as this pointed towards a total reincarnation of the town in the years shortly to come.

For the few years in the middle of the 1960s there was a genuine sense of optimism in the nation. Britain had lagged far behind other developed nations economically ever since the war, and had watched with indignation as the defeated nations of Germany and Japan had advanced far ahead. But for a little while now things seemed brighter. Frank's zoo would do great business all through the 1960s, not because it was an outstanding zoo (for it was not) but because the nation as a whole was learning how to enjoy itself through passive, relaxed entertainments.

Chiefy with film actor Stewart Granger in around 1962, at the premiere of *Sodom and Gomorrah*, in which fellow zoo animal Kinna had appeared. (The London News Agency)

The Carolines were merely the most high-profile additions to Colchester Zoo in 1964 – Frank was continuing to expand his collection on all fronts. Of the large number of new animals coming into the park, some of the most fascinating included a ring-tailed lemur, adjutant storks, a pair of tayra, a number of douroucoulis and an Indian mongoose called Rikkitikkitavi. A pair of chimps, Jill and Maggie, arrived straight from Africa, and an ancient giant tortoise, born in about 1860, was also brought in around this time, roaming freely in the grounds and giving rides to children. The zoo was also showing signs of becoming a busy breeding centre, with new arrivals among the Ankole-Watusi cattle, the agoutis and the spider monkeys.

The big cats remained the stars of Colchester Zoo, however. Rajah seems to have retired from the screen by the early 1960s, with at least seven major films to his name and a fame second perhaps only to Leo, the MGM lion. Chiefy, the zoo's tame male leopard, had since served as Frank's bankable star and had more than earned his keep by making many media appearances, which paid for a great deal of the works at Colchester Zoo. Since coming to live with Frank and Helena (at first in Southport) he had been shown in countless television adverts and programmes. He had also appeared in many films, including *The Cool Mikado* with Frankie Howerd and *Sammy Going South* with Edward G. Robinson.

Chiefy was, however, about the same age as Rajah and was beginning to show his age too, having started to develop joint problems. The new kid in town was Cliff Fairweather's friend, young cheetah Kinna, who went on to assume the greater burden of artistic duties. She had been born in 1960 and was hand-reared by a game warden in Kenya. In 1962 the warden had moved to Tanganyika; he could not take her with him and so he had sold her to the Farrars.

Kinna was one of the tamest of all the big cats Frank and Helena had, and was soon making all sorts of media appearances. She attended many London film premieres and starred in television programmes such as Anglia's *Weavers Green*, and a BBC adaptation of the Sherlock Holmes tale *The Speckled Band*. Kinna was also sought by television advertisers and appeared in offerings such as the iconic Fry's Turkish Delight television commercial. By the time Colchester Zoo was up and running she had played a part in several movies, starring alongside John Wayne in the minor classic *Hatari!*, and with Stewart Granger in *Sodom and Gomorrah*.

Kinna quickly found many cautious admirers in Colchester, given Frank's habit of walking her around his zoo on a lead and introducing her to visiting children, just as he had always done with Chiefy. She went on to attract even more attention when Frank started taking her into town. During their first Christmas in Colchester, Kinna helped to raise a record £744 (£13,000) for the Rotary Club's annual charitable fundraiser, meeting and greeting yuletide shoppers in Trinity Square. Kinna was a friendly cat, but she could be a little rough at times. She had given Frank a nasty amount of scratches to his face earlier in the year, when he had taken her along to Colchester's Carnival Queen Ball at the Red Lion Hotel on the High Street and she had been alarmed by a spontaneous round of applause. Nevertheless, for years afterwards, Frank, Helena and their animals were much in demand in the borough to open village fêtes and charity events.

Other animals became nationally known – Frank's bear cubs won the hearts of the country when they began to appear in long-running television adverts for Sugar Puffs breakfast cereal. One of Stanway's elephants went on to appear in *Dixon of Dock Green* in an episode called 'The Night of the Fog'. One of Helena's big cats is even said to have appeared in an episode of *The Avengers*.

Left Chiefy parked at the Savoy Hotel, London, in the 1960s. (Fred and Joan Honisett)

Below Frank in his Stanway Hall study with cheetah Kinna, in the mid-1960s. (Keystone Press Agency)

Stills montage from Fry's Turkish Delight television advert featuring Kinna, from the 1960s. (Cadbury Ltd)

Joey the kangaroo showed up in films and at events such as an Australian motorcar show at Earls Court; he was also borrowed by the BBC for a publicity stunt during the launch of their second television channel in April 1964, for which they had created a pair of cartoon kangaroo mascots called Hullabaloo and Custard. Joey might have become even better known when, in 1966, national hero Johnny Morris arrived at Colchester Zoo for two days of filming for his wildly popular television show *Animal Magic*. Joey was meant to have taken part in the shoot but he became rather too excited and kept knocking off keeper Morris' hat, so the film crew had to be content with clips of Kinna, the gibbons and the ducks instead.

Colchester Zoo was certainly attracting a lot of visitors but, even so, it struggled to make ends meet through 1964. The raging heat of June 1963 had just about allowed the zoo to put down its roots, but the loss of that first Easter holiday had certainly hurt. Visitor numbers had generally been excellent up to the end of the first season, but an unwelcome dent had been made in July, which had been a total washout with huge summer rainstorms and floods all over the borough.

There is no doubt that Colchester Zoo's initial years were successful, but it was really through the television and film appearances of its animals that it was carried safely through its earliest hours. The revenue from the media engagements also drove forward Frank's international animal dealership, which in turn helped him to build up the collection at Stanway Hall, completing the circle by allowing the taming of new animals for further media engagements. Although the new zoo had not yet made a profit, Frank knew that that time would come and spared no efforts to turn it into the major attraction of which he had dreamed at his desk back at Knights National.

Frank's grandiose ambition for his park and its desperate need for large amounts of money were both matched in 1965, when Colchester Zoo's

Helena with leopard cubs at Colchester Zoo in the late 1960s. (Fred and Joan Honisett)

animals and keepers were selected to appear on the Covent Garden stage. This is an event that many of Frank's old staff members look back on with the deepest pride. In the spring of that year, Frank announced to everybody that the Royal Opera House had offered £4,000 (£68,000) for his animals to appear in the first British production of Arnold Schoenberg's opera *Moses und Aron*. It was to be produced by Peter Hall, director of the Royal Shakespeare Company, and conducted by Georg Solti, arguably the greatest conductor of the day.

Frank set about organising everything straightaway. The animals briefed for Covent Garden included Frank's two white Arab horses – a twenty-three-year-old mare called Seagull and her stable mate Linkie. Boris the camel, Flora the Highland cow, seven goats and two donkeys were also put down for the London performance. George the gardener was given the job of making noise in the paddocks for weeks in advance, such as playing LPs on an old wind-up gramophone, in order to get the animals used to loud and unusual sounds.

June soon came and stage rehearsals were well underway in London. A convoy of city-bound vehicles full of animals and keepers was headed up by Frank in his Colchester Zoo van which he had painted all over with zebra stripes. It turned many heads along the way and even the great Peter Hall himself was overheard saying upon their arrival that Frank's van ought to be regarded as a notable piece of early Pop Art.

Frank's readiness paid off. The RSPCA were in attendance at rehearsals and were satisfied that all was in order. His animals were calm and well behaved throughout rehearsals, though one of his keepers had to follow them around with a shovel and a spray bottle full of apple scent all day. One reporter said that Flora and the other animals learned their steps quickly and that soon it was the human performers who were getting in the animals' way and not the other way round.

The only auditionee who did not make it through the earliest rehearsals was Boris. His keepers took one look at the tilted stage and refused to allow him to take part for fear he would hurt himself. Chessington Zoo later supplied another smaller camel called Sheena, but it seems Sheena had been insufficiently prepared for she knocked down part of the stage and fell through some scenery. Camels were removed from the bill.

The rehearsals were, by this time, making headlines everywhere on account of a notorious blood-soaked semi-nude sacrificial orgy scene in the opera's second act, for which Peter Hall had engaged the services of a number of Soho strippers. One of Frank's old zookeepers remembers that whenever the first act was being rehearsed the stage wings would be quite empty, but as soon as the time came to rehearse the orgiastic second act there would be crowds of electricians, carpenters and stage-hands who had suddenly remembered jobs in the stage wings that simply could not wait, accompanied by all kinds of other well-heeled hangers-on who had come to praise the tenor's firm diction or Solti's rousing manipulation of the orchestra.

Frank's animals provoked almost as much public interest as Peter Hall's chilly ladies, even to the point where Solti himself complained, 'We want music publicity, not zoo publicity.' Unfortunately for Solti's ideals, but fortunately for the show's reception, Frank was an expert publicist, making the most of every press and photo opportunity in London and Colchester for his famous livestock, and so helping in his own small way to turn this production, long-expected to be a financial flop, into a popular and critical victory.

Frank's staff also worked hard to make the six performance nights flawless. Gillian Tucker, Frank's twenty-year-old bear keeper, recalled that it was 'hot work' passing goats to cast members on the stage, then leaping down some steps, crawling through a shallow tunnel backstage and bounding up a staircase in the opposite wing in time to collect the animals again.

It was an experience that left varying impressions on those zoo staff members who found themselves turned into the children of Moses on these nights. Sixty-three-year-old gardener George had lived in Birch on the outskirts of Colchester all his life, and most people believed the furthest he had ever travelled was to Colchester Zoo. Suddenly here he was, an ancient Israelite leading Flora the cow around the Queen's stage, surrounded by a chorus of 200 singers and watched by a pan-European audience, including Maria Callas, Zoltán Kodály and Sir William Walton. Afterwards, George would remark that it had all seemed like just a lot of singing and fuss, though the post-show buffet had been good.

Some people today, feeling safe in the knowledge that Frank's story was safely forgotten and would never be told, have since painted him as a man who knew little about animals. *Moses und Aron* proves otherwise: it was an exceedingly difficult work to produce and its first performance, in Zurich in 1957, had required more than 300 rehearsals. Given even a hint that Frank did not have the fullest control over his part of the operation, neither Peter Hall nor Georg Solti would have wasted five seconds in dismissing him. Indeed, the Colchester Zoo cast returned to Covent Garden in 1966 for the triumphant revival production to reprise their roles.

6

THE ZOO OF THE FUTURE

B Y THE MID-1960S, Frank was making huge amounts of money from his showbiz bookings and a great deal of that money went into building up the animal collection back at Colchester. In 1965 there were the additions of a pair of binturong, three alpaca, a large monitor lizard, capuchin and squirrel monkeys, a three-toed sloth, a Chartley calf, a pair of civets and a trio of ten-week-old bears from Whipsnade, who took over the Sugar Puffs duties, and the number of gibbons rose to eight.

The number of cheetah in the park grew to three with the arrival of a new female called Pussy, along with a male in the following September. Frank hoped his zoo would be the first in the world to breed cheetah but the keepers at Whipsnade appear to have been the ones to make this particular breakthrough, beating Colchester exactly two years later, in September 1967. Indeed, it would seem that although many cheetah cubs were bought and hand-reared by Colchester Zoo, the Farrars never successfully bred this species.

Between January and March 1965, Caroline III had moved on and had been replaced by two new elephants – a pair of Asian elephants named Moto and Toto. The collection was growing very large indeed and new facilities were going up accordingly. Frank had made plans for a purpose-built elephant house for the two newcomers (just inside the front gate on the right-hand side), which would include a parade ground surrounded by a dry moat to separate the elephants from the public but leaving no obstacles to viewing and photography. A pool had already been constructed for Colchester Zoo's four new Jackass penguins, and work would begin later in the year on a 'futuristic' glass-fronted monkey house. A huge glass case would also be built for a 25ft sacred python which Frank had bought in

Left Asian black bear cubs at Colchester Zoo in around 1966. (Colchester Zoo)

Below Frank's purpose-built elephant enclosure from the 1960s. Frank is pictured in the foreground. It is not clear which elephant is pictured, but it may be Moto or Toto. (Film, Photographic and Sound Services Ltd)

Malaysia after it had outgrown the altar in a temple in the state of Penang, where it had lived.

But Frank had bigger ideas than simply putting animals on show; many other attractions were appearing throughout the 1960s at Colchester Zoo. He applied for planning permission for a lecture room, to be used by the many teachers that brought school parties, and by the late 1960s he had also constructed an artists' studio, a Japanese garden and two exhibition halls. Furthermore, there was a large parade of amusements in the zoo, including mechanised rides for children and slot machines on a plot of land that Frank had leased to the Harrison family who would later own Clacton Pier.

By far the most spectacular of the non-zoological additions to the park was advertised as 'The World's Finest Model Railway'. This was the brainchild of one Bertram Otto, who had recently constructed the largest model railway ever assembled for the New York World's Fair of 1964. It had so impressed American President Lyndon B. Johnson that he had personally presented Mr Otto with a gold tiepin. Otto later sold the layout to a buyer for £15,000 (£250,000).

Otto's new project, at Colchester Zoo, opened to the public on Good Friday 1966. This model railway was an ambitious layout, measuring 72ft by 15ft, with one-and-a-half miles of track. Having taken two years and £6,000 (£100,000) to build, it showed an imaginative panorama of Western Europe, with 400 items of rolling stock buzzing about between scale models of iconic international landmarks such as Christopher Wren's Cathedral of St Paul in London, Gustave Eiffel's tower in Paris, and Frank Farrar's zoo in Colchester, all set amid farms, factories, towns, villages, mountains and rivers. There was a permanent controller in the form of one Arthur Pulfer, who would work on this railway for years, but there were also rows of buttons for children to press that worked certain parts of the landscape.

Also part of Bertram Otto's layout was a 'City of the Future', showing what Colchester and the rest of the world would look like in the distant year 2000. In the booklet that Otto produced to accompany the exhibition, he explained his prophecy. His future city stood on stilts, allowing trains and road traffic to pass freely underneath all the buildings and leaving plenty of space for parking, and there were helicopter and rocket-launch pads all over the cityscape. As part of the visionary theme of the display, a bridge joined England and France over the Channel. Mysterious rotating silver spheres were also seen all over the layout, which Otto said would control the weather, as well as absorb nuclear fallout and germs. Money would be

The 'France' section of Bertram Otto's 'World's Finest Model Railway' at Colchester Zoo in 1966. (S.C. Kershaw)

The final section of Bertram Otto's 'World's Finest Model Railway', showing 'The City of the Future' in Colchester Zoo, 1966. In Otto's own words: 'The City of the Future is no utopia: it is the logical extension of today's methods.' (S.C. Kershaw)

obsolete. Crime, too, would be a thing of the past in Otto's scheme since (rather alarmingly) the death penalty would be instantly applied for the slightest transgression.

Despite Mr Otto's personal quirks, his 'City of the Future' won the admiration of zoo visitors for it struck directly upon the mood of the moment. Colcestrians of the middle to late 1960s were looking forward to the coming years with a rare optimism. At about this time there was a popular exhibition running in the town centre, which was making all kinds of predictions about what Colchester would be like in a few hundred years. All that was required was to endure a short upheaval in the borough and eventually everyone would be consigned to a life of ease and comfort for all time. Colchester seemed to be moving forward and there was a genuine sense that it was people such as the Farrars who were taking it there. Just as Albert Sloman was building the university of the future on the east side of the town, so Frank was building the zoo of the future on the west.

Towards the end of the 1960s, Frank was putting the finishing touches to his great masterpiece that surrounded Stanway Hall. In 1966, as the collection began to expand into a truly regional attraction, the zoo ceased

The 'futuristic' monkey house at Colchester Zoo in the 1960s. (Colchester Zoo)

Helena appears with Joan Honisett and tiger cubs Tank and Rebel on television, probably in the 1960s. (Fred and Joan Honisett)

to describe itself as a 'twenty-five-acre' park and became 'forty-acre'. Throughout 1966, '67 and '68, Frank continued to draw huge crowds with each deluge of new inclusions to his collection. Among the hordes of newcomers were a new pair of orangutans from Borneo, Malabar giant squirrels, talapoin monkeys, moustached guenons, bateleur eagles, anacondas, Victoria crowned pigeons, Formosan sika deer, a toco toucan, a breeding trio of black leopards, a kinkajou, rheas and Cuban flamingos. New bears arrived, including a pair of week-old Asian black cubs called Dot and Dash, and a quartet of bear cubs from Whipsnade named, inevitably, John, Paul, George and Ringo.

These bear cubs provoked delight when they appeared in the new children's animal petting corner, which also contained creatures such as rabbits, miniature donkeys and prairie dogs. Many more animals were born at the zoo and shown off by Frank, including four skunks, a camel and a ring-tailed lemur. Old Chiefy became a father at the age of twelve with mum Winny to a pair of leopard cubs in October 1966. The big news at Colchester Zoo in 1966, however, was the arrival of Colchester Zoo's first tigers – a pair of female Bengals called Ranee and Ranjit. This was followed by the purchase of three tiger cubs around New Year 1967.

Next came the purchase of two lion cubs called Chinky and Buster, who were hand-reared by Helena through the early months of 1968. Zoo visitors

A lion cub at Colchester Zoo, probably in the late 1960s. (Fred and Joan Honisett)

Colchester Zoo's elephant enclosure, 1968. The animals pictured are Asian elephants Moto and Toto (a second is just visible on the extreme left). Both would soon leave the Stanway Hall collection. (V. Gray)

were later amused to see Helena looking like the ultimate mad cat lady as she sat with Chinky and Buster in their cage, which she had furnished with the sofas and carpets from Stanway Hall's living room, trying to ease the transition for them from house to cage. Helena had hoped to undertake a huge cleanout of the Hall after Chinky and Buster had been weaned. However, within weeks she had a new-born puma called Mogi living in the house, scrambling all over her chairs and tables and attacking her telephone and indeed anything and everything else.

These were blissful days at Colchester Zoo. Old friends and family started to come down from Southport to help out at the zoo. Frank's sister Mabel had started to visit in the holiday periods to see the animals again and work in the café, as had Frank's niece Angela who was by now a young woman. Joan and Fred Honisett had also by this time moved down from Southport to be near the Farrars again.

Right and below Christmas
with tiger cubs Tank and Rebel,
1960s. (Fred and Joan Honisett)

The good old days at Westbourne Road even seemed to put in reappearances, for Frank and Helena went on to spend every Christmas Day afternoon with the Honisetts in the well-to-do Colchester suburb of Lexden. Helena no doubt loved pulling up in her enormous Rolls-Royce and watching all the curtains twitch down the road as she and Frank jumped out with a chimp or a young lion, or whatever else happened to be bottle-feeding at the time and could not be left alone at Stanway Hall.

Frank was determined to see out this decade, which had been so good to him, with a bang. He finally stamped his mark for good on the borough with a giraffe house at Easter 1969. He had gone to Uganda in 1968 to locate some animals and had chosen a male Rothschild giraffe and a female Masai giraffe. By November, work was underway on their tall new brick and glass building with a fenced outside run, all said to cost £8,000 (£110,000). On 30 March 1969, visitors were introduced to Frank's pair of three-year-old giraffes as part of a gala event that lasted for most of the day. Frank had invited down two celebrities from Anglia's popular *Try For Ten* quiz show, Roz Early and David Hamilton (who later became a host on *Top of the Pops*). The crowds applauded and news cameras rolled as Miss Early, balancing on a ladder, pronounced the giraffe house open and promptly christened the male Roz and the female David.

Later that day, Colchester Carnival Queen Vivienne Bigg-Wither christened a pair of chimpanzees Boco and Coco. A well-known local naturalist called Joe Firmin also opened Colchester Zoo's large new aquarium, designed, built and stocked by keeper Ivor Williams, on the same day. People thought particularly highly of this new feature of the zoo, with its beautiful tropical fish collection which included vividly coloured fire eels. On this grand day, Colchester Zoo declared itself a place to be reckoned with. Having started life as the mealy-mouthed Stanway Hall Zoo Park, its official title was now the straightforward and bold Colchester Zoo and Aquarium.

This period saw the place start to bring in truly substantial numbers of visitors, which would result in the beginning of Frank's 'coffee mornings'. This was a private joke between Helena and Joan, for whenever they awoke to find forty packed coaches muscling their way into the car park, Frank would start hopping and fussing about everywhere with a frown on his face and generally making a nuisance of himself. Helena would give the nod and Joan would quietly make up a cup of coffee secretly laced with valium for Frank. After this, he would be out at the front, happily waving hello to everybody and letting half of the visitors in for nothing.

Joan Honisett outside the new giraffe house in 1969 or the early 1970s. (Fred and Joan Honisett)

The zoo's parrot aviary in the late 1960s. (Colchester Zoo)

Helena with a tiger cub in around 1969. (Joan and Fred Honisett)

From the late 1960s onwards, the zoo was making more than enough money to allow Frank to indulge in many acts of more sober generosity. Each year he would liaise with the London cab drivers' association to sacrifice a working day in order to bring poor children from the city up to Essex for a free day out with the animals. The spectacular sight of fifty black cabs drawing up on a hot summer's morning and disgorging hundreds of thrilled kids, with all the Cockney cabbies cheerfully failing to organise them, was a highlight of the zoo's calendar for many years.

Frank believed in the value of zoos for the wellbeing of children. One of his stated aims was that Colchester Zoo might one day form part of the education of every child in East Anglia. In this way, as in many others, Frank was somewhat ahead of his time. This was a period in which almost no one was demanding that zoos be places for conservation or education. Yet Frank, from the very moment of Colchester Zoo's inception, was repeatedly talking to the public about rare animals which were under threat from extermination, and trying to inform people about problems such as over-hunting, the ivory trade and even plant-life extinctions. He once killed stone-dead one of his many parties in Stanway Hall when he insisted on showing everyone a film he had made about whale hunting in the Far East.

A wishing well stood near Stanway Hall, from which all the coins were donated to animal charities. When a local branch of the World Wildlife Fund was set up, Frank ran a campaign day at the zoo for them at which more than £100 (£1,300) was raised, including a portion of the gate takings – not a bad sum considering that rain and high winds battered Colchester all that day. Frank had even gone on to raise funds to donate a jeep to the WWF.

He was also ahead of his time in being far more suspicious of animal circuses than most people of the day. Frank had certainly made a fortune out of his animals' film and television work but he was, as a general rule, against the idea of performing animals. A typical example of one of his animals' appearances can be seen in Walt Disney's *The Moon-Spinners*, a film in which cheetah Kinna simply lounges on a cushion in a couple of scenes with Hayley Mills.

Frank had dealt with circuses in the past, but into the 1960s and '70s he increasingly came to dislike anything that demeaned or excessively humanised animals. It is notable how little evidence there is in the history of Colchester Zoo of the kinds of costumes, tea parties and circus tricks that could be seen elsewhere in zoos all over the country. Such things were

Eight-year-old visitor Stephen Blaxland on the children's amusements on the eastern edge of Colchester Zoo, taken in the mid-1960s. Now retired from a career in the police service, Steve works as a train driver at the zoo today. Frank's zebra-stripe van is visible in the centre background. (Stephen Blaxland)

Helena with a lion cub in the late 1960s. (Fred and Joan Honisett)

much in demand, yet Frank's somewhat more enlightened approach was working nonetheless well. The crowds now pouring into his zoo had never been greater and the local reputation of the park was high.

This was the consummation of his life and work – a testament to what could be achieved with dogged determination and not a little audacity. Frank owed nothing to anyone save Helena. He had recently become a millionaire (at a time when £1m was a very serious quantity of money, perhaps equivalent to over £10m today) and had made it all through his own ingenuity, foresight and sheer hard work. Everyone who knew Frank says he gave the impression of being plugged directly into the mains, having the energy of three or four men. The characteristic image of him is of a man scurrying all over his zoo with his baggy old cardigan hanging round his knees, interfering in all the keepers' and builders' work, telling daft stories to his visitors, fetching out his animals from their cages for all the children to have a closer look, and generally coming up with new larks and schemes which would maintain Colchester Zoo's place on the map.

Frank understood his audience and knew that they wished to come to the zoo not only to look at animals, but also to feel that they were getting a good day out with many subsidiary diversions. One of the more impressive

The penguin pool at Colchester Zoo in the 1960s. Note the species sign that reads 'Humbolot's penguins' instead of Humboldt penguins. King penguins shared the pool with the Humboldts in the late 1960s. (Peter Jennings)

The tiger enclosure at the zoo, in around 1970. (Colchester Zoo)

Zoo visitors near the hornbill cage. (Peter Jennings)

of these sideshows, for instance, was a permanent exhibition that he later opened, comprising eleven paintings by local artist Charles Debenham (showing scenes from the Siege of Colchester during the Civil War) along with related historical artefacts.

Colchester Zoo had many such secondary attractions besides the animals, but the strangest of these was a replica blacksmith's shop, built near the zoo's entrance and produced with the greatest love and care. This new building was constructed around the trunk of a chestnut tree. Inside were lots of nineteenth-century tools and other equipment that Frank had collected, along with a bellows, anvil and fireplace. On one wall was a fixed plaque bearing Henry Wadsworth Longfellow's poem, 'The Village Blacksmith'. In March 1968, Frank invited Lord and Lady Hill of Wivenhoe to open it officially.

Colchester Zoo had other similar attractions but these were either of general interest, such as the main exhibition centre with its antique bicycles, guns and preserved butterflies, or had been entirely created and run by other people, such as the model railway and the children's amusements. Why were none so specific and carried out with such attention to detail as this smithy? Frank was a well-read man; he was keenly interested in history and in the usage of words, and would have been quite aware that the name Farrar derived of old from the profession of farrier, or horse-shoer, which was at one time identical to that of blacksmith. Frank had, in effect, autographed his masterpiece.

In 1970 everything came together for one perfect season at the zoo; visitor numbers had been rising year on year and media interest was stronger than it had ever been, thanks to the new tigers and giraffes, as well as a huge number of novel additions to the animal collection, of which the most intriguing were a snake-necked turtle, a tamandua and a welter of truly stunning birds, including hornbills, a trio of king penguins, a vermilion cardinal and the charismatic red-crested turaco. Many births, including three puma cubs, attracted much attention at this time. Suzie, a black leopard, had also given more than one litter through 1969 and 1970, of which some of the cubs had been raised by Helena in the Hall, including

Baby African elephants Moto and Toto in around 1969. They are not to be confused with the Asian elephants of the same names that they replaced at the end of the 1960s. (Colchester Zoo)

Joan Honisett with a lion cub on the Stanway Hall lawn in the 1970s. (Fred and Joan Honisett)

a pair called Princess and Whiskers who had been rejected by their mother in May 1969.

But the real headlines were grabbed by a new guest of Frank and Helena – named Nyoka – whose arrival early in 1970 made Colchester Zoo one of the hottest tickets in East Anglia. And it certainly was hot. An intense summer heat settled over Essex into May and beyond, which would soon leave farmers praying for rain. The previous April had been the wettest for thirty-eight years, and people were more than eager to take advantage of the fierce sun and were attracted in droves to Colchester Zoo to see the enigmatic 'Jungle Man' Nyoka, who was receiving wall-to-wall coverage in local newspapers and television programmes.

Visitors were amazed by this broad-shouldered, muscular man, with a carefully honed 'white hunter' image, who would some days appear to his audiences as a hulking figure in a torn black trench-coat and wide-brimmed hat. Sometimes he would appear in leather boots, gold-trimmed jodhpurs and colourful, loose shirts with striking patterns. On the hottest days he would be naked but for a pair of trunks and a long ceremonial dagger hanging from a wide belt. Nyoka was an imposing character with distinctive features, a finely clipped pencil moustache and long, jet-black

'Jungle Man' Nyoka, Easter 1970. (Sheila May)

hair slicked back with oil. To a 1970 eye, he was a fascinating creature, perhaps animal-like himself and certainly reeking of exoticism and danger.

He had been in residence at Colchester Zoo since March, unaccountably having had to leave the Isle of Wight's Sandown Zoo in a hurry. He had brought with him his personal collection of animals, including an alligator, five leopards, two pumas, an ocelot, a margay, a civet and eight snakes, including a 27ft python called Cassius. Of all of Nyoka's animals, the one to win most interest was Simba, a male lion that Nyoka had caught as a six-month-old cub on the Serengeti in 1959. Simba had since grown into an extraordinarily large beast and Frank was quick to get the Guinness World Records team down to the zoo. In July that year, Simba was recorded as weighing nearly 60 stone and standing over 3ft at the shoulder – he remains in the record books to this day.

By this time, Frank and Helena were tied up with a lot of administrative work. Their park was receiving thousands of visitors each month. Like many towns in the area, the population of Colchester was continuing to explode, having risen by nearly 2,000 people every year for the last seven years, and many newcomers to East Anglia were finding their way to Stanway Hall. Car culture was also beginning to take over Britain. When Colchester Zoo

Nyoka's lion, Simba, who came to live at Colchester Zoo at the start of the 1970s. (Fred and Joan Honisett)

opened in 1963, over 60 per cent of households had no car at all; in 1970 the law now stated that each new-built house had to include parking space for two cars. As new and superior roads opened up, visitors were found to be regularly coming to the zoo from distant, alien places such as Bedford and King's Lynn.

It was rare that Frank or Helena any longer found time to show off their animals personally as they had done in years past. Nyoka filled this gap. He entertained endless crowds all through the summer, playing his African drums, telling stories about his jungle travels and frequently entering the cages of his animals to play with them. Various films of Colchester Zoo at the time show Nyoka hugging his pumas, or wrestling with a pair of young adult tigers, or crouching while a black leopard leaps on his back. A BBC news clip shows him kissing Kinna, playing with Helena's tiger cubs, showing off one of his smaller snakes and standing in Simba's cage, feeding him milk from a bottle, all the while surrounded by amazed crowds of people.

Nyoka caused a sensation. Across four days over the Spring bank holiday in late May 1970, Colchester Zoo boasted record crowds of almost 45,000 – perhaps about a third of all the visitors it had received in its entire first year. There was a permanent queue of cars for a mile in each direction. Frank later told the papers that, but for the help of the police that year, the zoo simply would not have coped with its own success.

7

HYBRIDS

NYOKA – REAL NAME Adrian Darley – presents a tragic figure in hindsight. Here was a highly intelligent, powerful personality with a ready laugh and an ingenuous love of animals and people. Yet he could not find his place in life. Having been born into a circus family he had one foot firmly in the past, in a culture that was, at that very moment, being swept away. On the other hand he was remarkably forward-looking, taking deep pride in his self-imposed ban on using force or weapons while working with his animals.

Had Nyoka been born forty years earlier he would have made a fine circus ringmaster. Had he been born forty years later he might readily have become an animal psychologist or slotted easily into a modern zoo with today's informed animal training methods. As it was, he was condemned to be neither one thing nor another and would continue to live an itinerant lifestyle, before demonstrating that a talent for animal-handling alone is insufficient for understanding the business of keeping animals in captivity. He ended his career running one of the most lamentable zoos in the country, at Knaresborough, and is said to have died in squalor.

Nyoka left Colchester for a zoo in Nottingham around New Year 1971. Frank was everyone's friend and had been happy to put up him and his wife and animals for a time at Colchester Zoo after they had left Sandown. Frank had predicted that Nyoka would provide excellent publicity for the zoo and had been proved right. He had, however, been uneasy about what Nyoka represented and had sent him on his way after about ten months.

The irony was that Frank was just as conflicted as Nyoka, but in different ways. Frank was happy to get the publicity accorded to reports of Nyoka walking around Colchester Zoo with Helena's tigers slung over

Nyoka in the late 1960s.
(Fred and Joan Honisett)

his shoulders, but still entertained ambitions that his park would become a highly respected conservation centre. Frank wanted his zoo to be the greatest in East Anglia, in Britain, indeed, in Europe, but he was not willing to re-invest the huge sums of money necessary to achieve this. He wanted his zoo to be educational yet lacked the necessary insight to achieve this with any consistency.

David Grist has since said that Frank seemed to be a man searching for something but who could never quite find it. He was still the dreamer sat at his desk at Knights National, imagining great things for his zoo but proving surprisingly unsuited to working out a structured plan of how he might achieve his goals. Frank was a man of impulse and action – a professional amateur whose hobby had grown out of all proportion. Though he was no one's fool and though his formidable instincts carried him far, he could never fully translate his ideas into reality and the results of his efforts often fell between stools.

Seemingly symbolic, now, of the beginning of the zoo's decline was the birth of the first of its three famous zedonks. Frank claimed that Colchester

An adult zedonk at Colchester Zoo in the mid-1970s. (Russell Tofts)

was the first zoo in the world to have this animal – others disputed this. Then again, other zoos with this type of hybrid variously called them zebra mules, zebra hinnies, even deebras and donkras, amongst other names. Moreover, some used the spelling 'zeedonk', so there is in fact a very good chance that Frank's zedonk was, after all, unique in 1971. Whatever the case, this hybrid was certainly unusual in the world and all but unheard of in Britain. There was a great deal of interest in the international press, especially in America. Television programmes such as *Blue Peter* are reported to have run features on this curious new Colcestrian.

Colchester's first zedonk appears to have been Sandy, born in April 1971, followed by Shadow in 1973 and Mary who was born in Christmas week 1975. Sandy had surprised and delighted everyone in equal measure. Staff and visitors alike were amazed at this fluffy, playful little brown horsey thing strutting about in two pairs of zebra-stripe stockings. She had been an accident: a zebra stallion had been put in the same pen as a donkey mare. Today there are controls on crossbreeding in British zoos, in order to protect conservation efforts. Ironically enough, Colchester's first zedonk appears to have been a side effect of this new conservation ethic that was then emerging in British zoology.

Up to this time, one John Knowles had made a very good living from chicken farming and had decided to use his money to preserve endangered species. While setting up his own zoo, Marwell, in Hampshire, in the first years of the 1970s, he developed close ties with Frank, spending a great deal of time working at Colchester Zoo and learning how to run a commercially successful park. (Both men were exceedingly wealthy and one of Frank's favourite games was to put a white coat on John and watch him argue over pennies with punters at the front gate.)

Those who were there at the time remember that Frank taught John a great deal about how to run a zoo, sharing his knowledge freely. John would later be critical of the Farrars but it is a fact that without a business-minded dealer like Frank (for all his flaws) who had the overseas connections, the handling experience and the space in his own zoo to hold animals temporarily, then a place such as Marwell Zoological Park would have found it harder to get off the ground.

John had decided that his new zoo was going to specialise in hoofstock, and he turned to people such as Frank to help him round-up endangered species from all over the world in order to create Marwell. It would seem that it was because space was tight at Colchester Zoo in these earliest years of the 1970s (owing to all the rare oryx, Przewalski's horses and suchlike who were passing through to Marwell) that animals like Frank's own zebras and donkeys, for instance, were forced to bunk up together – with odd results like little Sandy.

The unseen truth lurking somewhere in all this is that it was gradually becoming apparent by this time that Colchester Zoo itself was turning out to be one big zedonk. As with little Sandy, the zoo had many admirers – people appreciated the novelty of it all and flocked to see it – but it was also becoming clear that the zoo, like Sandy (and Nyoka and Frank), was a hybrid. It remained principally a tourist destination but would increasingly fail to cater for these tourists, who would start to drop away through the 1970s. Some of John Knowles' idealism evidently rubbed off on Frank, for in 1973 Colchester Zoo would start to advertise itself briefly as a 'game reserve', but attempts to move in this direction were half-hearted at best. Furthermore, Frank wanted his zoo to be a serious conservation centre, but had no clear scheme in mind, nor even any system by which breeding was properly organised.

The lower end of Colchester Zoo at Easter 1970. (Sheila May)

More significantly, just like Sandy and the other two zedonks, Frank's zoo proved ultimately to be sterile. After a spectacular birth in the 1960s, the 1970s at Colchester Zoo were an anti-climax and a time of recession, as the diminishing returns of mere novelty started to dwindle away. But just as the days continue to grow hotter for a while after Midsummer's Day, there remained, for a short time at least, the illusion that Frank's zoo had not already passed its best.

In 1972 there was renewed interest in the zoo, when it received its first rhinos. Since 1963, Frank and Helena had been promising the town that they would bring in this species. In 1967 they had been offered a pair for £12,000 (£170,000), which seems to have been slightly too steep a price at the time. The Farrars later went to inspect a rhino herd in 1968 but the search for giraffes seems to have taken precedence by that time. At last, after an eighteen-day visit to Africa at the invitation of the South African authorities, the summer of 1972 saw Frank undertake perhaps his largest-ever animal deal, as he shipped fifteen white rhinos out of Africa and into London.

Frank had lost none of his ability to catch people's attention – a national dock strike was running and hardly any cargo was being moved at Britain's ports, so Frank's rhinos were now stranded in the Thames. Newspapers were reporting that it would not be possible to get enough food out to them by helicopter. It was, in Frank's own words, a 'massive problem' (quite literally). But the nation's 42,000 picketing dockers had clearly not bargained on the word-wise Frank, who managed to persuade a sufficient number of them to open the London docks just long enough for all the rhinos to get safely to shore.

Most of them were bound for other zoos, but a pair named Malinda and Gigantus (possibly along with one other young rhino – maybe Flossy), arrived in Colchester Zoo on the evening of 7 August 1972. On the following day they were introduced to their public; 250 balloons were released as the rhinos were let into their new enclosure, which consisted of a brick hut and a low fence running around the outside, and allowed for visitors to stroke them and feed them grass from the opposite bank.

Among the other interesting new species to come to the zoo in 1972 were Malaysian flying foxes, knife-fish, two Chinese water dragons, a moray eel and a group of six-legged tortoises. There was also talk of receiving turtles, seahorses, sea bats and an octopus, but international diplomatic problems with the supplier country of Malta seem to have prevented this. The new rhinos were, however, the last real coup for Colchester Zoo. The whole project had gone about as far as it could under Frank's vision and the freshness of the zoo was beginning to fade.

The visitor amenities remained basic and many of the original buildings, which had been quickly knocked together in the spring of 1963, were starting to show their age. Larger numbers of 'repeats' crept into the collection such as new cheetahs, lions, monitor lizards and so forth. Some interest was raised by a new 28ft python which Frank claimed was the longest ever shown to the world's public, but people had already seen all this sort of thing at Colchester Zoo and, having come to expect endless novelties there, were beginning to wonder about the point of returning from season to season. Frank tried his best to drum up renewed interest but since he was offering no new ways of seeing or understanding his animals, his public were slowly becoming bored.

A rather pathetic note is now struck in the story of Colchester Zoo. Crowds continued to come to the zoo into the mid-1970s, but Frank seemed to realise that numbers were dropping and that he was running out of striking new species to show off. He then forced himself to pursue the impossible and, late in 1972, he began writing to China's leader, Chairman Mao, asking for giant pandas. There had been no such animals in Britain since Chi-Chi had died at London Zoo in the previous July, and Frank knew that a pair of these animals at Colchester would keep feet passing through his gate. He did, however, humbly admit that he would probably be put behind Moscow Zoo and London on the waiting list.

Frank received no reply but was undaunted and continued to write to Mao. By 1974 he was appealing to Mao's communist sensibility by pointing out that it would benefit the people of Colchester, who he described as being mainly working class, and that he was even willing to negotiate the allowance of free entry to pensioners and children on Mondays. Mao was unfortunately still rather tied up with producing China's first generation of orbital satellites and nuclear submarines, and Frank continued to receive no reply.

In July 1974, Frank began to plan a trip to south-east Asia and told the Colchester newspapers that on his way through he would drop by to see Mao, saying, 'As I am going to Indonesia anyway, I could easily pop into China and see if I could chase them up a bit.' Those who knew Frank say he would have pestered God himself on the telephone if only someone might have given him the number.

In fairness to him, Frank seems to have been quite serious about the idea, having ear-marked £50,000 (£500,000) for payment. It is nonetheless inescapable that his desire for pandas was poorly considered and stemmed from an unsound aspiration. Frank gave himself away in a statement to the press when he said his motive for wanting giant pandas was because Colchester Zoo had 'got just about everything else'. In other words, the sticker album was nearly full. There were few options remaining among the kinds of animals people wished to see and Frank had no will or capacity to recast the purpose of his zoo from the bottom up.

Frank never did get his giant pandas. These animals were (and still are) given as diplomatic gifts by the Chinese authorities to world leaders and nation states, and not to people such as Frank Farrar. His futile attempt speaks volumes about Colchester Zoo in the 1970s. In one respect his energy and determination had played against him. Had Frank been a slower and less enterprising person it might have taken him twenty years or more to work his way through all the most visually striking members of the animal kingdom, which might even have been sufficient time to start another round of the circle of life afresh. Instead, he had been down to the end of each avenue of his limited ambition within just a decade at Stanway Hall. At least one national zoo reviewer in the late 1970s remarked on the speed with which Colchester had amassed its enormous collection of animals. There was nowhere left for Frank to go.

Even though the zoo's star was falling, its reputation would remain, for a time, artificially high, simply for the reason that it was falling more slowly than other parts of Colchester. In the first half of the 1970s the zoo was one of the few parts of the town that the majority of Colcestrians could generally agree was a source of civic pride. Whether fair or not, the long-revered garrison was the subject of some discord, as Colcestrians divided over the local army's real and perceived connection to the military mobilisation in Northern Ireland from 1969 onward. The garrison became the target, rightly or wrongly, of considerable anger from certain quarters after Bloody Sunday, when more than a dozen unarmed people were shot dead (and many more grievously wounded) in Ireland by British soldiers in January 1972.

Before the mid-1970s, the University of Essex had suffered much bad publicity year after year, as endless reports emerged about student disorder – rumours, as well as confirmed stories, emerged of brawls during meetings and lectures, of staff strikes, of sit-in occupations, repeated invasions of the vice-chancellor's office, widespread drug abuse, arson, terrorist bomb plots and even Satanic rituals.

One day, 600 University of Essex students clashed with 250 police officers, who then went on to make ninety-four arrests for affray. A local newspaper carried a photograph on its front page of a student punching a professor in the face. By 1974, one MP was suggesting that the place ought to be shut down for two years and turned into an agricultural college. If anyone could have foreseen that the University of Essex would, by the twenty-first century, come to be ranked officially among the very best educational establishments in Britain and seen as a world-leader in academic research, it might then have seemed like a very long time away. Indeed, had anyone in the 1970s been able to see that Colchester as a whole would, towards the end of the century, become a hugely prosperous town with the lowest crime rate in the country, it would have seemed laughable. Many of the great schemes for the town's regeneration, dreamed up in the 1950s and '60s, had run out of money by the 1970s – but not before lots of building sites and major roadworks had been started and then abandoned. An editorial in the *Essex County Standard* in 1972 read: 'Not since Boadicea left the place a smoking ruin has the Colchester area been such a depressing mess.'

At this time, Colchester Zoo was one of the few exceptional places in the town. It was able to trade on its original (if waning) glories as 'East Anglia's

Own Zoo' and attendance was still good, if increasingly intermittent. At Easter 1973 the zoo received a record number of visits, with a tailback of cars stretching from the zoo's gates to halfway down Straight Road in Lexden, and the place remained profitable.

Nonetheless, Colchester Zoo could not forever avoid the miseries of the 1970s, which eventually contributed to slowing down its existing rate of activity as Frank, Helena and their staff struggled, like everyone else, to simply keep things going. The refusal of Middle Eastern oil-producing nations to provide certain Western nations with oil, along with related price hikes between October 1973 and March 1974, quadrupled the price of petrol almost overnight and caused a serious upset in the international economy. This situation posed stern logistical and financial problems for Colchester Zoo and Frank's animal trading business, just as it did for everyone else in Britain.

The many power cuts, which Britain endured in the early 1970s due to industrial protests, were also affecting everyone. The people of Colchester, like all other Britons, were frequently forced to shop by candlelight and to eat cold dinners in the quiet and the dark, wrapped in woollen layers. For many it felt like a return to the privations of the war years, only without any of the proud sense of national purpose and sacrifice that Winston Churchill had inspired.

All the wonderful electric stoves, radios, televisions, lamps and heating systems which had been bought in great numbers in the 1960s, with the promise that such things were the way into the future, were now lying useless for much of the time in people's houses. Factories, like Colchester Lathe, were having to leave their machines idle, and the university was forced to reschedule a great number of lectures and other events. For many people it was simply a case of waiting in boredom until the power returned. Patience, however, meant nothing at Colchester Zoo, where animals that depended on strong heat for their survival were under threat of suffering and death.

There was particular concern for the tropical fish in Ivor Williams' large, twenty-four-tank aquarium, for their survival relied not only on heaters but also on electrical water pumps. It was ironically fortunate that the power had accidentally been cut off to the zoo briefly during the winter of 1970-71, due to bad weather, for Frank now happened to be fairly well prepared for a repeat. From 1972 onward, when the electricity started going off for up to thirty-six hours a week at various times, Colchester Zoo had a ready

Helena with a cub, possibly in 1975. (Photocall Features)

stock of emergency gas tanks which could be placed strategically in and around the houses of the various animals who were likely to suffer most from the cold, such as the giraffes and the small mammals.

Other animals received extra-deep bedding and hot-water bottles. By the mid-1970s, Frank's staff were experts at warming animals and had become adept even at giving warm baths to the reptiles. Such things were doubtless a drain on the energy of Frank and Helena, who worked no less hard than their keepers to deal with these sorts of problems. Such was their devotion to their animals that they even took to sleeping with the lights on in Stanway Hall during the 1970s so that they would know straightaway if power was lost, and so get up and start creeping about in the cold dark, lighting the paraffin heaters under the fish tanks and so forth.

There were many other challenges to be met as the zoo moved towards the end of the decade. The most grievous for the future of the zoo was the fact that Frank no longer had a captive audience. National changes were each causing slight reductions in the zoo's visitor numbers and cumulatively were resulting in considerable loss.

Screen culture in particular was beginning to take hold, prompting people to stay indoors at the slightest hint of wind or rain to watch the box instead. Television went colour in 1967, and there was a continuing growth in the number of programmes available. Television sales had received a considerable boost during the preparations for the moon landing of 1969, for no one wanted to miss seeing that event. When Colchester Zoo had first opened, there had been only two television channels in Colchester and they were closed for much of the day. But by the late 1960s, one began to see references to the 'box-ridden' (an early version of 'telly addict'), as television sets began to become commonplace and broadcasting became more diverse and widespread.

Another of the 'new' Colchester's deadly forces working against Frank's zoo was the final victory of consumerism: shopping as a pastime or a way of life. Mass consumerism had already flourished briefly in the 1920s (satirised mercilessly in Aldous Huxley's novel, *Brave New World*) before being intruded upon by economic problems and war. It had then started to make a comeback in the 1960s, but was once again thwarted by recession and widespread industrial action in the 1970s. Consumerism began to make its final, victorious push after the economically morale-boosting commencement in 1975 of extraction from the vast Forties oil field in the North Sea, upon which Britain became an oil-exporting nation for a time.

The resultant British consumer boom, which would last almost uninterrupted until the global crash of 2008, first began to show its head in Colchester in 1978, with the opening of the new £7m (£36m) pedestrianised Lion Walk shopping parade in the town centre. Such places would eventually present a serious problem for Frank and Helena, for lengthy shopping excursions were starting to become a new form of entertainment for people who might otherwise have spent their days off at the zoo. There remained some comfort for the Farrars, inasmuch as most shops were then still forbidden to open on Sundays. But it meant that another portion of their old captive audience was steadily being nibbled upon.

Other features of the 'new' Colchester (which were snapping up money and time that would otherwise perhaps have been spent at the zoo) included the Mercury, a first-rate hyper-modern repertory theatre, which had opened in May 1972 and was receiving a very positive reaction. Another major addition to the town, which would jostle with Frank's zoo for trade, arrived in February 1975, when Colchester's first proper public swimming pool finally opened. It was a huge hit and was receiving 1,000 people each day by March.

And there were other forms of competition for people's time and money appearing. Having collectively vowed never to endure another winter like 1962-63, people had begun to explore air travel package holidays, which had been on offer for some years. To their delight, they found that such things were cheaper and easier than they had imagined, and they started to flee abroad in the following years. A further catalyst came at the end of the 1960s, when the British government suddenly scrapped the limit on the amount of money a person could take out of the country on holiday. By the mid-1970s, Britons had even started taking sunny foreign holidays during summer. This was not good news for provincial places like Colchester, which have never received a compensating number of foreign tourists, with incoming visitors generally remaining in international centres such as London and Edinburgh.

Any benefit Frank might have had after 1966, when it had been announced that two-and-a-half miles of Clacton seafront were to be closed for a couple of years while new sea defences were built, was no longer extant. Indeed, by 1971 Frank was actively losing visitors to Clacton, which by then boasted a dolphinarium which Reg Bloom had built on the pier and which had quickly become an essential part of the itinerary of many holidaymakers in north-east Essex in the 1970s. Bloom's ability to make headlines as far away as Colchester rivalled Frank's own talent for publicity, and Clacton's dolphin pool would become one of the most obvious sources of competition for Colchester Zoo for many years.

Clacton Dolphinarium was only one of Frank's zoological headaches, for there was a plethora of zoos now available to Colcestrians besides the one at Stanway Hall. When Colchester Zoo had first opened, its only direct competition had been the Natural History Museum at the bottom of Colchester High Street, which had a collection of live animals on show, including, from time to time, eels, frogs, toads, newts, adders, grass snakes, slow-worms, woodpeckers, grey squirrels, ferrets, mice, a mole rat and a badger.

By the end of the 1970s, however, there were much more serious zoological threats to Frank's zoo everywhere. Some of these places had long been around but higher numbers of car ownership and enhanced road connections saw Frank's old audience being able to pick and choose. Vange Zoo, Mole Hall Wildlife Park, Linton Zoo, Banham Zoo, Cromer Zoo, Chessington Zoo and others were now tapping freely into this particularly dense base of punters at Colchester on which Frank had so efficiently been drawing in the 1960s. Even places such as Royal Windsor Safari Park on the other side of London were now advertising in north-east Essex.

When Woburn Safari Park, less than two hours away by car, opened in 1970 with widespread and robust marketing, even those Colcestrians merely reading the newspaper adverts over the following years would have started to recognise what a truly provincial little park Colchester Zoo now seemed in contrast. Where Frank had Stanway Hall, they had Woburn Abbey; where Frank had a couple of neat little exhibition halls filled with the things which had caught his eye on his travels, Woburn had exhibitions of fine paintings, porcelain, silver and furniture; where Frank had tropical fish in tanks, they had a dolphinarium; and where Frank had a little franchised gift shop, an amusement arcade and an electric train set, Woburn had a garden centre and a model village, as well as a boating lake, a children's playground, a cable lift, a golf course and even a miniature railway exhibition of its own. Moreover, Woburn had just about all the animal species Frank had, but housed in what was advertised as Europe's largest drive-through game reserve.

Putting all of this together, one may say that by the end of the 1970s Colchester Zoo was starting to look like yesterday's news. Life in the 1960s for the Farrars had been easy by comparison and their zoo had been successfully swept along by the sheer exuberance of it all. The fact that they had made no serious attempt to develop the zoo wholesale after it had been founded was now starting to become all too clear, and the project became hampered by decreasing footfall at the gate, set against a backdrop of some serious economic difficulties in the country at large.

The opportunity to make a substantial reinvestment in the zoo had been missed, and now the park would find itself locked into a spiral of falling revenue, falling standards, falling reputation and, most significantly of all, the retreating vitality of the ageing Frank and Helena. Unfortunately, the decline was just steady enough to go all but unnoticed by the people working there, for whom each little drop in quality or interest in Colchester Zoo would be successively accepted as the normal way of things.

However, just as the world was turning away from Colchester Zoo so, too, was the zoo turning its back on the world. In the late 1970s, Frank allowed his memberships of the British Federation of Zoos and of the National Society of Zoos to lapse. He referred obliquely in a statement around this time to having lost patience with a spat that had been going on between the Federation and the Society, and having therefore left both by choice. Some people contrarily accused him of having been kicked out. Whatever the case, it is clear that Colchester Zoo was becoming isolated and introverted at the very moment when it was starting to need all the friends it could get.

8

BREEZE BLOCKS
AND CHICKEN WIRE

RANK'S FAVOURITE ANIMALS of all in the 1970s were three sweet-natured adult orangutans called Guy, Prissy and Lola. He would often go into their enclosure to play-wrestle and roll about with them. Film footage shows Frank walking them among zoo visitors around Stanway Hall's lawn. This species had lived at Colchester from the very beginning, but had always been housed in a building more suited to small monkeys rather than great apes. If any animals in the park were going to have their accommodation improved, it was these orangutans.

Frank completed and opened a new building for them in the summer of 1972. A young zookeeper called Jeremy Keeling came to work at the zoo shortly afterwards, and remembers that this new enclosure seemed rather futuristic and was adequate, by the standards of the day, for both the animals to live in and for the keepers to work in. It gave the animals more space to climb and was fronted with expensive toughened glass instead of bars. (This was, incidentally, Jeremy's first contact with orangutans, which led, in part, to his co-founding of the remarkable Monkey World animal sanctuary in Dorset.)

Sadly, even this seems to have been one of very few examples of Frank replacing and upgrading an existing major structure at Colchester Zoo, when, in fact, the whole park badly needed rebuilding. The zoo had been built in a hurry as the awful snows had begun to melt in early 1963. Moreover, most of the town's builders and plant machinery had been otherwise occupied building the university on the other side of town around that time. Many of the zoo's buildings appear, therefore, to have been created as temporary structures, simply thrown up to get the park going. Certainly, there had been very little attempt to make the buildings either suitable for the animals or attractive to the eyes of passing visitors.

Members of Colchester Zoo's orangutan family, in around 1971. It is impossible to identify them specifically. (Colchester Zoo)

Rajah's lion house was a bare breeze-block cube standing in a flat, empty run. The leopard enclosure looked like the concreted backyard of a pre-war terraced house. The areas for Frank's hoofstock at the lower end of the park were somewhat more satisfactory, with large spaces for grazing, but the fences were shallow, weak and unsafe.

The conditions under which Frank's builders had to work were frequently far from ideal. A carpenter named Maurice Birch once found himself up a wobbly 18ft ladder in one of the animal cages, trying to knock some nails through a panel of wire mesh that had come apart, while a pair of amorous gibbons sat on his shoulders, rubbing themselves vigorously against his neck. Frank was merely in fits of laughter at the bottom of the ladder: 'You're doing a grand job, love!'

COLCHESTER ZOO

Souvenir with plan

Cover of a Colchester Zoo guidebook of about 1977. The identity of the orangutan pictured is not known: the late 1970s saw a number of males enter and/or leave the collection, including Guy, David and Adam. (Colchester Zoo)

This sort of thing was common and meant that Frank's men were often forced to produce sub-standard work in a hurry. Cliff Fairweather remembers Frank asking him to build a den for Kinna inside her enclosure. Cliff had already met Kinna on the opening day some time previously but did not consider her a boon companion and was wary at the prospect of having to work with her inside the open-top cage. Cliff was digging out a hole in the ground, over which he intended to construct a timber platform that would offer Kinna shelter from the sun and rain, when he noticed out of the corner of his eye Kinna suddenly crouch down, looking straight at him. Cliff knew of her temper and imagined that his final hour had arrived. He could see Kinna's shoulder blades rippling up and down as she crept forward an inch and then another inch, preparing to pounce. He knew if he tried to outrun Kinna to the cage door she would be on him in seconds and so he froze, kneeling, with his grip tightening around the shaft of his spade. Then, before Cliff could react, Kinna shot out and jumped clear over him, snatching a golden pheasant cleanly from out of the air over his head.

These kinds of experiences were not conducive to building a zoo slowly and with care. Furthermore, Frank was always looking for ways to cut building costs. Roland Touzell remembers the first home Frank provided for the sea lions. He simply hired a mechanical digger, dug a huge pit in the ground and filled it with water. Roland, scratching his head, expressed reservations: 'Surely we should concrete the pool, Frank?' Frank replied: 'No, no; that'll be alright, love.' Of course, when the sea lions were released into the enclosure the first thing they did was dive straight into the water and thrash about with glee until the whole thing looked like a gigantic mug of frothy hot chocolate. It never seemed to bother the sea lions much but all their visitors could often see was the odd whiskered nose appearing briefly above the surface of the muddy water.

Frank did eventually concrete the pool and there was no real harm done but this type of thriftiness caused more serious concerns elsewhere. When they were first constructed, buildings like the giraffe house were considered acceptable for animal habitation by visitors, but Frank's contractors had a different point of view. For instance, instead of wasting money and time on buying girders of the right length for the construction of such buildings, Frank would make his men weld shorter, salvaged girders together – an almost hilariously dangerous practice and not in the least justified once the early years of penury at Colchester Zoo were over.

Kinna's enclosure at Colchester Zoo, November 1963. (Sheelagh Marron)

The first sea lion pool at Colchester Zoo, October 1963. (Sheelagh Marron)

One ought not to be overly critical of Frank in this respect, for, again, he was very much a product of the age. Building regulations were comparatively loose in those days and many of the other new buildings put up around the Colchester area during the 1960s and 1970s turned out to be expensive follies. (One thinks, for instance, of the vast and penetratingly ugly Queen Street multi-storey car park which was opened to great fanfare in 1972, declared unsafe within just a few years and pulled down in 1995 after many years of dereliction.)

Frank was different in one important way, however. Unlike the public coffers of bankrupt 1970s Britain, his own personal wealth was considerable. Sadly, his money was not going into the zoo in the way it ought to have done. His makeshift structures had come to be thought of as permanent. He had created just enough new buildings in the 1960s and into the early 1970s – one or two of them being fairly impressive, such as the extensive monkey house – to give the impression that serious reinvestment was going on, but even that money should really have gone into upgrading or replacing the existing, unimaginative compounds in which so many of his creatures had been living for years.

Frank's false economies meant that after just a short time many of the buildings in the zoo were starting to fall apart. One of the results was a huge number of animal escapes in the 1960s and 1970s, for the enclosures were simply not strong enough to contain them, nor designed according to the abilities of the animals in question. A porcupine that had burrowed out of the zoo in late 1964 eventually turned up three miles away, in a front garden in Monkwick Avenue. There were mysteries, too. One morning it seemed that Nellie the emu had simply melted away into the air overnight. Frank was at a loss to explain it – theft would have required a truck and a team of men with access to the zoo. Yet, Frank asked, if she had simply escaped, how could a 6ft flightless bird depart the district with no one spotting her? (The mystery was never solved.)

Again, in the early days, Colcestrians looked upon many of these escapes with good humour. One of the most celebrated fugitives was Wally the wallaby who disappeared from the zoo in October 1963, and it was not long before he was seen munching on grass near Mersea Road. By May 1964 he had been sighted in Fingringhoe. For years afterwards, Wally was spotted at random intervals by surprised locals, eventually becoming quite well known in the area. When he was finally killed by a car full of party-goers late one night near Abberton, locals seemed disappointed – not because of the zoo's cool attitude to security, but because it meant the end of tales of Wally ambushing the army on manoeuvres in Friday Woods, or throwing the Essex and Suffolk Hunt off their trails.

Some of the escapes were regarded with similar bemusement, such as in August 1973 when a flamingo flew away before its wing had been clipped, and Frank ended up chasing it in a blow-up dinghy around a lake in a Mersea Island caravan park. It is not uncommon for a bird to miss being clipped and vanish, but this sort of thing was routine at Colchester Zoo in those days. Other examples of a lack of proper planning led to unexpected dramas: despite all the careful measurements which Frank had made to ensure that the new orangutan enclosure would be secure, he did not, it seems, account for the eventuality that Guy, Prissy and Lola would work together, giving each other a leg-up to get out.

Despite the comedy pertaining to some of these chaotic stories, many escapes ended in sadness, such as when a six-month-old pygmy donkey named Michael disappeared from his enclosure in March 1974 and was found much later elsewhere in the zoo, in a large hollow tree stump into which he had fallen and broken his neck. Other animals came to similarly unpleasant ends, but some escapees presented a serious danger to the people of Colchester themselves.

In May 1978, a big stir was caused when a 1,600lb young male American buffalo called Bill escaped from the zoo. His accomplice, a younger buffalo, was rounded up before long. Bill was more elusive, evading capture and spending the night in the Gosbecks fields. He turned up in the morning, walking about in the large new housing estate of Prettygate. Zoo staff, local vets and the police (along with hordes of children) were soon swarming in the area, with Frank advising everyone to shut the curtains on their French windows when Bill was found roaming through some back gardens in Cotman Road. There are experienced people in the zoo world who say they would be forced to shoot to kill such a powerful animal under such circumstances, but this case saw Bill darted with a crossbow tranquiliser. However, tranquiliser darts rarely work with the quickness and sureness that one sees in the movies – if they work at all – and he continued to wander for some time.

Large groups of people watched from a distance, laughing when a crawling chase given by a Mini full of policemen went into a slow reverse when Bill turned and started walking back towards them. He eventually ended up in Nash Close, where he was blocked in by a mechanical digger and took to munching the flowerbeds in the front garden of Mrs Joy Wells. The vets used more darts, and the zookeepers were able to edge towards Bill as he lay down and went to sleep, before they loaded him onto a lorry. All the policemen had meanwhile shut themselves in their cars – seemingly unaware that Bill could easily have turned them over – leaving a lone, young policewoman to assist in the capture.

Frank made his usual sort of excuse that no fence could have stood up to Bill. It is true that animals in zoos will escape from time to time (just like farm animals and domestic pets) and none of these events, taken individually, could be considered proof of the zoo's failings. Yet, taken together, these and other comparable tales suggest that Frank's zoo was suffering from a lack of general preparation. This was buffalo Bill's third escape. Today, Colchester Zoo takes an exceptionally strict approach to its safety procedures relating to its large or dangerous animals, but things were much more lax in Frank's day and, with only minimal security devices on enclosures and a casual approach to security, sometimes even a big cat would get out into the park.

Escaped American buffalo, Bill, in a suburban back garden in Prettygate, May 1978. The crossbow tranquiliser dart can be seen in Bill's left shoulder. (Peter Jennings)

The rushed and cheap infrastructure at the zoo also led directly to rather disturbing mishaps, such as the death of an alligator in 1964. The creature was electrocuted while lying in his pool, after a large snake in the adjoining enclosure managed to dislodge a power cable which then fell into the water. The simplistic nature of many of the enclosures, at which one stood against a sole row of bars and could readily put one's fingers through, also resulted in many human injuries. On one occasion in 1966, Frank and Helena were successfully sued in the High Court for £400 (£6,500) after one of their monkeys had bitten a boy.

Colchester Zoo's simple fences and poor security also meant that the animals, in turn, were not safe from the public. A local man named John Plunkett, who had recently donated his pet boa constrictor to the zoo, decided to pay a visit to his old snake one night in 1974, after an evening of heavy drinking. It was not until well after ten o'clock on the following morning (many hours after the keepers ought to have done the rounds) that Plunkett was found asleep in the reptile house, having caused hundreds of pounds' worth of damage.

It seems that Frank did not learn his lesson, for a black leopard was stolen from the zoo a year later, in January 1975. Named Czar, he had been born in a litter of three in the middle of the previous October. Czar was handed to the RSPCA the following week, safe and sound, by a rather surprised fisherman who had found him wandering along the banks of the Medway in Kent. A group of suspects were eventually brought before the Magistrates' Court, which heard the charge that a seventeen year old by the name of Roy Kearney had let himself into Colchester Zoo and then into the leopard enclosure, where the mother was sleeping with her three cubs. Roy Kearney (who was already serving a maximum borstal sentence) pleaded guilty and a truly wretched story emerged.

This was in fact the second time Kearney had broken into the zoo. A week before the theft of the cub he had stolen a pair of barn owls with a mind to sell them. One of the owls had simply flown away but as soon as the other had successfully been sold, Kearney had returned to the zoo to steal a cat. Kearney went on to sell this leopard cub, then worth £600 (£5,200), for £40 (£340) to a pair of youths who found it to be 'not very friendly' and let it go. Dismay was expressed when it transpired that Kearney had even left the leopard cage door open at Colchester Zoo on the night of the theft. The mother was not counted among Helena's tame cats and would have been quite capable of hurting someone very badly. Nevertheless, many locals still found this sort of thing amusing – after Frank announced that he was tightening security with canine patrols, a cartoon appeared in the *Standard* of a chirpy little guard-dog reassuring a disdainful lion that he would be safe from now on.

One of the park's senior members of staff expressed bafflement that a stranger such as Kearney could have separated a young leopard from its mother without receiving so much as a scratch. What was not so baffling was why Kearney was able to take his pick of the animals with ease. Colchester Zoo had the aspect not of the tightly controlled rare-breeds centre that Frank was always banging on about, but rather of a glorified farm. For a glorified farm was indeed what Colchester Zoo was and always had been, and most of its keepers were glorified farmhands. It was a rough and ready sort of a place in which the staff obviously loved their animals but there was very little in the way of security procedures, professional animal handling operations, structured breeding programmes, or even a great deal of consideration given to the safety or welfare of the animals, staff and visitors in the park.

Despite all this, Frank tended to get away with it and his staff respected him. He himself took more hooves to the groin, was kicked over more fences, and had his arms and eyes slashed by more claws and teeth than anyone else at Colchester Zoo before or since (simply because he was always right at the centre of all the action); he probably didn't think anyone else should much mind the prospect of the same happening to them. Jeremy Keeling remembers an incident which, with hindsight, sums up Frank completely. He and Frank were sitting in the zoo's zebra-stripe van while a large tiger behind their seats was, worryingly, chewing its way through the crate in which it had been placed. Frank was simply laughing about it and happily stuffing up the holes with wads of the Colchester Zoo leaflets which he carried on his dashboard, and which he was always putting up everywhere (and getting fined for).

Jeremy, who learned a great deal from Frank in a short time, testifies to Frank's fearlessness and his uncanny, if improvised, abilities to deal with individual creatures. In fact, he holds that Frank's empathy with his animals was where the real strength of Colchester Zoo lay in those days, and has since said that in terms of hands-on husbandry, Frank was a true 'animal man' of a type now probably almost extinct. Indeed, the departure of men and women such as Frank and Helena and their zoos was well underway by the 1970s, but had been coming at least since the 1930s when writers and broadcasters, such as the popular Naomi Jacob, began extensively to criticise the ethics of zoos in far harsher terms than opponents of zoos had used previously. Movements such as these were firmly sidelined during the Second World War but steadily began to resurge in the 1960s, as people began to find more time and energy to think about such matters in detail.

Any objections the sniffy and aloof in Colchester might have made against Frank's new zoo in 1963 had nothing really to do with philosophical questions about animal captivity and everything to do with the fact that it was supposedly the sort of carnival attraction one expected to see in *simply dreadful* places such as Chelmsford and Clacton, and most decidedly not in the ancient and venerable fortress city of Colchester. Nevertheless, the whole town had since been won over and (after the dramatic 1970 season with Nyoka) few suspected that Frank's time was passing.

It came as a surprise to Colcestrians in 1971 when a national report on zoos seemed to suggest that their zoo was not as good as they imagined. An animal welfare organisation called UFAW had prepared a secret survey of seventy-two British zoos, rating them as 'very good', 'good-fair' or 'poor-bad'. Only those zoos which fell into the highest bracket were explicitly named in the report which hit the newspapers. Many of Frank's competitors, such as Chessington, featured among the identified twenty-four best zoos – Colchester Zoo's name was missing.

Frank was usually able to talk himself out of any predicament but here he was put in a very difficult position. He had been telling Colchester for years that his was one of the finest zoos in the country, in Europe even. Should he go openly on the defensive? There were over 300 zoos in Britain at the time; perhaps Colchester Zoo had not even been inspected? Might it seem questionable if Frank and Helena were to start protesting too loudly about the report? UFAW refused to comment, and Frank saw that his wild claims about the centrality of his park's position in British zoology had come back to bite him hard.

In a resultant statement to the local press, Frank pointed to his zoo's breeding success and to the fact that his membership of the British Federation of Zoos had required careful checks by vets and the Board of Trade, which was all true. A statement was also given by Grahame Clarke, an RSPCA inspector who had recently visited Colchester Zoo to investigate a (groundless) complaint by a member of the public. Clarke said he had been impressed by the standards at Colchester Zoo and that the animals he had seen were in 'extremely good condition'.

Frank usually managed to bluff his way through tough situations, but this UFAW report was something different, something new. For one thing, it was perceived as a possible criticism of his whole project, not just a part of it. It also portended a new way of doing things in Britain generally, something for which a man such as Frank Farrar was quite unequipped. What we now call 'health and safety culture' was starting to creep in, under which every little aspect of every part of working life would be scrutinised and regulated. The world was gradually starting to catch up with people like Frank who had made the very most of the unparalleled personal freedom which the post-war years had afforded.

We do not know exactly what Frank's private reaction to the UFAW report was, but from what we do know of his way of living, one imagines that he laughingly made light of it to the people around him. Still, the questions remained. The mood of the nation was changing: the happy-go-lucky Beatles were gone and something darker and stranger had already begun to appear in popular culture through figures like Arthur Brown, David Bowie and Syd Barrett, who were singing openly about sex, madness and suicide. The early 1960s promise of an eternal consumer heaven for all was beginning to falter as Britain's economy stumbled into the 1970s.

The rhinoceros enclosure at Colchester Zoo, 1970s. (Richard Martin)

For many, the clean and easy 'City of the Future' was remaining too steadfastly in the future. People were growing disaffected, becoming more political and rejecting the established way of life more aggressively. The animal welfare political movement, for its part, had gained new momentum as a result of increased mobility. Mixed up with protests against farming, the meat trade, the fur trade, hunting and baiting, as well as vivisection, animal circuses and even the keeping of pets, was increasing opposition to Frank's zoo. In the 1960s, people had sometimes complained to the authorities or written letters to the press expressing concern over Colchester Zoo's small and bare cages, the frustration shown by its animals, and the collection techniques that people such as Frank used in the wild. Many made sensible and pertinent accusations against Frank. However, these had generally been lone voices who usually received rebuttals from other locals and strong denials from Frank himself. Moreover, Frank had been ahead of his time in many ways up to about 1970, which helped to disguise the problems from which his zoo was suffering.

But if this old man had ever been ahead of the game, the world was now accelerating past him. John Knowles was enjoying considerable success with his new conservation-based zoo at Marwell. People like John Aspinall would shortly begin making great strides in the treatment, nutrition and

African elephant Moto or Toto, 1975. (Susan Wilson)

housing of animals at zoos like Howletts in Kent. Other zoos of a similar age to Colchester, such as Jersey and Twycross, had been working hard for many years on improvements in enclosure design for the benefit of their animals. Animal parks such as Woburn and Longleat were setting new standards in the ways in which animals were presented to the public.

If anyone was talking about Colchester Zoo by this time, it was often to ask questions about the purpose of such a zoo, whose message remained only that it was a cheap and fun day out for the family. Any debate would now have concerned not whether Colchester Zoo was up-to-date but whether it had ever been up-to-date. Had it always really been a 1920s zoo, like Frank's father's, but with added electric gimmicks?

Colchester Zoo had once appeared to be ultra-modern and futuristic but the mask was slipping and the park was starting to look very old-fashioned. Once all the extraneous things the zoo had previously offered had ceased or lost their lustre – the glamorous Hollywood appearances; the tales of foreign expeditions; the cabaret acts; the up-to-the-minute machines, gadgets and gizmos – what was left but some rather bored-looking animals in small cages? Frank was running out of energy and ideas. Perhaps he had not realised that the park would grow so rapidly; that he would so soon fulfil every small businessman's dream of making his millions and go on to lose the sense of urgency so critical to the ongoing success of a project?

It had been much too easy for a man like Frank. His interest in everything and his fascination with novelty had led him to triumph in the 1960s, but his lack of any central idea which could maintain the zoo, after everyone had seen what once seemed like each of the world's species, was now showing it up as an enterprise without a valuable purpose. The old idea of zoos as animal encyclopaedias was falling away and the eyes of professional critics were on Colchester. Frank had only expanded, not consolidated. The cracks, literal and metaphorical, were showing. He was now well past his sixtieth birthday and was finding that whatever work he undertook at the zoo now seemed to require twice as much effort.

And then there was Helena. She was a predator: she and Frank still loved each other, but she was pitiless and brooked no admission of failure or cries for help. Frank continued his work as breezy and cheerful as he had ever been. But along with all the llamas, donkeys, sheep, capuchins, tigers, leopards and baboons raised at Stanway Hall in the 1970s, Colchester Zoo was also raising many questions surrounding its future.

9

THE ZOO OF THE PAST

MORE AND MORE concerns were voiced about Colchester Zoo as it steadily declined through the 1970s. If Frank and Helena ever doubted themselves, they did not show it and, in fact, seem to have been delusional about the park's future. At no point did either of them appear to have recognised that they were mortal. Perhaps this was to be expected; after all, both had cheated death many times. While at sea during his first animal-collection trip abroad, Frank had fallen more than 30ft through a hatch into the ship's hold and had at first been given up for dead, but eventually came away with nothing more than some nasty bruising. He was also frequently savaged by cats and bears on such journeys, and on one occasion he was nearly killed by two wild leopards during a voyage back to Britain. He had gone below deck to check on these new cats for his zoo but found that their cages had sprung open. When the ship's crew responded to Frank's calls for help, the first thing they did was lock the cabin door, not realising that Frank was still in there with the two animals loose. He later recalled that the leopards were both frantically climbing up him in the dark and that he was saved only by the fact that the crew realised quickly enough to open the door by a fraction to allow Frank to slip out, badly scratched but still in one piece.

Helena likewise carried about her an air of indestructibility. One of her lions, for example, had once charged her. She did not believe in corporal punishment for her animals but on this occasion had simply stood firm and punched him squarely on the nose. Men now in their nineties confess to being still somewhat scared even of Helena's memory, and many people around her at the time had their own suspicions that she was invincible.

If Frank or Helena sensed that their bodies would one day fail them, they did not reveal it in their attitude towards the future of the park. None of their three grown-up children had ever showed any interest in animals and had played almost no part whatsoever in their zoological adventures. This might have prompted them to consider the ultimate fate of their zoo a little more closely. In reality, they were surprisingly lackadaisical about what might happen to their life's work.

They announced in 1978 that they intended to negotiate with the authorities in order to hand Colchester Zoo over to a charitable trust. Frank, at this point, does seem to have been thinking about the legacy he would leave behind him. He wanted to ensure that the zoo would not be broken up, nor become subject to certain types of taxation that might jeopardise its continued existence. It seems as if the plans were reasonably serious. Frank revealed that there would be fifteen members on the board as well as a general manager. Nevertheless, perhaps he never really believed he would actually die, for nothing came of these plans and they do not seem to have been mentioned again.

Worse still, not only did Frank and Helena fail to put in place a contingency plan for the zoo, but even began to slip into semi-retirement without making any serious decisions about how the park would continue to run. It did not seem absurd at the time. Their live-in head keeper, Reg Howe, was not the brightest of men nor was he exceptionally gifted in the handling of exotic wild animals, but he had been at the park for many years and made a very reliable caretaker of the zoo; and when the new position of assistant manager was filled by one Ian Lockwood, the Farrars found themselves free to take regular holidays.

Activity at Colchester Zoo was slowly running down and perhaps it seemed like a good time for Frank and Helena to enjoy some of the fruits of their labours. Their days in the media world were largely behind them. It steadily became the case that when opportunities did arise they tended to involve people coming to them instead of the other way round. (Television comedy legend Ronnie Barker, for example, came to film a scene with one of Helena's tame lions in the early 1970s, for which twenty BBC crew members built a full set inside Colchester's lion enclosure.)

Frank's collecting trips also became fewer as he got older, and more health and safety regulations began to restrict the movement and keeping of wild animals. The animal trade in Britain shrank after the passing of national legislation, such as the Dangerous Wild Animals Act of 1976, and the signing

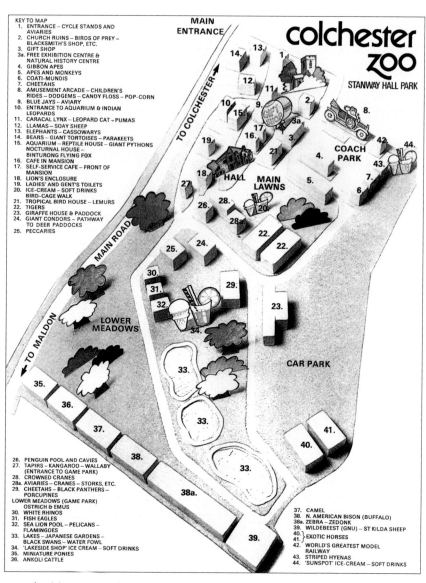

KEY TO MAP
1. ENTRANCE – CYCLE STANDS AND AVIARIES
2. CHURCH RUINS – BIRDS OF PREY – BLACKSMITH'S SHOP, ETC.
3. GIFT SHOP
3a. FREE EXHIBITION CENTRE & NATURAL HISTORY CENTRE
4. GIBBON APES
5. APES AND MONKEYS
6. COATI-MUNDIS
7. CHEETAHS
8. AMUSEMENT ARCADE – CHILDREN'S RIDES – DODGEMS – CANDY FLOSS – POP-CORN
9. BLUE JAYS – AVIARY
10. ENTRANCE TO AQUARIUM & INDIAN LEOPARDS
11. CARACAL LYNX – LEOPARD CAT – PUMAS
12. LLAMAS – SOAY SHEEP
13. ELEPHANTS – CASSOWARYS
14. BEARS – GIANT TORTOISES – PARAKEETS
15. AQUARIUM – REPTILE HOUSE – GIANT PYTHONS NOCTURNAL HOUSE – BINTURONG FLYING FOX
16. CAFE IN MANSION
17. SELF-SERVICE CAFE – FRONT OF MANSION
18. LION'S ENCLOSURE
19. LADIES' AND GENT'S TOILETS
20. ICE-CREAM – SOFT DRINKS BIRD-CAGE WALK
21. TROPICAL BIRD HOUSE – LEMURS
22. TIGERS
23. GIRAFFE HOUSE & PADDOCK
24. GIANT CONDORS – PATHWAY TO DEER PADDOCKS
25. PECCARIES

26. PENGUIN POOL AND CAVIES
27. TAPIRS – KANGAROO – WALLABY (ENTRANCE TO GAME PARK)
28. CROWNED CRANES
28a. AVIARIES – CRANES – STORKS, ETC.
29. CHEETAHS – BLACK PANTHERS – PORCUPINES
LOWER MEADOWS (GAME PARK)
OSTRICH & EMUS
30. WHITE RHINOS
31. FISH EAGLES
32. SEA LION POOL – PELICANS – FLAMINGOES
33. LAKES – JAPANESE GARDENS – BLACK SWANS – WATER FOWL
34. 'LAKESIDE SHOP' ICE CREAM – SOFT DRINKS
35. MINIATURE PONIES
36. ANKOLI CATTLE

37. CAMEL
38. N. AMERICAN BISON (BUFFALO)
38a. ZEBRA – ZEDONK
39. WILDEBEEST (GNU) – ST KILDA SHEEP
40.
41. } EXOTIC HORSES
42. WORLD'S GREATEST MODEL RAILWAY
43. STRIPED HYENAS
44. 'SUNSPOT' ICE-CREAM – SOFT DRINKS

MAIN ENTRANCE

colchester
ZOO
STANWAY HALL PARK

TO COLCHESTER

MAIN ROAD

TO MALDON

GIFT SHOP

HALL

MAIN LAWNS

COACH PARK

LOWER MEADOWS

CAR PARK

Map of Colchester Zoo in the 1970s. (Colchester Zoo)

of international agreements, like CITES, from 1973 onward. Life was simply not quite as busy as it had been in previous years. There was little or no construction work going on at the zoo and, though the place remained profitable, visitor numbers were continuing to decrease as the 1970s ended. As the 1980s began, fresh attractions were emerging which drew more people away from the zoo. In 1980, for example, work would begin on Colchester's Culver Square precinct – a second major consumer attraction in the town centre, which would feature at least one huge department store amid everything else.

Now and then a burst of visitors would swamp the zoo if the weather was particularly good. Colchester Zoo probably also benefited from a 70mph storm which swept the area in January 1978 and ripped a 100ft hole in the Clacton Dolphinarium, forcing its temporary closure. However, the zoo seems to have been ill prepared for large crowds of visitors on the occasional days when they did come in these later years. In April 1979, over 25,000 people were received across the four-day Easter period. This was excellent news for the gate takings, but the old days of an organised park in command of itself had clearly ended.

A letter appeared shortly afterwards in the *Essex County Standard*, from one Beverley Austin of Assington. She complained of revolting conditions at the zoo, suggesting that it was under-staffed and so dirty that visitors would be well advised to wipe their feet on their way out. Mrs Austin also raised animal welfare issues, mentioning that all the animals seemed to live on diets of ice cream, popcorn and peanuts, and that the penguin pool was full of litter, cigarette ends and pieces of wood. This was, however, mild criticism when contrasted to the attacks which came next year.

In May 1980 a prominent article appeared in the *Standard*, drawing attention to allegations of neglect and cruelty at Colchester Zoo. A West Bergholt nurse named Vera Brown had taken a group of her hospital patients to the zoo and had been shocked at what she had seen there. She protested of animals living in confined spaces, many of which looked unwell or poorly nourished. She said the primates had nothing to stimulate them and that the penguin pool remained polluted. She described it as the worst zoo she had ever visited.

The Farrars, having been invited to comment, heatedly denied the accusations. Peter Scott, the RSPCA inspector for Colchester, offered tentative support for the zoo, saying that its animal care had always been good in the past. This was to no avail: the touch-paper was lit. Nurse Brown's complaint set off a string of letter bombs which exploded across the pages of the *Standard* for weeks afterwards. She had clearly articulated what many people had gradually come to feel about the town's zoo, and other local people were quick to toss oil on the flames.

A reader from Great Bentley, a Mrs J.A. Pinney, endorsed Vera Brown's letter a week later, repeating the accusations that the enclosures were much too small, the pools were filthy and that the zoo carried a general 'air of neglect'. Mrs Pinney appears to have had genuine concern about the state of the zoo (rather than any grievance to redress) for she signed off her letter by saying that it was a shame since everyone at the zoo was surely trying very hard to make it work. Whatever the case, her additional comment that she could no longer visit the bears while at the zoo, finding it much too upsetting, was a stark reproach no matter how one looked at it.

Another letter from a Mr Beales of Bures agreed with Vera Brown, having recently been likewise aghast at seeing animals in bare cages with muck everywhere and very little opportunity for play. He similarly rated Colchester Zoo as one of the worst he had ever visited. Again, the Farrars were given space in the newspaper to rebut these accusations, but next week there were more complaints. Karen Wolton of Lexden questioned whether or not the council was aware of what she called 'the situation' at the zoo. Next week there followed a letter from Kathleen Mitchell of the Captive Animals Protection Society, which criticised RSPCA Inspector Scott as well as Colchester Zoo and broadened the complaint to cover what was described as the disgraceful state of British zoos at large.

Mitchell's letter went on to mention circuses, whereupon the continuing correspondence diverted away from Colchester Zoo, but the foregoing letters, as samples of public feeling towards Frank and Helena at the start of the 1980s, were a powerful indictment of the pass to which the Farrars had come at Stanway Hall. Comments from letter writers that they had seen boys entering the rhino enclosure to throw rocks at the animals, unchallenged by staff, were seen as withering accusations against the state of the park.

Significantly, people had also made the point that, even aside from the animal welfare problems, the zoo was no longer much fun even purely from the visitors' perspective, with litter thick on all the lawns, paths and lakes. In all respects the park was failing. A high-ranking and dispassionate member of the international zoo community would later describe the conditions at Colchester Zoo in these years as 'despicable'.

Above Stanway Hall, Colchester Zoo, in the mid-1960s. (Susan Wilson)

COLCHESTER ZOO
AND AQUARIUM

Right Colchester Zoo guidebook from the early 1970s. The two giraffes pictured are likely to be Colchester Zoo's first pair, Roz and David. (Colchester Zoo)

Colchester Zoo's wishing well, opposite the elephant enclosure in around 1970. The money collected from the wishing well always went to animal protection charities. Frank's imitation blacksmith's workshop is seen here in the background on the right. (Colchester Zoo)

The exhibition hall at Colchester Zoo in around 1969. (Colchester Zoo)

Keeper Peter Zwitser with Kinna. Colchester Zoo, 1969. (Peter Zwitser)

Fred and Joan Honisett with tiger cub Tank or Rebel, in about the late 1960s. (Fred and Joan Honisett)

Nyoka with Simba the lion in the late 1960s. Simba, to this day, remains in the Guinness Book of World Records as the world's largest captive lion. (Fred and Joan Honisett)

Zedonks Sandy, Mary and Shadow with their mother (far right). Colchester Zoo, late 1970s. (Colchester Zoo)

Joan Honisett with tigers Tank and Rebel at Colchester Zoo in the early 1970s. By the end of their first decade at Colchester, the Farrars no longer had enough spare time to keep their cats sufficiently humanised, and their practice of free handling therefore began to cease altogether. This picture shows the last day Tank and Rebel had direct contact with zoo staff, and as such is representative of the end of a phase in the Farrars' and Honisetts' lives. (Fred and Joan Honisett)

Frank and Helena Farrar on holiday in the 1970s. (Fred and Joan Honisett)

Dominique Tropeano with a young chimpanzee at Twycross Zoo in the late 1980s. (Sarah Knuckey)

Sarah Tropeano with Nia the sea lion, 1994. (Colchester Zoo)

The new entrance hall at Colchester Zoo, 2000. (Colchester Zoo)

Keeper Clive Barwick with a trio of snow leopard cubs, 1990s. (Colchester Zoo)

Left The main viewing area for the indoor enclosures within Chimp World at Colchester Zoo, around the turn of the twenty-first century. (Colchester Zoo)

Below Keeper Kate Broad performs a routine dental check-up on the sea lion Winnipeg, 2011. (S.C. Kershaw)

The Kingdom of the Wild complex seen from the west, 2012. The building has almost remained unaltered since 2001. (S.C. Kershaw)

A giraffe at the UmPhafa Private Nature Reserve in South Africa, 2011. (Amy Sutcliffe)

Dominique Tropeano at the UmPhafa Private Nature Reserve, South Africa, in around 2008. (Colchester Zoo)

Opposite Project co-ordinator Liam Westall in the field with hand-reared warthog Spike. UmPhafa Private Nature Reserve, South Africa, 2012. (Nicole Sharpe)

Sarah, Dominique and Anthony feed red-ruffed lemurs in the new Lost Madagascar enclosure in October 2012. (S.C. Kershaw)

In her complaint, Vera Brown had suggested that too much cost cutting was going on – a fair criticism. Frank and Helena worked hard at the zoo, but they also played hard. It is alarming to think that while many of their animals were living in gimcrack structures and staffing levels were far from adequate, Helena refused ever to drive anything but Rolls-Royces (of which she bought several over the years) and Frank constantly indulged a passion for natty sports cars, including many E-type Jaguars and an XK150S which had once belonged to the pianist Semprini. Frank and Helena also owned a condominium in Florida, in the rich coastal city of Boca Raton, to which they often retreated.

Perhaps one could justify these considerable luxuries by pointing to the fact that Helena and Frank had worked like fury for decade after decade, hand-raising sick animals, sitting up with the snakes at night to make sure the heating did not go off during power cuts, dealing with arson attacks on the zoo as well as thefts in the shops and museums, racking up thousands of road miles while hauling back and forth to quarantine centres and other appointments and even, at one point, tramping around the Himalayas in search of evidence of the Yeti (as Frank had once been commissioned to do by a national newspaper).

Without doubt, Frank and Helena had earned their comforts and holidays. Then again, one cannot escape the accusation that as soon as they were minded to drift into retirement, they ought to have been far quicker either in selling the zoo or at least in ceding control to a charitable committee, as they had announced in prior years. For time was now up at Colchester Zoo. A new, fatal threat was now hanging over the park – a threat with which Frank was utterly unfit to cope.

In 1981, the Zoo Licensing Act was passed by Parliament. It was a landmark piece of law making. There had already been plenty of ground-breaking animal welfare legislation created in Britain since 1822, when the Cruel Treatment of Cattle Act had been produced. In 1981 there was now a special requirement for local governments to ensure that their zoos met certain standards peculiar to zookeeping alone, as a response to the uncontrolled explosion in the number of public animal parks across the country since the war.

The ZLA required, for the first time, that zoos had to acquire temporary licences, subject to major inspections as well as periodic inspections for the life of each licence. The Act made a special provision that the quality of staff, management and animal quarters had to be of an adequate standard. It stated that a licence could be refused if the health and safety of local people was at risk. A licence could be refused if a zoo employed anyone who had been convicted of animal abuse. Local councils were given the power to alter the licence arrangement of a zoo at any point during the licence period.

This was not some piece of pettifogging bureaucracy. Though it had been drawn up by people who were broadly sympathetic towards zoological parks, this Licensing Act was strong stuff. Failure to comply with every condition was an offence, and disputes arising from an inspection could be referred directly to the Secretary of State.

Britain's burgeoning new health and safety culture of inspection and litigation was alien to Frank, who had no way of relating to any of this. He had grown up in the world war period. It had been a hard time but it had also been a much freer time. For most people life had been a case of simply 'make do and mend' – if a person went on to show real initiative and created wealth and new affairs with gusto, it was all to the greater good. People had looked up to imaginative persons like Frank Farrar during the grim times during the First and Second World Wars and the economic depression of the 1930s. If anyone chanced to bring amusement into people's lives by starting up, say, a zoo, then most people would respect them for it (almost regardless of the methods used) for adding to what used to be called the gaiety of the nation. Such an effort would almost have been seen as an act of British patriotism by helping to maintain industry as the old Empire melted away.

Notwithstanding the suspicions among Colchester's traditionalists, the sense of popular excitement in Colchester in 1963 had been palpable, as news reports had circulated of a fearless man coming down out of the North with his lions and leopards; a martial hero who was travelling to the ends of the earth to bring back strange, unimagined creatures; a mercurial man with learned words, able to convince anyone of anything; a jovial man, able to make everyone love him and who mingled freely with foreign heads of state and legends of the silver screen.

In the early 1960s Colchester had been a strongly rural community of limited horizons, which could still produce newspaper headlines such as 'POWER CUT AT FETE: TEAS AT STANDSTILL'. When Frank turned up, the common man saw his new zoo as being immensely impressive and a jewel in the crown of local public life. But by 1981 the character of the town had changed. The new tendency for well-travelled, ambitious urban people and their families to buy up second homes and dormitory houses all over

Colchester had taken hold. Frank's rather grotty little animal compound on the western fringe of the town was now conflicting badly with the borough's upwardly mobile aspirations.

The vast changes in Colchester, which the zoo ironically had presaged, had come swiftly over the twenty years since the Farrars first came to town. It had been predicted in the early days that Colchester Zoo would make a huge contribution to the sophistication of north Essex. Indeed, the zoo had been thought sophisticated for a time, but the goalposts had since been moved. Frank had not learned the rules of the new game, and what had once been seen as sophisticated had fallen behind. He was still in perfect command of his mind at the age of seventy. The tragedy was that he was now too old to understand, in the deeper sense, that he had outlived himself.

Instead of passing the zoo on to someone else post-haste, Frank's response to the criticism was to throw himself into his work with what remained of his dwindling energy. And it appears that he made some headway. Those who were there at the end remember that the zoo did once again start to look tidy and attractive, as in the old days, and that some efforts were made to improve the lives of the animals. But it was not enough. The Zoo Licensing Act was an untried piece of legislation and few zoos felt completely confident of their own futures. The signs were exceptionally bad for a place such as Colchester Zoo, for the Act appeared in conjunction with a wider political movement which had, as its aim, the outright and immediate abolition of all zoos.

By 1981 unemployment in Britain was soaring to almost the highest levels in living memory, and was continuing to rise, with unemployment among young people especially high. These idle youngsters became progressively more radical as, throughout the 1980s, the number of people out of work continued to swell to a greater size and for a longer duration than anyone could remember. The boredom and resentment engendered by mass inactivity, inflamed by a small but conspicuous new class of impossibly rich young men and women which had emerged as a result of the Conservative Party's blanket deregulation of the banking and finance industry, led to widespread disaffection with the British establishment as a whole.

The millions of people left out of the 1980s' economic boom found an outlet for their frustrations by joining various pressure groups that had formed since the war to campaign for widespread changes in the nation, from a ban on nuclear weaponry to equal rights for homosexuals. Among those causes which advanced in the 1980s were sundry animal protection groups, such as Lynx, the Captive Animals Protection Society, the Crusade Against All Cruelty to Animals, Stop Animal Suffering, The Animal Liberation Front and, as an example from closer to home, Colchester Action for Animals.

Many people may have joined these animal rights groups with the intention of righting certain wrongs in the treatment of animals, but for others it was equally as much a case of trying to find ways of exercising some kind of personal authority after their power had been stripped away in other areas. Even some people in forward-thinking zoos such as Chester, Marwell and Whipsnade were concerned about the severity of the anti-establishment reaction against British zoos in the 1980s. There was no hope for Colchester.

Positive local press interest in Frank's zoo had all but dried up. It was now receiving, at most, 150,000 visitors a year. This was enough to maintain the business but it was far lower than in previous years. In a park that had grown so complex with such a large collection of animals, there was a distinct impression of public desertion. Everything was going wrong. Frank finally fell to a stroke late in 1981, just before Christmas. His health had not been terribly good for quite some time and everyone agreed that he had simply worked himself much too hard in the months previously.

It came as a terrible blow to Helena. She and Frank were well known for having lots of furious rows, with Helena often shouting at him in front of hordes of holidaymakers in years past and throwing his belongings out of the first-floor windows of Stanway Hall, but they still loved each other deeply. Helena might have been tough, but she was not that tough. Running Colchester Zoo on her own, as well as tending to a sick husband, was far too much to take on and the park was put up for sale a month later. Frank was well enough again to speak to the press by the end of January 1982. He said that the reality of the situation had not yet sunk in – words which were truer than he may have imagined. The Farrars still seemed to have failed to grasp the gravity of the matter. Though they had quickly received perhaps as many as thirty purchase enquiries, they were still considering their options and trying to find a buyer who would maintain Stanway Hall as a zoo.

By May 1982 the zoo remained unsold. Helena had been running the zoo alone for six months by this point and things were going from bad to worse. As if to give flesh to the saying, the principal proof that Helena gave for the high quality of her zoo was that it was being repainted. Helena

Most of Colchester Zoo's staff in January 1982. L-R: Helena Farrar, Joan Honisett, head keeper Reg Howe, unknown, Clive Barwick, unknown, Glyn Evans(?), unknown, Gordon Pennington. Background: African elephants Moto and Toto. Note the absence of Frank Farrar. (Fred and Joan Honisett)

was fooling herself if she thought that Colchester Zoo's growing problems could be solved with a splash of fresh colour. She was also fooling herself that she had all the time in the world to select a buyer.

She said in a statement that although the (now forty) prospective buyers had been winnowed down to two, she still had not selected to whom she would 'like' to sell it. The fact is that Helena simply could not let go of the zoo. She went on to say that she was not about to let thirty years of hard work be lost. What does not seem to have occurred to her is that, in the new climate that was brewing, those thirty years of work at Southport and Colchester now counted for nothing. All that mattered was the direction in which zoos would be moving in the future.

Helena, locked in her own secret hell, aged terribly in 1982. She was no longer the spry bombshell she had been in 1950, nor the fearsome force of nature she had been in 1970. Could she admit to everyone – to herself – that she was now an old lady who could not cope? Frank remained ill and she was doing all she could to help him. Some of their keepers were still working hard and Joan Honisett, as ever, offered all the support she could, but it was becoming impossible to keep up with everything. Some staff members were clearly taking advantage of the situation, with much apathy and theft in evidence.

This was not how it was supposed to have happened. Helena and Frank had planned a retirement together. They would surely have sold the zoo sooner or later but had kept putting off the day for they could not bear to leave their animals behind. Helena had blinked at some point and 1972 had become 1982. Suddenly, the zoo was old-fashioned in all the wrong ways and bang-up-to-date in all the wrong ways.

Giving up Colchester Zoo was not, for Helena, giving up a business: it was giving up her whole life. She knew the end had come and it was time to leave. When Frank had been well, something had always turned up. Helena was used to doing everything her own way, but now her hand was being forced.

10

ARRIVALS

I N EARLY 1983, a light green Peugeot 505 entered the gates of Colchester Zoo. Inside was a young family who had just bought the park and were coming to live with the animals. We have met the mother before: it was Angela, Frank's niece, who had grown up next door to Sammy and Rajah at Westbourne Road in Southport. By then in her early forties, Angela had been, in one way or another, a part of the story of Colchester Zoo since its earliest origins in Lancashire. Frank and Helena had become too old and ill to continue running the zoo as well as they had done in the past, and they had sold it to Angela and her husband, Dominique Tropeano.

Until 1983, Dominique worked as a hotel consultant and ran several of his own small businesses. His career began when he came to England as a language student from his native France. He and Angela met each other at Southport's vast Birkdale Palace Hotel in the 1960s, where she was working as a receptionist. It had been love at first sight for Angela and Dominique, who had been inseparable from the start. Angela had still been in the habit of spending time at Southport Zoo, which had by then been bought by Douglas and Carole Petrie, and she had taken Dominique there. Her boyfriend had been happy to walk about seeing the animals and had observed Angela's delight with interest. He listened with amusement to her excited stories of larger-than-life Uncle Frank with his tame cheetahs and fast cars. But from Dominique's perspective, Frank was only a name and his legacy at Southport nothing more than a small and unremarkable seaside zoo.

Dominique had previously visited Colchester Zoo before 1983 and had even stayed overnight at Stanway Hall on occasion, but never once did he imagine that he would ever buy this zoo, or any zoo for that matter. He and Angela had, however, been looking for a new life. They had been considering opening their own hotel in the Lake District before Colchester Zoo had come up for sale in 1982. At first it had seemed like a ridiculous idea, but the more they had thought about it and the longer the zoo had stayed on the market, the more the prospect of the purchase appealed to them as a unique opportunity. Dominique and Angela had been looking for a big change in their lives and this was about as big as any they might have found.

The greatest attraction of Colchester Zoo had been the idea that their little family might be together at last, living and working in Stanway Hall. They had both been working horrendously long hours over the years; and, with Dominique often away from home on business, he had, to date, missed out on much of the lives of his young son and daughter, Anthony and Sarah.

At this point, Anthony was thirteen years old and it was becoming clear that he had inherited his mother's fascination with animals. He had come to view David Attenborough as an idol since the landmark nature programme, *Life on Earth*, aired on BBC television in 1979, and he already had many animals of his own, which included tropical fish and breeds of grasshoppers. A few years previously he had been thrilled when the mysterious and animated Uncle Frank had come up to Southport and, along with many tales of his adventures in the deserts and jungles of the world, had offered Anthony a pair of black axolotls. Despite her love of animals, Angela had not been too sure about these exceptionally weird creatures with their bulbous heads and staring eyes. Indeed, Angela and Dominique had tried to dissuade their son's ambitions to work with animals, for, as they had put it, there was no money in such a career.

Also in the back of this Peugeot, buried somewhere under the family's two German shepherd dogs, Mopsy the cat, Anthony's fish tanks and all the belongings which the family had not sold or given away, was Anthony's sister, eleven-year-old Sarah. Although quiet, she was quite possibly the most excited of them all. Utterly obsessed with equine creatures, she could not wait to be with all the horses, ponies, zebras – and zedonks – at Colchester Zoo.

The thrill for every member of this young family would, however, start to pall almost as soon as they disembarked from the car and crossed the threshold of Stanway Hall. For Angela, the coming years were not to be a repeat of the carefree days with Rajah in the 1950s. For Anthony, life at the zoo would prove very different to the safe and ordered experience of watching a nature documentary. And although Dominique was looking for a new challenge, he would soon find that he had accepted an exceptionally

Anthony Tropeano with Napoleon in Southport, October 1982. (Sarah Knuckey)

formidable one. Perhaps the most difficult fight for him would be trying to put on a brave face for the sake of his family as it began to dawn on him that he had bought what was said to be the worst zoo in Britain.

The Tropeano family soon realised that much of Stanway Hall itself had not been used or looked after properly for maybe thirty or forty years, and was badly in need of clearing, cleaning and decorating. This large house full of junk and peeling paint would soon, however, seem nothing; worse surprises by far lay in wait. The family shortly came to realise that they allowed the presence of a few impressive animals at the zoo to blind them to the fact that the animal collection bequeathed to them by Uncle Frank was largely worthless. Many animals had died in recent years and had not been replaced. Many of the more valuable creatures had been sold to compensate for falling revenue at the gate. There were still a few high-profile exotic species such as elephants, rhinos and chimpanzees, but a large proportion of the collection was comprised of animals such as ducks, hens, geese and other creatures of limited zoological interest and no conservation value.

The financial prospects were no better. On his visits to the zoo before the purchase, Dominique had seen visitors in the park, but at close range he came to see that their numbers were far from high. Frank and Helena seemed to have picked the number of 100,000 out of the air, and it soon became apparent that even if this number had been accurate, it was steadily dropping.

Worse still, Frank and Helena were unable to produce for Dominique and Angela a single book, account, calculation or record of anything that had ever happened at Colchester Zoo. It was impossible even to establish precisely of what the animal collection consisted. Few knew where a particular animal came from, to whom it was born, or even what species it was.

Dominique and Angela soon realised that running Colchester Zoo was going to be even harder than the work they had been doing previously. Angela had known Southport Zoo well, Dominique had grown up on a farm in France, and the two of them had a proven talent for running businesses in general, but neither of them knew a huge amount about looking after exotic animals. When turning to their staff for help and guidance, they were met with wary eyes and contempt for their lack of specialist skills and knowledge.

Little Sarah was too young to comprehend the family's coming struggle, but one day soon after they arrived, she found herself sitting on the staircase at Stanway Hall, and her father Dominique came through the door, shut out the zoo behind him, and told her that coming to Colchester Zoo was a terrible, terrible mistake.

PART TWO

ALWAYS SOMETHING NEW

Six thousand miles over flames the noon:
The arrowhead the earth has flung in shade
Has dipped to fall; a change in heaven's heart
Effaces star, then two, and stars the more …

– Dante (1265-1321)

1

THE TO-AND-FRO CONFLICTING WIND AND RAIN

B Y THE MID-1980S, Colchester Zoo was falling apart. What its new owners, Dominique and Angela, really needed was a large team of dedicated workers to help them rebuild it. What they had instead was a small, rag-tag staff of jaded older boys who did not much care for Dominique, who had no background in zoology, and younger men whose experience did not equal whatever enthusiasm they may have had for their work.

A number of Colchester Zoo's staff members were not over-exerting themselves and had become used to working days full of tea-breaks and sitting around eating ice cream from the kiosks. Most of the animals were living in filth as a result – one of young Anthony's earliest memories of the zoo was seeing that a lush green lawn had grown over the mound of excrement in the bison stable. Nevertheless, Dominique and Angela had to recognise that the existing staff knew the park far better than they did and had to make the best of an unsatisfactory situation. Dominique knew he was no zookeeper; nor was Angela, despite her previous time at Southport Zoo. They could not afford to bring in extra people to supplement the half-dozen existing full-timers. The only option open to the Tropeanos was to immerse themselves in a crash course in running a zoo alongside the staff as it stood.

Dominique quickly realised that he would not win the respect of his staff nor be able to keep Colchester Zoo running without becoming a keeper himself. He quickly began to spend all his time working with, and learning from, the keepers around him – helping with feeding, mucking out, cleaning the animals, moving them about and assisting with veterinary procedures. This was not an entirely alien world to him for he had grown

Angela Tropeano with Bonaparte by All Saints' Church, 1983. (Colchester Zoo)

up surrounded by livestock and wild animals on his father's farm in Nice in the south of France. Yet this was the first time he had worked directly with exotic animals day in, day out.

Training as a zookeeper is hard work and more than enough for any person to take on at any point in their lives. But the zoo was short-staffed everywhere and Dominique soon found that he was not going to have the time to learn to become a keeper at his leisure. He would carry out keeping duties for many years to come but at any given moment he might just as easily have been found selling tickets on the gate, clearing tables in the cafés and washing up in the kitchen, parking cars, or meeting visitors and talking to them about the animals. He might have been meeting with the director of another zoo one minute and the next picking crisp packets out from under the bushes on the lawns. He was determined that no worker in his zoo should ever have to do what he himself had not done. On one occasion, the visitors' ageing and decrepit toilet block became completely obstructed and started to spill human waste onto the ground around Stanway Hall.

Without a thought, Dominique opened the drain and plunged up to his neck into liquid filth to remove the blockage himself.

Adventures such as this were merely revolting – often the work at Colchester Zoo was downright dangerous. Many of the cages and enclosures at the zoo were badly decaying, with rusting grilles and precarious fences everywhere. Many were totally unsuitable for each animal in question. The old giraffe house, which had been opened with such fanfare hardly more than a decade previously, was already coming apart at its joints. The building had been cheaply made and many holes had since been knocked through the walls to make new doors and windows, without concern for whether the building might fall down as a result.

The several generations of Frank's giraffes had long since died or departed, and this cold and draughty house had been turned over to the zoo's family of chimpanzees in the late 1970s. It was not a strong and secure enclosure such as is required for chimps and, in October 1984, three of them broke out. Very young chimpanzees are playful, cuddly creatures, and have long been popular in mainstream culture as the very image of entertainment and sentimentality. It is surprising how few people, even now, realise that a change tends to come over these animals as they get older and that adult chimps, like their close cousins man, can become very dangerous indeed.

Police riflemen were called as soon as it was realised that chimps Billy Joe, Jenny and Tiger had managed to work loose a section of mesh surrounding their enclosure and had disappeared into the zoo. The park was immediately closed and visitors were advised to leave the premises or, failing that, to lock themselves in their vehicles in the car park.

Tiger, the big male, was the most tractable of the three escapees. He did nothing other than climb a nearby tree, collect a lot of leaves and then descend to push the leaves one by one through the bars of the jaguar cage. It then started to rain; Tiger decided he did not much like this and shortly returned to the ex-giraffe house of his own accord.

Billy Joe took a full tour of the zoo and was seen everywhere. The Tropeanos' son, Anthony, fourteen years old and armed with nothing but a broom, froze with fear when he saw Billy Joe coming straight in his direction. Luckily, she darted off again and was later found in the kitchen eating bananas. Fat with fruit, Billy Joe was thereafter walked back to the old giraffe house with little fuss.

The most aggressive of the three chimps that day was Jenny. Dominique found her near the gift shop and cautiously tried to corner her. Other staff members looked on with fright as Jenny picked Dominique off the ground as if he were light as a feather and hurled him through a large glass window. Fortunately, Dominique did not sustain any serious injury. More fortunate still was the fact that the closest anyone came to using a weapon was when Jenny was struck with a tranquiliser dart.

Angela, in particular, was troubled by this event; she had already instituted a new policy of double-checking locks and security on all animal cages and this now became stricter yet. It was, however, only a short time later when Billy Joe escaped a second time. Once again she traversed the whole zoo, this time taking along her ten-month-old baby, Tara, for company. On this occasion, the zoo was sealed even more swiftly and heavily than before. For safety, 200 visitors were locked inside various empty cages, sheds and even the rhino house for nearly an hour; a group of visitors were shut by the keepers inside the guinea fowl hut – one among them recalled the little birds peeping in at them through the windows with curiosity.

Happily, when a keeper named Julie Turner found little Tara and her mother in the education hall, she was greeted with a big hug from Billy Joe and was able to walk hand-in-hand with them back up to the old giraffe house. But Dominique had no time for cute stories like this. He was appalled that the same thing had happened twice in his zoo and ordered a staff inquiry. It emerged that one of the keepers had regularly been going into the cage with the chimps (forbidden by Angela and Dominique) and had been leaving the door unlocked.

Animal escapes remained common in these years, as Colchester Zoo continued to cave in on itself. The third major escape happened when six wolves ran loose in October 1986. Four were quickly recaptured inside the zoo itself, but two managed to get out into the surrounding fields. One of these was no more than a cub that returned the following morning after the pack had been howling all night. The sixth wolf, by contrast, had become tangled in a barbed-wire fence in nearby Birch and had been shot in the head by a startled gamekeeper who had chanced upon him. The sad irony is that, exactly opposite to chimpanzees, healthy wolves are not nearly as dangerous as is commonly supposed and will usually flee given the choice, but it was clear that this rotting zoo, in a roundabout way, posed as much of a threat to its animals as it did to the zoo's staff and visitors.

Colchester Borough Council undertook an investigation at the zoo, for this had been the second wolf escape that year. It was, however, understood that the escape had been under exceptional circumstances. The enclosure

Dominique Tropeano at Colchester Zoo in around 1985. (Newsquest)

had been poorly placed by Frank and was susceptible to ground erosion. Freak rainstorms had dumped 60mm of water on the town of Colchester that week, which, at the zoo, had washed away earth from underneath the fencing. The authorities were also satisfied by Dominique's new plan to reduce the number of wolves and to limit the amount of burrowing they were doing by digging ready-made hides for them.

Frank's old enclosures were also dangerous for the keepers who had to work in them every day. The fact is that most of the enclosures were much too basic, often being no more than a blank, square cage with a hut in the centre. Such a design does not give a zookeeper many options if they want to get in to clean. Often keepers would have to distract an animal with food at the far side of an enclosure while another keeper dived in and breezed through their work as quickly as possible.

In the earliest days, on one occasion, Dominique and a couple of members of staff were with the lions inside their cage when the male suddenly began to get very excited and started to face the men down. Dominique and the others urgently started removing their outer clothing to throw to the lion to distract him. They had just enough time to call for help on their new walkie-talkies before dropping everything and fleeing to shut themselves in the lions' indoor enclosure, leaving outside nothing but a pile of radio equipment and uniforms for the other, horrified, keepers to find in the cage as they rushed down from other parts of the zoo.

Beside the personal danger to staff and visitors, or the headline-grabbing break-outs, the worst thing about most of the existing buildings was that the animals were suffering as a result. Many of Frank's enclosures had not needed to be elaborate and comfortable. Some of his animals had been tame and had often gone into their cages only to sleep at night. Some enclosures were nothing more than holding pens for animals passing through the international dealership Frank had been running at the zoo in years gone by. Yet, gradually, Colchester Zoo had evolved into a more hands-off, fixed collection, and many of the animals were now languishing permanently in tiny, featureless enclosures.

One of the worst in the park was the elephant enclosure. Frank, in his inimitable way, had placed it right at the entrance to the zoo, in order to make the greatest impression upon incoming visitors. This had worked a treat in previous times but the eyes of visitors had since changed and now the first thing they saw when coming into Colchester Zoo was a pair of adult African elephants (named Moto and Toto after their predecessors) imprisoned on a small concrete podium, fronting a hut which looked like nothing so much as a garage. As the saying goes, one has only a single chance to make a good first impression, and this impression was not good.

The question of captive elephants was an exceptionally hot one in the 1980s. The death, in late October 1983, of a young elephant called Polé-Polé at London Zoo had caused sadness and outrage in the nation and fomented a strong and organised protest against all zoos, particularly against the keeping of elephants. With dreadful synchronicity, Colchester Zoo suffered the loss of one of its elephants at precisely the moment when this protest was reaching boiling point.

Dominique has since said that the death of Moto was simultaneously the most impressive and the most desolate thing he has ever seen. Early on the morning of 24 September 1985, Dominique happened to be standing near the elephant pen. Moto had seemed fine that day but suddenly she stumbled to her knees and crouched for a short time. She then hauled her great weight back up again. No sooner had she done so than she crumpled and fell a second time, dead.

Dominique was stunned. The Tropeanos had been at the zoo just over two years and had already come through a number of struggles but this was of another order altogether. What was the reason? What should be done? The first thing Dominique did was close the zoo for the day. The few visitors who had already arrived that morning were refunded their ticket money, but Dominique was subjected to abuse by other people arriving at the gate, who cared nothing for his explanation that one of the elephants had just died.

Elephants are immensely sensitive animals who grieve at death. The vast body could not, however, be moved, and Angela was able to do nothing but watch as Moto's life-long friend Toto stroked her dead companion gently with her trunk and nudged her with her feet in an attempt to wake her. The keepers were deeply affected too by this sudden death of Moto. Long-time keepers such as Gordon Pennington were devastated. A younger member of staff named Richard Spurgeon lost an expensive holiday he had arranged in order to stay with the bereaved Toto, even to the extent of sleeping nights in his car next to the elephant pen.

Anthony seems to have taken it hardest of all. His parents could preoccupy themselves with making arrangements for Moto's body and feel they were doing something proactive. His sister Sarah was upset but was perhaps a little too young to understand fully what was going on. Anthony, on the other hand, was fifteen years old by this time and had already started to work with the keepers on weekends. His idealistic dream of living with the animals at Colchester had already been dealt a few blows but this was exceptionally difficult to accept. To this day he remembers with chilling clarity the great carcass hanging from the crane which transferred it from the enclosure to a waiting truck.

A high-profile, hard-line anti-zoo organisation named Zoo Check (today a part of the Born Free Foundation), which had attacked London Zoo for the death of Polé-Polé, now turned its attentions to Colchester. A national newspaper printed a report by Zoo Check which complained that the elephant enclosure at Colchester was too small, that it lacked proper drainage, and that the animals were being fed mouldy food. It also claimed that the RSPCA was concerned about the goings-on at Stanway Hall.

African elephants Moto and Toto in 1977. This enclosure was exceptionally dangerous for the animals: they are seen here in a characteristic pose reaching out for food over the deep dry moat that surrounded their yard. (Colchester Zoo)

It would appear that at no point did anyone from Zoo Check talk with the zoo. Essentially it was an opportunistic 'hit-and-run' attack, which offered no positive help and did not recognise that Angela and Dominique were as horrified as anyone at the death of Moto. Zoo Check's failure to observe that the Tropeanos themselves wanted nothing more than to change the zoo led to some bitter retorts in the press from the family. There were certain legitimate defences to be made. For example, though the drainage was indeed poor in the elephant pen, Zoo Check's representative had visited on one of the wettest days of what was one of the wettest years in Colchester for nearly sixty years, with the worst local harvest since 1900. (As the *Essex County Standard* weatherman, Terry Mayes, later put it: 'All in all it was a summer most people would like to forget.')

Yet, though it came as a shock at the time, the Tropeanos now see that it was small wonder that Moto died. The post-mortem, carried out at Braintree, concluded that this mere teenager had died of a heart attack.

The poor conditions under which she had lived with Toto were bound to have resulted in something like this. Their indoor quarters were far too small – as a result the elephants had, for years, often been forced to stand outside in the wind, rain and snow. The outdoor paddock was also too small and gave little opportunity for exercise, which was another obvious culprit for Moto's poor health.

Furthermore, over the years both elephants had frequently fallen into the deep dry moat that ran around their paddock while reaching over for food from zoo-goers. (This was especially common in British zoos in those days – a young elephant called Diksie had even died at London Zoo in 1967 after her forelegs were crushed when she fell into her moat.) The whole situation had not been helped by the fact that this food had always consisted of copious quantities of sugary and fatty treats, which Moto and Toto had been fed all day, every day, since they had arrived as babies in the late 1960s.

This all added up to a bad state of health. Yet neither Moto nor Toto had ever been properly trained by Frank and so no one had been able to do anything with them. Moto had essentially been a dangerous wild elephant living at Colchester. No one had been able to take blood samples from her or even carry out proper physical inspections.

If there was one saving grace, it was that this painful episode was soon over. Moto was gone and Toto, within a matter of weeks, had gone elsewhere, originally to Longleat and then to a zoo at Wroclaw in Poland. Very different was the story of Colchester Zoo's bears; perhaps the saddest and most protracted story of all.

Colchester Zoo had two pairs of adult bears when the Tropeanos arrived in 1983: two Syrian brown bears and two Asian black bears. They were housed along the northern edge of the zoo, between the llama and the pygmy goat enclosures, in a couple of small, bare, concrete-based cages with no drainage facilities. The old male brown bear, Big Man, seems to have died not long after the Tropeanos bought the zoo. The other three bears – Big Man's mate, Susie, and the two black bears, named Mandy and Bruno – lived for many years longer. As cubs they had been freely petted in the zoo and had often been taken out to local functions by Frank and Helena, and one or more of them may have been among those animals that had appeared in the Sugar Puffs television adverts.

They had, however, long since grown up. For years, they had all been entirely confined to their tiny cages facing Maldon Road with little to stimulate them. Bears are inquisitive creatures and need things to occupy

The Syrian brown bear enclosure at Colchester Zoo in the 1970s. Either Susie or Big Man is pictured. (Richard Martin)

their time or they will begin to develop psychological problems. All through the 1970s and early 1980s these bears had steadily become disturbed in one way or another. Yet this disturbance was not immediately evident and the complaints coming from visitors about the state of the bears tended to pertain only to the bleak character of their enclosures rather than to the animals themselves.

The secret fact was that the bears were being occupied (during opening hours at least) by the constant stream of chocolates, nuts and sweets which were thrown to them by the visiting public. By 1983 the bears were all desperately overweight and in poor condition as a result. Dominique and Angela knew that this had to change. Early in 1985 they replaced the bars on the front of the bear cages with toughened glass. The bears were now bereft of the entertainment of public feeding, and all the mental problems they had quietly developed became agonisingly obvious overnight.

The one thing the bears had ever really had in their adult lives was the pathetic joy of sitting with their mouths open by the bars of their cage, begging for titbits from zoo-goers. Once this was taken away from them, the three of them took to walking up and down their little cages in constrained little circles, unable to understand why the generosity of zoo-goers had suddenly stopped. Susie, the brown bear, was the least affected of the three. She showed a little odd behaviour but was a fairly relaxed character and did not appear to suffer much. The two black bears were another matter.

Bruno was the most distressed of all, incessantly pacing in tight and repetitive circles, exaggeratedly weaving his head with a glazed look in his eyes and showing many other classic signs of aberrant bear psychology. The staff did their best to offer new diversions to the bears, such as giving them things with which to play. Susie and Mandy often responded well to this, but it appeared after a time that very little could be done for Bruno. His abnormal behaviour was hard-wired into him and it was doubted that anything could be done to assuage it.

The people of Colchester reacted with shock. One person, who today works at the zoo, recalls coming to Colchester Zoo as a visitor in the mid-1980s. Chancing upon the bears immediately after having seen the condition in which the elephants were living, he simply broke down in tears and had to leave the park immediately, vowing never to return. Even zoo-goers who were very young at the time recall visiting the bears and, despite enjoying seeing these animals, somehow knew that something was very, very wrong, even if they could not quite put their finger on it. The outcry was amplified by the fact that the bear cages were clearly visible from the busy main road and so anyone passing by in those years would see Bruno sitting in his cage, rocking ceaselessly from side to side.

When he had first arrived at the zoo in 1983, Dominique had announced his plans for instantly expanding the collection with unseen animals such as sharks and albino wallabies. He had quickly learned that the real way forward for Colchester Zoo would have to be the commercially risky but necessary strategy of actively reducing the collection to a more manageable size.

Many animals were leaving the park for other zoos by 1985. No zoo, however, would touch Colchester's ageing and mentally and physically unwell bears. Should they be destroyed? Dominique certainly considered it. There would surely be ever-more vociferous calls for the zoo to be closed down if it were to be said, as it no doubt would, that the Tropeanos were sending their animals insane and then killing them off. Should they then allow free public feeding to recommence? The zoo had scraped through its first licensing inspection in 1984, for the inspectors had recognised that the place had recently come under new management. However, many conditions had been attached to the licence, including that no animal feeding should occur unsupervised and that diets ought to be healthy and appropriate. To allow the bears to go back to eating salted nuts and chocolate bars all day could, likewise, potentially lead to the closure of the zoo.

A decision had to be taken at last. Dominique and Angela resolved to let the bears live and to try to improve their lot as best they could. The keepers began to give the bears a more interesting and varied diet. It meant a great deal more work but their cages began to be regularly filled with fresh hay. Some entertainment was offered to the bears, such as the novel idea of giving them their food frozen into giant ice blocks in order to keep them busy.

The sad fact, however, was that the zoo simply did not have enough staff members to give the bears the continuous attention they deserved, nor the resources to build new enclosures for them. Admitting that the zoo had no spare money, the Tropeanos launched a public appeal in July 1985 to raise funds for the rebuilding of the bear cages. Angela told the press that she ultimately wanted to do more for the bears than the licence conditions demanded. Her stated intention that the bear enclosures should be completely replaced with larger enclosures, with water pools for the animals and extra facilities for the keepers was, sadly, not realised: there was simply insufficient money and time.

Some alterations were eventually made to the existing enclosures and extensions were added. These gave the bears some private space to retreat to, as well as more sunlight and longer sightlines out over the countryside. Still, the issue would drag on for years as accusations of having sent their bears mad continued to be directed at the Tropeanos.

As it happens, much of Bruno's head-rolling in later years was actually caused not by the 'mental agony' which was reported but by the fact that his teeth were ruined after a lifetime of eating sweets from the hands of East Anglians (for which he went on to receive much expensive dental treatment). His intense pacing was also aggravated by the recurrence, after repeated surgical removal, of corns and ulcers on his feet as he got older. Though Bruno's mental condition, against all predictions, did actually improve slowly over time as more and more was done to alleviate his problems, to outsiders the strange behaviour which continued as his physical health deteriorated through age often appeared to be irrefutable evidence that he had been sent permanently insane. But as long as groups such as Zoo Check continued (as indeed they did for many years) to film places such as Colchester Zoo secretly and then call for inquiries in the press, there was little opportunity to discuss such details properly.

Sometimes the attacks even emerged from within. In the early 1990s there came the public resignation of two members of Colchester Zoo staff in protest at what they said was maltreatment of Bruno. These two girls had never, however, worked directly with Bruno, and did not seem to acknowledge that the zoo had in fact been acting at the time on the advice of an internationally respected veterinary consultant by giving mild sedatives to him and by experimenting with temporarily keeping him in his private quarters, away from zoo-goers, during opening hours to see if his mood improved.

Bruno died on 18 November 2001 and even to the very end the zoo was receiving allegations of abuse and threats of violence. Susie had already passed away, on 12 October 1998. Mandy, the last of these troubled bears, died a few months after Bruno on 10 April 2002. The years with the bears had been traumatic, with real tears of anger and frustration shed by people on all sides. Even random and accidental events, such as when a keeper named Terry Halls exposed his hand to the bears and ended up in hospital with nasty injuries, contributed to the lasting sense among the public that the bear situation at Colchester Zoo was out of control. Strictly speaking it had never been out of control. It was simply a tragic situation – tragic in the proper and ancient sense, in that no matter what decision might have been made, it would have been the wrong one.

Yet even those who insist on apportioning blame must accept that the Tropeanos' hard decisions in the early years were often made harder still by desperate bad luck. Many of the efforts to which they had gone to improve the park were ruined in October 1987, when the worst English storm for nearly three centuries swept through the country. The Home Counties were hit harder than any others and Colchester Zoo was not spared an inch. On the night of 15 October, Dominique and Angela happened to be away in Germany, having gone to meet with other zoo directors. Anthony and Sarah, still teenagers at this point, were alone in Stanway Hall. Jo Wheatley, a young keeper who lived in a caravan on site, was woken up by another keeper in the small hours as the storm raged, and remembers fighting her way up to the Hall to check on the youngsters. Each person there, including Anthony and Sarah, downed a shot of whisky to sooth their nerves and decided between them to complete a circuit of the zoo in order to assess the situation.

Anthony and Lee Thomas, a keeper in his late forties, armed themselves with shotguns and stepped outside with the others. Anthony recalls the dark and deafening scene outdoors, which seemed as if the very winds of hell had found their way to Stanway. Gales were shrieking and carrying everything in the park with ease. Anthony remembers roof tiles, heavy bins, and plates of sheet metal blowing freely around the zoo – just standing out in the open was potentially fatal.

No one knew what animals might be loose in the darkness. The little group reasoned that the worst situation imaginable would be if the bears had got out of their cages and so they headed there first. Thankfully, the bear houses were intact; they were among the few enclosures that had been built for posterity, giving the impression of having been modelled on Soviet nuclear bunkers.

It was a different story with the big cats. Falling everywhere were the majestic, colossal Lebanon cedars which had been saplings at the birth of Great Britain and which had so attracted Helena to Stanway Hall in the 1960s. One had landed over the fence of the tiger enclosure, offering a handy escape route for the animals inside. Anthony and the keepers were, however, quick to lever the whole tree over the fence and no tigers escaped that night. One of the zoo's pumas had already escaped from her cage, which had been crushed by another fallen giant. (She reappeared some hours later, stalking a member of staff, and had to be shot dead on sight by keeper Lee.) There were other escapees, including a pair of hyena (who were rounded up fairly easily) and a wolf called Josie who had been raised by hand and who was of no worry to anyone. Things could have been far worse – the only other fatality that night was a raven, which had been crushed in its aviary.

The zoo was forced to close for several days afterwards and there was no mains electricity for more than a week, but the summer season was long-finished and not too much revenue was lost. The main issue was the damage done to everything. Fifteen million trees had been blown down across Britain and more than a few of these had landed in Colchester Zoo. The beautiful old cedars for which the park had always been known had at last proved a liability.

A thousand local soldiers were deployed in the area, many of them coming to the zoo to clear the deadwood. This helped enormously, but did nothing to save the many structures that had been destroyed. One of the most galling pieces of damage was that done to a brand-new and costly cheetah enclosure. The cats had all been in their indoor quarters that night and were fortunately unhurt, but their outdoor area had been ruined. Such an exhibit – one of the very first built by Dominique and Angela – represented a major investment for Colchester Zoo at the time, an investment that had been quite lost.

The destruction across the rest of the park was considerable – vehicles had been damaged, windows had been smashed, the roofs had blown off the elephant house and the gift shop, and much of the zoo's outdoor furniture was wrecked, including its benches, tables, signposts, information boards and so forth. For the town of Colchester as a whole, the storm's aftermath required the biggest clean-up operation since the Second World War and cost the borough £750,000 (£1.8m). For Colchester Zoo, the 1987 storm was a calamity that undid much of the initial renovation work which the Tropeanos had been desperately trying to carry out with limited funds over the previous few years.

This was money the zoo could ill afford to lose. Its financial position was not good in the mid-1980s and it was this that was of the greatest cause of anxiety to Dominique, who had come to recognise that although money was a poor source of motivation in its own right, it was the route to achieving the ambition he had set for himself. Of all the struggles and indignities of his first years at Stanway Hall, Dominique today identifies the most disquieting experience of all as the moment at which Colchester Zoo's finances reached breaking-point: his bank manager came to speak to him and ordered him not to pay anyone unless it was strictly necessary.

Dominique could absorb the hatred and contempt which many people had for his zoo. He could cope with the accusations that were levelled at him personally, fairly and unfairly. He could cope with the long hours and the possibility that it all might come to nothing in the end. He could bear the personal threats he received by telephone from members of the public. He even shrugged off the time when a national newspaper took his photograph in front of Stanway Hall and went on to publish a lot of nonsense about how he and his family were living in luxury while their animals suffered, failing to note that the Hall was, in fact, by that time a complex of offices and storage space which afforded the Tropeano family no privacy and functioned for them as little more than a place to sleep. But for a man such as Dominique, who takes such pleasure in his working life, the idea of being unable to support his staff carried with it the prospect of the greatest humiliation. He could accept the fact that he could not afford to pay himself a proper wage in all these years. Nonetheless, he knew that he could not for a moment ask the same of his staff, without whom nothing could be achieved – for what would happen to the animals then? Another person might have given up at the moment bankruptcy loomed. Yet it only steeled Dominique's resolve that he would never again be in this position and that Colchester Zoo would be reborn.

2

NEW ZOO ORDER

FRANK FARRAR HAD the heart of an artist, working by feeling and intuition. Life for him, zoo and all, had been one big, uproarious game of blind man's buff and everyone around him had been carried along with the intoxicating, directionless fun while it had lasted. Dominique Tropeano, by contrast, has the head of an architect. Like Frank, he is a man of intuition, but a very different type of intuition – one possessed of a guiding will to organisation. Frank was a man of funny ellipses and impossible corners; Dominique, by contrast, is composed of clear sightlines and even planes.

Under Frank, Colchester Zoo had been a place without order and without duration, like a musical suite that sought to convince people, not with any kind of central message or sustained development, but with the delightful exuberance of each of its components. With the arrival of Dominique in 1983, a framework of time and space was newly thrown around Colchester Zoo. For the first time, the zoo became subject to the ministrations of a patterning mind which divided its future into three parts. These three parts were Dominique's short-, medium- and long-term plans for the zoo.

Despite the enormity of the problem that faced them, Dominique and Angela felt confident of their ultimate ambition for the zoo, for they knew they could rely on each other's determined support. Together they wanted to create a conservation and education centre which would raise money to help the wild cousins of the exotic animals with which Angela had grown up. They reasoned that there was only one way to reach this long-term goal, and that was through a medium-term strategy of rebuilding the zoo as an array of modern facilities allowing teaching, charitable fundraising and controlled animal breeding.

The only way, however, to start work on this medium-term strategy for the zoo was to embark on a short-term strategy of bringing large numbers of visitors back, in order to raise the necessary funds. Yet even before this short-term strategy could be initiated, an immediate rationalisation of the park was required. Dominique himself has said that in his early years at Colchester Zoo he had to be dictatorial. Certainly, it must have seemed that way to some of the members of staff when suddenly they found themselves invaded by this tough and energetic Frenchman.

If Dominique was dictatorial, he did not, however, act stubbornly, nor did he jump to conclusions. Another person observing the crippled state of Colchester Zoo at the beginning of the 1980s might have charged in and blindly divided everything into good and bad, according to personal whim. Dominique, on the other hand, did not truly begin to direct events until the beginning of his first summer at Stanway Hall, having spent his first few months there simply working on the ground with his staff and watching how the park functioned. The first objective was to simplify the whole park. From an evolutionary point of view, the Colchester Zoo of 1983 was a body of vestigial limbs, redundant organs and permanent parasites. Dominique was, however, now flexing his surgeon's knife. Within a year the structure of the park would be quite different.

In the early days of Colchester Zoo, Frank had leased out space for each of the zoo's kiosks, gift shops and children's amusements to other local businesspeople in return for a small rent. This had made very good business sense in the 1960s and 1970s. Frank and Helena had been completely engrossed in their lucrative film and television appearances and international animal deals, and never knew when they might have to leave the zoo for the other end of the world at a moment's notice. They had neither the time nor the interest to set up and maintain sideline attractions at the zoo, and it had been wise for them to allow others to build and run such things on their land in return for a fee.

By the time the Tropeanos were running Colchester Zoo, exotic animal dealerships were closing in Britain and few zoos here were hiring their animals out for media and circus performances. This meant that money was much tighter than it had been in Frank's day. The only real income the zoo had in 1983 was the gate money, and, since visitor numbers were miserably low, there was no question of raising the ticket price by any significant amount. (The first ticket prices set by the Tropeanos were £1.40 for adults and 70p for children – about £3.50 and £1.80 in today's money.)

The large amusements area on the eastern edge of the zoo, with its dodgems, one-armed bandits and children's vintage-car rides, was a very nice little earner for the Harrison family who also ran the zoo's gift shop. The rent they were paying in 1983 for these pitches was still, effectively, at a 1963 rate and the zoo itself was receiving a pitiful slice of these considerable sources of revenue that it so desperately needed.

The Harrisons had a number of other business concerns elsewhere and it was galling for the Tropeanos to see them come and go in their expensive cars while the zoo could barely scrape together enough cash to pay the mortgage each month. As soon as the Harrisons' contract was up, the amusements and the gift shop were taken back. The same went for all the other kiosks and suchlike which were run by outsiders. This caused some resentment: many were honest people who had been coming to Frank's zoo year after year and did not appreciate Dominique and Angela's attempts to streamline the business.

Also to go was 'The World's Finest Model Railway', which, after twenty years, was starting to look like it would only just about win the title even of Colchester Zoo's Finest Model Railway. The axe was dropped on Frank's museum rooms, too. In the time since Frank's stroke in 1981, many of the museum items which had been of any value or interest had grown legs and vanished. One John Malseed, whose collection of rare vintage bicycles had been on show at the zoo since about 1965, now recalls wishing he had been sufficiently light of finger to help himself to some of the scale-models of planes, African musical instruments and Second World War weaponry, which all went walkabouts in the early 1980s.

By 1983, the main museum at the zoo was a history lesson in leftovers. Little remained besides some old hand-farming tools, some unremarkable spears and an elephant howdah no thief had been able to fit in his pocket. Also on show were a couple of fake shrunken heads Frank had once brought back from a visit to South America and a sculpture of a lion, claimed as Roman but most likely bought from a local junk shop. John Malseed's bicycles were still interesting, but the time had come for a major spring clean and it all had to go.

Colchester Zoo steadily began to become profitable once again in this way, by slimming down overhead costs and redirecting streams of income straight back into the zoo. Many problems were still waiting in the wings, but these would be mitigated thanks to this early, rather brutal, severance of the park's flab.

Similar surgery was performed on Colchester Zoo's staff. Reg Howe, of limited ability with animals and a rather grouchy old soul to boot, was relieved of his position of head keeper. His loyalty to the zoo was, however, recognised and he was kept on for many years as a full-time driver until his retirement in about 1990. Gordon Pennington, too, was removed from the keeping staff, for his way of dealing with exotic animals was likewise outmoded. Yet he also had an old-fashioned talent for hard work. Indeed, there have been few people at Colchester Zoo who have worked harder than Gordon, and for many years up to retirement he served as the head of Dominique's in-house team of construction workers.

Some of the old guard left for new prospects of their own accord on good terms. A young keeper named Glyn Evans left for Cotswold Wildlife Park in about 1986. Joan Honisett, who had been with both zoos at Southport and Colchester for nearly thirty years, also left at about the same time. Joan and the Tropeanos knew and liked each other well. She had known Angela as a girl in Southport in the early 1960s, and she had also known Angela's children since the early 1970s when they had first come to visit Uncle Frank at Colchester. Sarah had, admittedly, then been no more than a bump, but Anthony had been just big enough to make a fine wreckage of Helena's living room at Stanway Hall. Joan worked in the mid-1980s under the Tropeanos just as assiduously as she had done under the Farrars and her contribution was valued. Still, for Joan it was never going to be the same without her beloved Helena and good old Frank, and she and the Tropeanos parted company after a few years, wishing each other well.

Other members of staff were simply not interested in the Tropeanos and even looked down their noses at these newcomers to the park and to the zoo world. These staff members were dispatched with some rapidity. But if Dominique was clear in his mind about who ought to be excluded from the park's future, he became, throughout the 1980s, rather more focused on who deserved to be supported, surrounding himself with younger members of keeping staff, such as Clive Barwick (today a curator at the zoo) and Richard Spurgeon (now the zoo's manager).

And Dominique certainly did surround himself. The most telling fact about Colchester Zoo as it moved through the 1980s was the steep rise in the number of workers. At the zoo's height in 1970 Frank had employed perhaps ten keepers. When the zoo was sold in 1983 that number was down to about six. However, by 1987 (even with a reduced animal collection) Dominique had twenty-eight animal keepers on his books.

The severe cuts performed during the Tropeanos' early years produced a single, simple entity, with every penny spent going into the zoo's own coffers. The realigned and expanded staff body was being worked extremely hard, with good results. The recovery from the operation was slow but steady and the zoo would, as a result, find itself well placed to start the work of attracting visitors back in. Now, and for many years afterwards, the greater part of the zoo's energy was turned to changing the perception of the zoo and improving the quality of visitors' days out in the park.

A coherent attempt was made to awaken the public to the fact that things were going to be different from now on. Perhaps the most confident and overt change was the official restyling of the park as 'The New Colchester Zoo', publicly signalling an intent to develop and modernise the park. The advertising also changed in the 1980s. Adverts for the zoo had often been fussy or gimmicky in the past. Under the Tropeanos they quickly became simple, bold and classy. Though Southport Zoo had been explicitly aimed at children in former years, Frank and Helena had directed their advertising at Colchester Zoo towards families in general. The Tropeanos now made their address much more specifically to young families.

The zoo's new promotional leaflets were glossy and colourful, showing pictures of sprightly, modern nuclear families in baseball caps, getting up-close-and-personal with parrots and other animals. A bright series of logos was developed, all based around a distinctive semi-circular pattern suggestive, perhaps, of a rising sun, and featuring smiling elephants and suchlike. Sometimes included in the later designs was a new mascot called Chester, a dapper cartoon tiger wearing a straw-boater hat. These efforts at re-branding paid off, with Chester the Tiger in particular becoming well recognised by Colchester's children over the years. The zoo again started to be mentioned in local newspaper articles with the kind of regularity it had known in the early days, as its profile rose and its new advertising began to draw larger numbers of punters back to Stanway Hall.

But the change would not happen overnight. From many potential visitors' point of view the Colchester Zoo of the mid-1980s, 'new' or not, remained a distinctly unappetising prospect. Opportunities for entertainment at the park were few and outdated. All the paths were dirt tracks, which became quagmires on rainy days. There was little shelter from the elements, and the shop, food and toilet facilities were exceedingly primitive by post-industrial Britain's new standards. Die-hard animal enthusiasts had always been willing to brave these discomforts but

The New Colchester Zoo logo, 1980s. (Colchester Zoo)

Dominique and Angela knew that, if their long-term goal was to succeed, Colchester Zoo was going to have to devote itself in the short-term to increasing its appeal to casual visitors.

The business of catering for tourism has a long pedigree going back many centuries, at least to the seventeenth century when affluent young noblemen invented the gap year as they roved aimlessly around Europe, in the awkward period between reaching adulthood and inheriting their fathers' fortunes. It had not been until after the Second World War that the tourist industry had begun to become a science. By the early 1980s it was becoming an art – something that had not gone unnoticed by the Tropeanos. Another person in Dominique's position in 1983 might have been minded to start touring other zoos in order to start copying how they conducted their business. This Dominique did, drawing much inspiration, for example, from Twycross Zoo. However, he also took the unusual step of visiting attractions such as Alton Towers, which had been growing soundly since 1980.

Intriguingly, Dominique went yet one stage further in his search for ideas. He considered nothing irrelevant; everywhere he went he closely watched how various institutions and organisations provided for their clients, even including railway stations, airports and motorway service complexes, which were starting to become ever more adept at presenting and selling their products and services. Dominique became particularly interested in the first generation of gigantic shopping malls which Britain was then starting to produce. He was struck with the force of revelation that people's consumption habits were altering out of all recognition. To him, these malls seemed more like theme parks than mere shops.

Seeing how such places recognised the needs of their visitors, Dominique realised just how far Colchester Zoo's provision for its own guests had dropped behind expectations. This was not, however, an issue limited to his zoo alone. By the mid-1980s most zoos in the country were laying on very poor fare. In 1984, an influential book by Jeremy Cherfas, *Zoo 2000*, happened to paint an unflattering picture of a lunch he had recently eaten at London Zoo. Cherfas described the restaurant itself as a filthy mess, with revolting food and headache-inducing décor and lighting. His book also suggested that the toilet facilities were inadequate and that a place such as London Zoo might do well to learn something about customer care from department stores like Selfridges.

It was not the case in all places, but there was a strong sense in many British zoos that the paying public were an inconvenience to be tolerated rather than accommodated. Facilities for them were poor, keepers generally avoided them, and zoo-goers were made to feel like outsiders. Dominique, also coming into the zoo world as an outsider, was able to see more clearly than many others the disparity between British zoos and tourist attractions such as Alton Towers and Pleasurewood Hills. In the latter venues, visitors were actively welcomed. Staff members ran regular shows for their visitors, engaged with children, talked and joked with the parents and generally made people feel at home. If a visitor had a problem, there always seemed to be a friendly helper available to lend a hand.

Frank's personal love of the general public had also inspired Dominique and Angela. They resolved that their park would be among those leading the way into a new and more open era in British zoos. The most important of the Tropeanos' early developments was a new policy that all keepers should actively seek contact with the public. This is something that has persisted to this day and has played an absolutely crucial part in Colchester Zoo's extraordinary success. Staff had always mixed with visitors since the earliest days of Frank's zoo, but there was no structure or purpose given to this. Under Dominique, keepers began to carry out routine talks and displays with their animals at specified times so that visitors could get to know the staff and begin to feel more emotionally involved with the zoo's animals. There were, for example, scheduled penguin parades, when the birds would be led out of their enclosure for a short walk around the zoo, accompanied by a couple of keepers to explain a little about their origins, behaviour and diet and to introduce them to people by name.

A large permanent marquee was set up which housed regular shows designed to demonstrate the learning capabilities of parrots, who would carry out things like simple counting tasks and talking sequences. These shows became comparatively complex, with little cars made for them to drive around in and even special bicycles which they would pedal along high-wires. Another major feature of the zoo's developing daily rota was the sea lion show, which the Tropeanos' daughter Sarah helped to develop. Three young South American sea lions, Pat, Ago and Nia (collectively

Keeper Lee Thomas in training with elephant Tanya or Zola outside Stanway Hall in around 1986. (Colchester Zoo)

named after their place of origin), came to live at Colchester Zoo late in 1986. Before long they were delighting audiences at their shows, having been trained to do some basic tasks – like clap their flippers together, and gather hoops around their necks that had been thrown into their pool – while their keepers talked about their individual personalities and the nature of the species as a whole.

Other important new additions to the park, which directed themselves squarely at public engagement, included in-house falconry displays which started at Easter 1987, organised at first by keepers Lee Thomas and Andrew Hulme. But the star attraction above all was the daily elephant walk. After Moto had died and Toto had gone to Longleat in 1985, Dominique and Angela had asked themselves if they ought not to be replaced. Then again, Colchester had been an 'elephant zoo' almost from the very beginning: would it damage the zoo's identity too grievously to do without this much-loved species?

A decision was made to bring in a new pair of elephants. This was a brave choice, for the headlines concerning Moto were still raw in people's memories. It then remained normal for zoos to buy and sell animals (but under much tighter laws than previously) and two young females were purchased from Longleat for £20,000 (£52,000). Tanya, born in about 1981, arrived at Colchester Zoo on Saturday 2 November 1985, and Zola, roughly a year younger than Tanya, made the trip on the following Saturday. These two girls seem to have been (in a limited sense) rescue animals, having been spared from a controlled cull on a game reserve in southern Africa.

Dominique, Angela and their staff were determined that the mistakes made by Frank should not be repeated. Colchester Zoo was to remain an elephant zoo and would atone for the death of Moto by proving that it could look after elephants properly. From the start, Tanya and Zola were closely and carefully trained by the Tropeano family and their staff so that the animals could be freely handled and medical checks carried out.

This hands-on approach meant that the public could also be invited into the elephants' lives in an appropriate fashion. A distance barrier was erected around the main elephant enclosure to put a stop to unrestricted public feeding, but outside the front door of Stanway Hall a special additional pen was created. The elephants would be walked there regularly to be petted and given good food by members of the public under the supervision of the keepers. These, and many more innovations, allowed the public to feel ever closer to the animals. Dominique also placed general entertainers among the growing crowds, such as fire-jugglers and musicians. Significantly, all these events and entertainments were free to anyone who had paid on the gate.

Other ideas for breaking down the divisions between the zoo and its public were trialled. Animal adoption programmes had long been running at other zoos. Frank had developed a very lukewarm animal adoption programme in 1974, which had petered out quickly. The Tropeanos reinstated the scheme in December 1983, recognising in it a chance not only to raise sorely needed money for the zoo but also yet another way for visitors to feel that they were making a special personal contribution to the park. The scheme was only a moderate success at first but it was obvious that persistence would pay off eventually. After one year, 150 people had each sponsored an animal in the collection. Dominique and Angela were happy with this figure: it was not going to pay for the rebuilding of the zoo, but it showed that, despite continuing attacks from various quarters, many people were appreciative of what they were trying to achieve.

As the years passed, the Tropeanos experimented with many other initiatives and attractions within their zoo, always with the aim not just of enticing the public back into the park, but also of making them feel that they were actually a part of life at the zoo. Colchester was at the very forefront of new trends in zoology, such as giving opportunities to members

Dominique bathing elephant Tanya in the new public arena outside Stanway Hall, in about 1988. (Marian and George Sayer)

of the public to work with the park's keepers for a day alongside the animals, in return for a donation to the zoo.

Footfall steadily increased as the zoo continued to embrace its visitors in such ways. In 1983, annual visitor numbers had been low, at around 100,000 or so; the figure for 1985 was 280,000. By 1987 it had risen again to 325,000. The short-term strategy for the zoo was working – the gate at Colchester Zoo was once again becoming a busy thoroughfare, and the gift shop and food outlets were also performing their reorganised functions admirably well. Budgets remained tight, but good money was finally starting to be taken.

Unfortunately, the path around one obstacle led directly into the face of another. In 1987 the zoo's licence came up for renewal. The team dispatched to inspect the zoo were not happy with what had been going on at the zoo in the three years since the previous licence had been awarded, just after Christmas 1984. This team included John Knowles who, the reader will recall, had worked at Colchester Zoo in the early 1970s and had known Frank well. Knowles had always believed that an insufficient amount of the zoo's profits had been reinvested in the park in previous years. Now it appeared that history was repeating itself under the Tropeanos for it seemed as if nothing had fundamentally altered. It would not become compulsory for British zoos to do education and conservation work until 2002, but Knowles and the other inspectors knew which way the wind was blowing and were not much impressed by this zoo, which seemed to be focusing its energies almost exclusively on entertainment and leisure.

In 1987, when looking at Colchester Zoo under the Tropeanos' command, the inspection team saw little evidence of noteworthy proceedings such as the birth of endangered and difficult-to-breed species, or widespread changes to the unacceptable animal cages. Some basic work had been done to improve the lives of some of the animals – there were new houses for the zebra, lemurs, wallabies, and various small and big cats, as well as a new reptile house – yet things were generally thought inadequate. The most high-tech recent addition to the park was running around the lakes at the bottom of the zoo: a larger and more elaborate miniature train ride to replace the smaller one which had been placed at the top end of Frank's zoo. The most conspicuous events under the Tropeanos had been such things as a motorbike stunt display by daredevil Eddie Kidd in the zoo's car park in 1983, and the time when pop stars Midge Ure and Paul Hardcastle had played a set at the zoo during filming for a children's Saturday live television show in 1986.

It is small wonder, then, that the conservation-minded Knowles and his fellow inspectors expressed dissatisfaction with the direction in which the

Michael Dean at the helm of Hercules, Colchester Zoo, 1980s. (Gordon Dean)

zoo appeared to be heading. There was some charity and education work going on, but even old Frank had managed this in one way or another. Indeed, by 1987 the whole thing seemed like nothing so much as a new version of Frank's zoo.

One sympathises with the members of the inspection team now facing Dominique, whose confidence in the future of his park was riding high on the concrete success of his short-term plan. Dominique knew that his strategy was working and that his medium-term plans would soon start to be put in motion. All he needed was a little more time – but to Knowles and the other inspectors it was just words. How could they be sure that enough money would eventually find its way to the right places? Dominique adamantly insisted that he was serious about restoring the zoo as a whole, but needed the benefit of the doubt for a while longer in order to shore up the park's financial security.

Knowles and his team had their own reputations to consider. Colchester Zoo was attracting more visitors now – so much was true – but its standing was still low and the verdict of their inspection report would be noted by many people. Could they sanction this defamed park which, even now, seemed to be placing the desires of its visitors above other considerations? And then there was the legitimacy of the licensing process itself. For years, zoos had been seeking to distance themselves from animal circuses, which were clearly dying a death throughout Britain. Yet Colchester Zoo was unabashedly putting on regular displays of animals demonstrating overtly 'circusy' tricks. To give a licence to such a zoo could potentially tarnish other licensees as well as themselves.

Disagreement was expressed at the meeting when the inspectors laid out their requirements for the immediate future. Dominique contested that their conditions were unreasonable. To his mind, at the time, it seemed they were asking for the near-total rebuilding of Colchester Zoo's animal facilities within three years. Where was the cash for the vast quantity of building material going to come from? Who would pay the construction workers' wages? And even given all the money in the world, would it not be physically impossible to carry out all this work within the given time limit while still keeping the zoo open to visitors? Hot words began to be exchanged. The licensing meeting broke down and was abandoned.

3

RESURFACING

EVEN AFTER MANY years of running his own zoo at Marwell, John Knowles had not forgotten what it is like to struggle through the first years of an enterprise. He saw something authentic in Dominique's protestations and eventually persuaded his inspection colleagues that the New Colchester Zoo ought to be given a little longer to prove itself, and the licence was granted.

Dominique now admits that he may have stuck to his early strategy too doggedly and that more might have been done for some of the animals in his very earliest days at the park. However, in the years of 1983 to 1986 there had been no real money for this. The family was already mortgaged for all they were worth and no more cash was forthcoming from the bank. Much of the little income the zoo was receiving in those days was going on loan repayments.

Maybe one could criticise the Tropeanos for failing to seek private backers. Then again, who would have been willing to invest in one of the most public embarrassments among British zoos? Many doors were barred. Colchester Zoo lacked the resources and manpower to perform the sort of revolution such as was going on at other zoos in the mid-1980s. There was not even a way for the Tropeanos to deliver some kind of grand one-off gesture that might have helped to win over a distrustful audience. Dominique remained something of a stranger to the zoo world and various people in the Federation of Zoos and in the charitable zoological societies viewed the New Colchester Zoo with misgivings, seeing it as little more than a money-making operation.

It is, in truth, to Dominique's credit, that he dug his heels in when challenged on his short-term strategy for his park. Without his singularity of vision, Colchester Zoo would have been finally damned during this second inspection. Dominique knew he was right and did not forget his self-imposed mission for a moment, even when many of the veterans around him were telling him he was, at best, following the path of good intentions. Dominique would doubtless have received lots of pats on the back from other members of the zoo community had he, from day one, blundered in and spent all his time working on time-consuming conservation projects and trying to provide all his animals with thoroughly modern enclosures on his initial shoestring budget. Dominique would doubtless have also received lots of cooing sympathy when his zoo came crashing down around him a few years later, as it certainly would have done.

While Dominique and Angela had, in reality, focused on making the zoo seriously profitable once again, it seemed to many outside observers by 1987 that little was being done to improve the zoo at large; a visitor could still walk around Colchester Zoo and almost imagine themselves to be walking around Frank's zoo in 1967 – if they ignored 'secondary' features, such as the new toilet blocks, the new zoo-themed items in the gift shop, the higher quality meals in the café and the daily events list. Many people continued to criticise the zoo, blind to what such changes portended and ignorant of many invisible things such as new staff training and management practices, new record-keeping methods, and new plumbing and electrical infrastructure. Regular critics of the zoo were effectively silenced from 1988 onward, as the zoo emerged from the depths. Criticism of the zoo would endure, but it was reduced to mere potshots about specific issues instead of broadsides against the whole park. And even this sniping would begin to fade away as the Tropeanos' medium-term ambitions for the park became startlingly evident as the 1980s ended.

In 1988, a superb new enclosure was constructed for two Diana monkeys who had recently joined the collection. It was to be the first vindication for the Tropeanos' vision. The Colchester Zoo of today dates from the construction of this enclosure. Admittedly, a number of new enclosures had already been produced in the previous five years, but these had been done quickly and cheaply. Several had also been badly damaged in the storm of the previous October.

The zoo had begun to set out its stall with an impressive new monkey complex (with a 47-metre viewing bridge) in March 1988, but it was the Diana monkey house which appeared in the following July which combined, for the first time, all of Dominique and Angela's future aspirations.

Dominique (right) in the New Colchester Zoo uniform, overseeing construction of a new spider monkey house, in late 1987. (Newsquest)

At £15,000 (£35,000), the cost of this enclosure was a considerable outlay for just two creatures, but the Tropeanos were determined to make a declaration of their belief in animal welfare and conservation. This large building was of a size that many zoos of fifty years previously might have filled with dozens of animals. It afforded abundant room for a mere pair of Diana monkeys. The enclosure was divided into two parts, with an open-air run and an indoor 'forest' area. This space inside was filled to bursting with carefully arranged tree trunks, branches and foliage that gave these monkeys plenty of opportunity for exercise and play.

This new enclosure also consolidated the continuing departure from the zoo's old aesthetic of mesh and concrete slabs. It presented to visitors' eyes the attractive and more homely combination of glass and diagonal wood panelling, which would become the zoo's visual signature all through the 1990s as the Tropeanos' medium-term reconstruction scheme began to be realised. Other features about the enclosure told of Dominique and Angela's ultimate ambitions and also of how people were starting to perceive their zoo. It was given, for example, a short opening ceremony conducted by

Brigadier Steve Goodall, a respected member of the zoo establishment. Across the front of the enclosure was placed a large and attractively painted educational board about Diana monkeys, detailing various facts about the species. The zoo, continuing to dream up ways of involving members of the public directly, also ran a competition for suggestions for names for the two new animals. (This idea has since become very fashionable.)

There was also, for perhaps the first time at Colchester Zoo, a coherent conservation message. Dominique passed a statement to the press about the decline of the species in the wild. The opening of the new enclosure also coincided with a month of events that were being run at the zoo in support of an overseas conservation project, which at that time was seeking funds to perform a survey of the declining habitat of wild Diana monkeys in Africa.

Just before the Diana monkey enclosure opened, the RSPCA had released a report about Colchester Zoo, criticising the sterility of the animal enclosures. An RSPCA spokesman did, however, admit that Dominique and Angela seemed to be trying to improve things. What the Diana monkey enclosure, then under construction, portended for the next ten years at Colchester Zoo makes this now seem like a considerable understatement. Though Colchester Zoo might have appeared to such observers to have been even more antiquated by 1987 than it had been in 1983, in terms of attitude and intent the zoo was, in reality, twenty years ahead of its time.

The zoo was only just shifting into second gear but its engine would be turning hard as the Tropeanos' short-term strategy segued into the medium-term. The following year, 1989, would see the opening of a huge new tiger garden. In another innovation considered unusual at the time, this enclosure was given an imaginative title, Tiger Valley. This name was part of an attempt, for the first time, to give an individual Colchester Zoo exhibit a general theme of some kind. Looking back now, Anthony considers the theme of Tiger Valley to have been rather crude and patchwork, with its ersatz Middle Eastern onion dome arches crossed with painted-stone balconies vaguely reminiscent of classical Asian architecture. Maybe it was crude, but whatever concessions might have been made to the orientalist fantasies of Home Counties zoo-goers, the central focus was upon providing Colchester's tigers with a plot of land considerably superior to the spartan cages to which they had previously been confined.

Like the Diana monkey enclosure, the size of Tiger Valley was ample for a pair. There was much foliage and many secluded spots to which the cats could retreat if they wanted privacy from visitors or from each other. The

The Tiger Valley enclosure in 1989 or early 1990. (Colchester Zoo)

new trend for zoos to allow their creatures to hide if they so wish has been, and remains, a difficult pill to swallow for those people who consider they are not getting their money's worth unless they see every last animal in a zoo in a single visit. Yet it was being pursued with conviction at Tiger Valley, even in the 1980s.

The ground of the enclosure was also varied. A large pool was let into the central lawn. This often afforded the tigers more entertainment than was expected: though it had been intended for the tigers, who as a species are good swimmers, it more often served as a favourite watering spot for some of Colchester's wild ducks, whose swiftness often had to match their courage. Further stimulation was provided by rocks arranged to break up the enclosure's landscape, as well as many tree trunks for the cats to claw.

New animal houses would now start to appear all over the park in a rash of glass and timber. There would be major new enclosures for the zoo's jaguars and beautiful maned wolves. The zoo's family of otters would also be provided with a new home named Otterama. As the 1990s dawned, Colchester Zoo's construction team, under Gordon Pennington, was beginning to hone its skill in providing new buildings for its animals. There had already been many successes, but by 1992 the time was right for the Tropeanos' first truly landmark addition to the park. Chimp World, as this

The main viewing gallery overlooking Tiger Valley. (Colchester Zoo)

new exhibit came to be named, represented an even fresher initiative in construction and animal care at Colchester Zoo.

At the time, Chimp World was the most advanced building ever constructed in the grounds of Stanway Hall by some considerable margin, and compared well with ape facilities in other zoos. Staff and visitors alike had always loved the zoo's chimpanzees, but life was miserable for them in the crumbling ex-giraffe house. Both Dominique and Angela sincerely wished to do something spectacular on their behalf. To this end, a 6,000-square-foot complex, costing around £300,000 (£500,000), was planned for Tara, Mandy, Billy Joe, Jenny and the others. Chimp World was to consist of three principal enclosures: day quarters with a waterfall; sleeping and feeding quarters; and large outdoor quarters. The whole complex was to be filled with ropes, artificial trees and rocks for the chimps to swing, climb and play upon.

By this time, a new policy known in zoos as 'environmental enrichment' had begun to be officially adopted by Colchester Zoo. 'Enrichment' refers to the extent to which zoo animals are mentally and physically stimulated in captivity. One form of enrichment is making animals work for their food. In 1991, Colchester Zoo announced that it would no longer always be offering easy meals to many of its animals, but, where appropriate, would be hiding food in boxes of straw, submerging it in pools, or suspending it from swings and ropes in order to exercise and entertain its animals. Chimp World, for example, boasted an artificial termite mound full of holes in which food could be hidden, in order to be teased out with sticks by the chimps.

The new enclosure also represented a new type of experience for the zoo's visitors. Instead of standing around the outside looking in, the design of Chimp World was such that people found themselves immersed within the complex, moving around the leafy covered walkway formed by the gaps between the animals' quarters. The animals were no longer simply housed in a box, to be passively observed like a television show. One had to search actively to find them and perhaps look around for another, hidden, window that might afford a better view.

Special attention was paid to the provision of education within Chimp World. A number of unpalatable truths were spoken unflinchingly. Visitors could read about the abuse of pet chimps by photographers on tourist beaches. Instructions also invited visitors to discover the identity of the planet's most destructive animal by opening a door, which revealed nothing more than a large mirror.

Chimp World was a hugely complicated exhibit. In former years, enclosure structures had generally contained one species, such as the elephants in the elephant pen. If they had contained more than one species, they tended to conform to a type, as in the large aquarium which Ivor Williams and Frank had built. Chimp World seems to have been the first structure at Colchester Zoo in which wildly different animals were presented side by side. Within the northern end of the building, directly adjacent to the chimps, was created, for example, a separate enclosure suitable for a pair of small crocodiles.

Much public attention was paid when Simon Mayo came down to open Chimp World in April 1992. As the long-time host of BBC Radio 1's prestigious breakfast show, which in those days received almost ten million listeners, Mayo was one of the biggest names in British show business. His appearance at Colchester Zoo made an appropriately big impact for what was in fact the most exciting opening ceremony at the park since Radio 1's 'Diddy' David Hamilton had opened Frank's giraffe house almost a quarter of a century earlier.

It was no coincidence that Chimp World was built on the site where old Rajah's cage had stood. That had been demolished and now, at the centre

Angela and Dominique Tropeano receive a UFAW award for the design of a new enclosure for colobus and black mangabey monkeys in 1991. (Newsquest)

of Colchester Zoo, stood instead this imposing modern building, which covered all bases at once. It comfortably balanced the needs of the animals, the expectations of visitors, and even the demands of the keepers, who were provided with generous service corridors and room for storage. For the first time since 1969, Colchester Zoo was running ahead of its time. Indeed, the zoo was pushing ahead so far and so fast that a little urgent diplomacy was required when one guest at Chimp World's opening ceremony, Conservative MP Anne McIntosh, publicly announced that she was looking forward to seeing chimps' tea parties there.

Anachronisms like tea parties could not have been further from Dominique and Angela's minds. After nearly ten years, their park was at last starting to look like a contemporary animal conservation centre. Not only was Colchester Zoo once again a member of the Federation, but Dominique had even been appointed to its education and marketing committees and now sat on the Federation's council. The first of many awards were starting to roll in for the zoo's breeding programmes and improvements to the designs of its animal enclosures.

And just as Colchester Zoo began to launch itself once more into the future, its past began to disappear behind it — its founder was dying. Helena Farrar had been gone for some years by this time. It had been an awful surprise to everyone when she had dropped instantly from a heart attack on 4 February 1988. By then, Frank had been in poor health for years and everyone, himself included, had been convinced that his wife would outlast him by decades.

Frank was lost without Helena. The two of them had fought endless battles with each other over the years but it was, as Dominique puts it, one of their ways of showing their affection for each other. Deep down, Frank's beautiful wife had been his rock for almost forty years. Together they had explored far-flung forests and jungles; together they had raised tigers and orangutans; together they had conquered this unforgiving world. In later years, Helena had patiently nursed him after his stroke. Despite all his faults and indiscretions, she had remained faithful to him always.

By 1988 Anthony was nearly twenty years old. He and Frank had long been good friends, ever since the day he had been given those axolotls back in the 1970s. Anthony vividly recalls the day of Helena's funeral and bodily supporting old Frank, who was all but blinded and lamed with grief. Dominique, like Frank and everyone else, had secretly believed that Helena, this strong, noisy, terrifying woman, would live forever and had been as shocked as anyone when she had suddenly vanished out of the world. Yet when he saw Helena lying in her coffin he was left with the unshakeable impression that she seemed far smaller than she had been in life. Her ashes were eventually returned to Lancashire where they were scattered in the Silver Birch Glade at Southport Crematorium in the following June.

For the five years since Helena's passing, Frank had lived alone on Layer Road in a house which they had, in former years, set up to Helena's liking, given that she had been due to live far longer than him. To live in solitude in a house in which everything reminded him of his dead wife was torture for him, but he still had many friends to distract him. Joan came to cut his hair most Saturdays, and Angela and the family often visited him. It was never enough, though. Frank was a person designed for the scrum and was only ever in his element at the centre of some great performance or ridiculous adventure. He was not suited to retirement, and he constantly craved companionship.

A younger friend of his, David Judge, remembers that old Frank would often set off his own burglar alarm on purpose and telephone David to ask him to come over and 'fix' it. Like everyone else, David never really minded, for Frank was excellent company and would always tell lots of fascinating stories about the old days; perhaps about the time he was ripped to shreds by wild lions in Africa, or the time he found himself in the midst of the terrible Portugal earthquake of 1969 while on holiday in the south, or, perhaps, about the time he somehow got caught up in the Invasion of Goa while in India in 1961.

But that had all been a long time ago. It was 1993; Frank was finally on to his ninth life and even that was now running out. Anthony recalls arriving at the old Severalls Hospital in Colchester to find the rest of the family standing around his uncle's bed on 2 April. Frank's sister Nancy, like Helena, had died, but the devoted Mabel was still there. Dominique and Angela were there too.

Dominique recalls that Frank had been lively enough that afternoon but suddenly seemed to become younger by twenty years when Anthony walked in through the door. The old Frank Farrar grin suddenly seemed to fill the room. 'There you are, love!' said Frank. 'Tell us now, who's won the National?' It was, however, only Friday – that year's Grand National would not run until tomorrow and Anthony told him as much. Frank turned away and died. On the next day, the National was declared void. Animal rights protestors disrupted the start of the race and a series of resultant misunderstandings meant that, for the first and (still) the only time since the first Grand National of 1839, the race was run but produced no winner.

Dominique Tropeano was done few favours by Frank Farrar – he was given no discount on the purchase of Colchester Zoo, and he was also left holding a great number of ticking bombs, many of which he had defused with only the most painstaking care. Yet Dominique, to this day, maintains respect for the memory of Frank, a man who himself had asked no favours of anyone and who had carved his own unique path through life's wilderness.

Nevertheless, Frank's route had proven a dead-end and it now fell to the second generation to forge a road in a different direction. For Colchester Zoo, this new path was to run out of the woods and straight through a building site. The years between the death of Helena and the death of Frank had already seen many new enclosures going up around the zoo. The new decade would see the park recast as an institution upon which the town of Colchester could look proudly.

4

ORANGE SQUASH
AND POPCORN

B Y THE END of the 1980s, Colchester Zoo was on a sound footing. In accounting, retail and catering, Angela was running a very tight ship and was more than a match for these challenges. Gordon Pennington was ably exercising routine control over the construction and maintenance going on in the park. In animal husbandry, Dominique had built a strong team of thirty zookeepers, now including Anthony who had recently given up the opportunity to read Law at the University of Nottingham.

Indeed, the foundations of Colchester Zoo were now strong enough for the park to offer aid to other zoos. In 1991, the closure of London Zoo was announced, after more than 160 years of business. Its visitor numbers had been dropping throughout the 1980s and the vast size of its animal collection was entailing costs that could no longer be met. Its collection had begun to be dispersed: no one could then have known that a ground-swell of public assistance would eventually enable its ultimate survival. In October 1991, Colchester provided homes for several refugees. Three species, in fact, were accepted, including a male caracal who had been alone at Regent's Park but who quickly settled in with Colchester's two females. Also from London came a troop of Mayotte lemurs and a pair of cream ponies.

This was, however, small fry in contrast to the assistance that Colchester Zoo had already started to lend to other zoos. Dominique had for some time been an active member in a new organisation named the European Association of Zoos and Aquaria (EAZA, known briefly until 1992 as ECAZA). The purpose of EAZA was to provide a network of support and co-ordination among European zoos. This purpose became all the more urgent as the Iron Curtain was lifted and it became abundantly clear how true were all the stories of economic and technological failure in the

Communist borderlands. To all countries, but especially to those who had suffered under Soviet rule, EAZA offered assistance and advice on how to run a zoo which worked from every angle: commerce, education, recreation, welfare and conservation.

Dominique's restoration of Colchester Zoo had been noticed by a number of important people in the zoo world and he had been invited to join EAZA's work. Dominique had accepted because his own park was now running well enough for Angela, Anthony and Sarah to be able to hold the fort while he travelled abroad. His work with EAZA would take him all over Europe and Asia for twenty years. As a member and, later, chairman of the Association's Technical Assistance and Animal Welfare Committee, he would go on to make perhaps forty formal trips to European and Asian zoos, in order to offer the benefits of his learning and experience, to help with legal problems, business and tourism planning, architecture and enclosure design, and to run workshops on animal nutrition, enrichment and safety.

His first visit took him deep into Eastern Europe, to the zoo at Latvia's capital, Riga. Together with a colleague from Cambridgeshire's Linton Zoo, Dominique was pleased, if a little embarrassed, to be received like royalty at the airport by a welcoming party bearing flowers. Upon arrival at Riga Zoo, however, it quickly became apparent to Dominique that this was to be no holiday. Soviet insularity had fostered an inward-looking ethos at Riga. Except for one young keeper who had been lucky enough to travel abroad, no one had learned much from zoos elsewhere in Europe. Many of the animal enclosures were of bad design, which caused many problems. For instance, though Riga's rhinos, hippopotami and elephants each had only the most limited indoor facilities, all were locked permanently inside every year from October to March.

More problematic was Riga Zoo's overall attitude. This proved difficult to alter, but they had asked for help, which suggested that there existed the will to change, and this gradually proved to be the case. For example, the directors of Riga Zoo were eventually persuaded to give up their beautiful and gentle bull elephant (who was something of a star in Latvia) when it became apparent that they simply could not provide him with what he needed. Riga acted upon much other advice regarding planning and restructuring at its zoo, and its staff members were even invited to Colchester Zoo in order to observe newer forms of animal keeping. Riga Zoo has since improved hugely and Dominique today points to it as a shining example of how an institution can turn itself around.

Many such inspections were hard work. Plenty of zoos were less willing to change than Riga. Many also thought that assistance from EAZA would mean lots of free money and new animals for their collections. It often came as an unwelcome surprise to them when they were advised to direct more of their own spare money into improvements to their facilities and even to reduce their animal collections where necessary. The misconception that the Association was an animal dealership was a tough one to break, especially after ECAZA had officially become EAZA in 1992 and incorporated the EEPs, through which zoos make animal transfers in an organised fashion to protect and optimise the gene pool of the international captive populations of individual species.

Dominique's work for EAZA was challenging for a host of other reasons. Language barriers sometimes posed problems. He also often found himself working in sub-zero conditions. During one inspection at Kaliningrad Zoo, north of Poland, the temperature dropped to -27 degrees, leaving him unable even to hold a pen to take notes. The widespread habit of drinking copious quantities of spirits at committee meetings was also hard going for Dominique in his early days in Eastern Europe. Even though he strictly limited his intake on such trips (drawing the line, for example, at drinking before midday), he has not been able to touch vodka since the mid-1990s.

Nevertheless, despite the various obstacles, small and large, advances were forthcoming at many zoos all over Eastern Europe and Russia after the collapse of Communism. Dominique had always loved solving problems. He was now being given the chance to do this on a grand scale for a cause in which he believed. Conscious of his own success at Colchester and of the appalling condition of some of the places he was now touring, Dominique grew bullish in his pursuit of improvements in Continental zoos. A series of sobering experiences would somewhat change this.

On one occasion he was invited to lend assistance to the zoo at Albania's capital city of Tirana. Dominique had already seen many dreadful things, both in Britain and overseas. At a zoo in the Ukrainian city of Odessa, for example, he had been gravely moved by the wretched sight of a female Asian elephant permanently chained to one spot, day and night. But his experience at Tirana Zoo was to be the worst of his career and one which he has never forgotten. None of the animals at Tirana had access to the outdoors. Many of them were kept in little boxes, with little space and no fresh air. Few had ever felt sunlight, wind or rain on their feathers, skin or fur. Not one of the keepers at Tirana appeared to have any kind of training,

The lion enclosure at Tirana Zoo, Albania, in the 1990s. (Colchester Zoo)

the zoo's electrical supply was poor, and there was not even any running water on the site.

In the discussion following his initial inspection, Dominique pulled no punches. He told the staff at Tirana that the conditions at their zoo were intolerable. At this moment, the translator seated at Dominique's side fell silent. Dominique asked her if she was going to translate what he had just said. He found himself unexpectedly shamed when she declined but apologised and quietly replied to him that if he thought Tirana Zoo was bad, he ought to see how the people of Albania themselves lived.

Dominique recounts that he learned a lot about himself during such trips. It may have been appropriate for him to pass judgement at his own zoo back in the wealthy developed world, where opportunities for change and advancement were many, but at Tirana he realised that it was quite another thing entirely for him to be marching around the poverty-stricken towns and cities of countries which were mired in shocking political and economic problems, or struggling to prise away the dead fingers of Communist rule. Dominique was being forced to confront the fact that willpower alone is not always sufficient: that no matter how hard a person may try there is sometimes simply no way out.

Dominique tells the story of a young woman named Alla whom he befriended. She worked at the bitterly cold and grey zoo at Kiev, the capital

A primate enclosure at Tirana Zoo, Albania, in the 1990s. (Colchester Zoo)

of Ukraine. This girl was so poor that she could not afford a place to live, and so she slept at night-time on the floor of the zoo's records office. Despite not being paid a living wage, Alla was devoted to her zoo and desperately wanted to improve things there. Such was her dedication, that she had recently returned straight to the zoo following several weeks in care after being horribly mauled by tigers when a colleague had mistakenly released them while she was cleaning their cage.

Alla was likeable and hugely intelligent. Her language skills were also good: she often served as a translator for Dominique and other members of EAZA, and was keen to learn about new developments in zoology elsewhere in the world. But she was unable to act upon her enthusiasm, for she was soon to be diagnosed with terminal cancer. Dominique was appalled at this penniless girl's plight and sent her some money so she could at least spend her last days in a hospital.

Such experiences left their mark on Dominique, who, then in his late forties, was becoming a more thoughtful man. His struggles in his own work had been considerable, but the problems which he saw others confronting in the East were something different. Other members of EAZA who travelled and worked with Dominique were also deeply affected, as were zookeepers from Colchester who were occasionally sent out to Eastern Europe and Russia to provide advice and hands-on training.

Perhaps the most emotional experience of all was the visit Dominique paid to Sarajevo in the wake of the Bosnian War. Sarajevo sits in the valley of the Miljacka River and is surrounded by hills. It was in these hills that Serbian soldiers set up a ring of camps in 1992 and blockaded the city. The terrible Siege of Sarajevo would last almost four years: the longest siege of a capital in modern history. In these hideous years, Sarajevo would be continually shot at and shelled by the Serbian forces. More than 60,000 civilians would be killed or wounded. Most of the city's buildings would be damaged in one way or another, if not destroyed. Parliament buildings, hospitals, schools, markets and museums would all be hit. Pioneer Valley Zoo, not far from the centre of Sarajevo and a great source of city pride, would be utterly ruined.

Sarajevo's giraffes, eagles and wolves would be among the first to die in the crossfire. Ponies, donkeys, deer, antelope, peacocks, goats, pheasants, buffalo and swans would all be grievously maimed or killed by shots and explosions. Animals would be used for aiming practice by Serbian gunners or would be caught in blasts from shells directed elsewhere. Animals not killed outright would eventually die of starvation. Their keepers would be largely unable to reach them or to carry enough food to them due to being targeted by snipers themselves. All the herbivores would soon be dead; the carnivores, such as the big cats, survived a little longer by eating each other.

In previous years, Pioneer Valley Zoo's male lion had been famous across Sarajevo for roaring loudly every morning before seven o'clock. His final alarm call would be heard on one morning shortly after Midsummer's Day. *The New York Times* would report on 4 November 1992 that the very last of Sarajevo's 100 zoo animals, a bear, had died, having somehow survived months of hunger and bombardment.

When the Dayton Agreement ended the Bosnian War three years later, Dominique was among the many people called upon to help rebuild this devastated city. He flew out to meet with the mayor of Sarajevo and the staff of Pioneer Valley Zoo, in order to help create a strategy for reinstating the zoo and for resuscitating the area's industry. Dominique recalls having an al fresco lunch with the mayor, early during this visit, eating delicious trout freshly caught from the Miljacka. Looking around at the sublime hills surrounding them, Dominique remarked that the city could quickly be regenerated by focusing on tourism and building strings of attractive hotels down the sides of the valley – the mayor shook his head. Dominique did not

Bosnian War gravestones in Sarajevo, 2006. (Christopher Charles)

understand exactly what he meant until he was taken for a walk with some locals up one side of the valley. The land to the very horizon was thick with landmines. As the walking group crested the hill, carefully remaining within a narrow path which had been mine-swept, Dominique suddenly found himself confronted with row after row of beautiful but bombed-out houses. Beyond these houses was one of many graveyards containing hundreds of fresh graves, a great number of which marked the resting places of children. The central city itself was a hellish ruin: this was common knowledge across the world. Dominique now saw that in truth the entire Sarajevo Valley had become a spectacle of death.

Nonetheless, life continued in and around the shattered buildings. The people of Sarajevo had much to teach about the real meaning of pride and fortitude. Dominique and his associates stayed for a short time with a surgeon who had been decorated for his work during the Bosnian War. While his city had burned around him year after year, this man had regularly risked his own life to help people with horrifying injuries and fatalities. He had seen some terrible sights. Yet, so he told Dominique, the very worst moment of the war, for him, had come when his little daughter, who had not left the family's flat for three years, asked him for nothing more than some chocolate and he could not oblige her.

On another occasion, Dominique and his colleagues found themselves being entertained by a lady who lived in a single room with her young boy and her dog. She fetched down her best glasses and set before them all the food she had: a feast of orange squash and fresh popcorn. Dominique remembers it as one of the finest meals he has ever eaten. This woman had almost nothing left in the world but her eyes were shining with the joy of giving it all to her guests.

Dominique had found himself among strong people who had stood firm while their world had fallen. Stories of the greatest honour and sacrifice emerged at Pioneer Valley Zoo. At least one keeper had survived a bad wound he had received under fire while trying to reach his animals in that first year of death. Another keeper, a young man named Esref Tahirovic, had been shot to the ground while running through no man's land in 1992, trying to take food to his animals in the zoo. It was not until the shooting had stopped two hours later that anyone had been able to reach him. Nineteen-year-old Tahirovic (an unpaid volunteer, like all the keepers at Sarajevo's zoo) had died on the way to hospital.

In this and in all his work in Europe and Russia, Dominique wanted to see such tragedies counterbalanced by restructuring and rebirth. This desire was often forcibly mixed with the profoundest frustration, for many of his plans seemed to come to nothing. At Sarajevo there was no money immediately available to put in action the scheme that Dominique and the others drew up for Pioneer Valley. Zoos in other nations were paralysed by politics and corruption or by a lack of foresight and open-mindedness. Dominique sometimes doubts whether any of his efforts to assist other zoos had much effect. Others flatly contradict him. His work as an international zoo consultant became, for example, a factor in the creation of the 1999 European Zoos Directive, which set minimum standards for education, conservation and animal welfare in zoos in European Union countries.

Koen Brouwer, the former long-time Executive Director of EAZA, readily describes Dominique's attitude towards those in need: if he recognised that assistance was needed and deserving, he would board the very next plane. Moreover, if Dominique could not help, he would find people who could and frequently drew on his many connections to help individual zoos. Late in 1995, for example, he undertook to secure a great deal of money from a multitude of other zoos in order to pay for an operation on the infected tusks of an Asian elephant called Boy at Kiev Zoo.

Those who travelled and worked with Dominique as part of EAZA's Technical Assistance programme also testify to the fact that his hosts in whatever zoo he has ever visited have always maintained great affection for him as a person and have had great respect for his work. Through such assistance and in helping with the creation of initiatives such as mentoring and a formal EAZA membership application process, Dominique played a part in fostering a sense of community and collective purpose among Europe's zoos. He must be counted among those people who have helped, therefore, to make possible such long-term programmes as managed international endangered species breeding.

The very fact that people like Dominique showed interest in places such as Sarajevo when they requested aid helped to inspire them to rebuild and improve, and even today he is only a telephone call away for such places. EAZA now has well over 300 member zoos and even Sarajevo has become an official candidate for membership – a fact which gives Dominique and others great pleasure.

Koen Brouwer adds that, in all his years of working with EAZA in zoos around the world, Dominique claimed not a single penny of the expenses to which he was entitled. Dominique simply says that his continuing efforts to assist others has been his way of showing gratitude to those people who believed in him when he was trying to rescue his own zoo back in Essex.

The early days at Colchester Zoo had been a difficult experience and had toughened Dominique Tropeano. But a person would be quite mistaken if they thought he might have been softened by the sights and stories of zookeepers lamentably wounded or killed carrying out their work for little or no pay. If anything, his work with people in places such as Sarajevo, Tirana and Kiev more tightly circumscribed any impulse he may have felt to accommodate those at home who showed little instinct for self-sacrifice or who could not reconcile themselves to work and privation.

Indeed, by the mid-1990s Colchester Zoo was, once again, in need of all the help it could find, and Dominique had time only for those people who wanted to see the park achieve great things. Throughout the remainder of the decade and into the new century it would be all hands on deck at Stanway Hall, for Dominique and Angela's zoo was beginning its transformation from a moderately sized provincial animal garden into a national-class zoological centre.

5

BEHOLD NOW BEHEMOTH

ARCHITECT PETER JOHNSON was used to building warehouses and supermarkets. It was he who, in the late 1980s, had helped to design the huge shopping park at Tollgate where western Colchester meets the A12. Peter was a little surprised, then, to receive a telephone call in 1992 from a stranger with a thick French accent who wanted him to build half a zoo.

Peter had been a life-long zoo-goer, but though he had often visited faraway parks such as Chester and Bristol he had never once visited Colchester Zoo, despite having lived nearby for years. He admitted as much to the man on the phone, to which Dominique replied, 'Yes, you and many others!' However, Dominique then explained that his zoo had been offered the chance to change this sorry state of affairs.

The land surrounding Colchester Zoo had long been owned by Tarmac, who had been working out gravel quarries in the area for years. The empty portion of land between Colchester Zoo and the village of Heckfordbridge to the west was, it seems, of no use to Tarmac, for the Roman River Valley had been designated a conservation zone in 1976. There was doubt that the authorities would permit the opening of new gravel pits so close to the protected river and so Tarmac had given Dominique the option of purchasing this piece of land. Dominique had agreed and was now inviting Peter to the zoo to talk about expanding onto this virgin plot.

Peter admits that when he first arrived at the zoo he felt Dominique to be rather arrogant, so full was he of big plans and confident that no one could possibly stand in his way. Peter soon realised it was in fact the sheer excitement talking. The Tropeanos had been walking against the wind for a decade at Colchester Zoo and still had managed to make things work.

This offer from Tarmac was, really, their first stroke of good luck. Both Dominique and Angela realised that with the wind at their backs for once there might be no limit to what they could achieve. It was Peter's unenviable job to calm everyone down and make them set aside their prophetic visions for a moment. He was an old hand at this sort of thing and knew from experience that the first thing to do was to clear the table in order to work upward from the known facts.

Building a new half to the zoo was going to be very different to the way in which Frank had built the existing park in the simpler 1960s. There were many struggles ahead: planning permission had not yet been given. Even if permission were to be given, there would surely be limitations imposed on the number and nature of potential buildings, as well as all sorts of other legal hurdles to jump. The more Peter examined the facts, the more apparent it became that Dominique had scarcely formed a solid idea of what function this expansion would serve. His enthusiasm was, however, infectious and in the end Peter's methodical positivism combined with Dominique's energy would prove to be a formidable partnership.

Their co-operation on this expansion of the zoo is something they both think of with the greatest fondness today. It was hard work but in many ways it was also like a holiday. For Peter it was an enjoyable relief from his daily workload – supermarkets may be necessary but do not offer much freedom to an architect's imagination. For Dominique it was a delight not to have to worry about first demolishing and working around Frank's old buildings and foundations, or to have to conform to existing routes around the zoo. This new twenty-acre development at the bottom of the zoo was a blank page and gave these two men many opportunities to act out grand Corbusian and Consular fantasies as they arranged and rearranged their *arrondissements* and *régiments* all over the map.

Their plans to turn Colchester Zoo into a leading British animal collection were publicly announced in April 1993. A front-page splash in the *Essex County Standard* described Dominique's intention to create a 'miniature Serengeti' at Stanway Hall at a cost of £2m (£3.5m). This plan probably came as a surprise to many people in Colchester. The statement to the nation by Blur singer Damon Albarn (by then verging on household-name status with the release of his second album, *Modern Life is Rubbish*) that his hometown was a den of mediocrity was still being discussed in local newspapers, almost two years after he had said it. With the borough yet to emerge from Britain's economic struggles of the early 1990s, many townspeople were rather inclined to agree with him that modern life in Colchester was, indeed, on the rubbish side.

In 1963 Colchester had initially believed itself not to be the sort of place that *ought* to produce zoos. In 1993 it seemed to many that Colchester was not really the sort of place that might be *able* to produce a miniature Serengeti. Those people who had stayed true to their vows and avoided the zoo since the dark days of 1980-86 would certainly have been mystified at these new and bold ideas emanating from Stanway Hall.

The highest priority for Dominique was to re-house his two elephants, Tanya and Zola. The girls were almost teenagers now. They had been at the zoo for nearly ten years, yet were still largely confined to the old enclosure that Frank had built. Once upon a time this elephant house had been considered acceptable but now it was a source of shame to everyone. Visitors coming into the zoo in the mid-1990s were less than impressed when immediately confronted by this miserable and frankly dangerous concrete podium and hut in which such lovely young ladies as Tanya and Zola were housed.

A new elephant house was at the top of Dominique's to-do list for strictly personal reasons, too. Zookeepers always maintain that they do not and must not have favourite animals, but Tanya and Zola represented – and still do represent – something very special to Dominique Tropeano. The arrival of these two girls late in 1985 had marked the moment at which Colchester Zoo had slowly begun to demonstrate that it could be made to work. A conscious decision had been made that every effort would be taken not to repeat the mistakes of the past. And, sure enough, life was much better for Tanya and Zola than it had been for their forebears Moto and Toto. Tanya and Zola had long been on healthy diets, were given plenty of mental stimulation and had always received the best medical treatment money could buy. They were the subject of a great deal of daily attention by the zoo's staff and were regularly exercised, being taken for walks around the zoo and even up and down Maldon Road.

Yet despite the fact that the time to build Tanya and Zola the house they deserved was long overdue, they would have to wait a little while longer. The old spectre of zoo traffic had returned to Stanway. With limited visitor numbers in the 1980s, it had never been a big issue for the Tropeanos. Now that the zoo was regularly receiving over 300,000 guests each year, the local roads were once again becoming clogged. The problem, as it had been in the 1960s and 1970s, was that Frank's old ticket office (hardly more than a

Keeper Richard Spurgeon with Tanya and Zola in the public arena outside Stanway Hall, 1990. (Colchester Zoo)

shed with a window) was an artless way of doing business, being set virtually on the main road. On busier days the stream of waiting cars would be split and tickets would be sold directly at car windows by several staff, but the whole set-up had always been far from adequate.

By 1993, Colchester Zoo had turned from a basket case into the fifth most popular tourist attraction in Essex. On busy days, zoo traffic was queuing down Warren Lane to the A12. Local residents were once again having their patience tested as they watched the resurgence of long, permanent, slow traffic jams, with the added modern delight of waterfalls of drinks cans and food wrappers spilling into their front gardens from the windows of stationary cars. The zoo was warned by the police that they would no longer be permitted to open on bank holidays in the future, unless something was done about the admissions gate arrangement. And if the zoo was serious about doubling its size, and thereby perhaps doubling the number of its visitors, there might be serious questions asked about its continued viability as a whole.

As much as everyone would have liked to see work begin right away on the new elephant enclosure, the first job had to be the construction of a proper entrance building. A new scheme was devised – Frank's old 'pay and park' system would be replaced by a 'park and pay' system. Zoo-bound drivers were to exit straight off Maldon Road and park up inside the zoo before paying on foot. In the summer of 1995 work began on what was, once again, the most impressive building Colchester Zoo had yet produced. This large new entrance hall, still in use today, was designed to resemble a traditional Essex barn, in keeping with the demands of the planning regulations. The underlying structure went up over the winter of 1995-6, topping out on 13 February 1996, when the distinctive roof turrets were lifted into place by crane. Inside the hall were provided a row of four modern pay desks, a conference suite and a large gift shop, as well as other amenities.

In the last days before these new ticket desks opened, zoo traffic, having threatened to do so at various times since 1963, finally achieved total gridlock across the whole of Stanway when 26,000 people converged on the park over the 1997 Easter bank holiday weekend. Easter Monday alone saw 8,000 people visit the zoo, with cars reported to be queuing into Eight Ash Green, two miles away. When the new entrance hall finally opened shortly afterwards, this zoo traffic, which had been such an infamous feature of western Colchester since the early 1960s, disappeared in an instant, passing into local legend. (It also confounded the long-standing dodge of children being hidden in car boots to avoid the purchase of tickets.)

The turrets on the new entrance hall are lifted into place on 13 February 1996. (Peter Johnson)

Dominique and Peter's attention had, however, already long since turned back to their new elephant house. Peter had never before designed an animal house of any kind and was keen to start as he meant to go on. Dominique, too, was determined that the new development should be completed to the very highest specification. The two of them together toured elephant houses all over Europe in order to study what worked and what did not. They observed the facility at London Zoo but found this to be of limited use to them. This classic early 1960s design, courtesy of architect Sir Hugh Maxwell Casson, was quite unsuitable for keeping elephants. (Only a few years later the decision was taken by London not to keep elephants there any longer.) They also visited Dominique's good friends Molly Badham and Nathalie Evans at Twycross Zoo. Their elephant house was better, but still not what Dominique had in mind. Twycross kept only cows; by contrast, Dominique intended to create an elephant-breeding centre at Colchester Zoo. Keeping a bull elephant is a quite different proposition to keeping a cow. For one thing, males go through periods known as *musth* (an Urdu word deriving from the Persian for 'drunk'). Often signalled by a strange treacly secretion from the sides of the head, in this period a bull's testosterone levels rocket upward and he becomes unpredictable and often highly destructive.

Peter and Dominique between them knew they still had much to learn before setting in stone their plan to keep bulls. They travelled to many elephant zoos overseas: they took notes from the layout of enclosures in some Irish zoos, and they learned much from Rotterdam Zoo in the Netherlands. Speaking with the elephant keepers there, they heard many stories about the power of bull elephants. For example, Rotterdam's elephant enclosure had originally separated the bull entirely from the cows. This had seemed a sensible decision for the protection of the females. The bull, of course, had known well that he was not alone in the zoo and had other ideas. During his *musth* he became so frustrated at not being able to get at the females that he charged the great steel gate which divided them, ripping the whole fitting out – wall, steel lintel and all. The staff at Rotterdam soon realised that if they allowed the bull to have a form of controlled contact with the cows, such as allowing them the opportunity to caress each other with their trunks through wide bars, the bull's violent response largely disappeared.

Dominique and Peter took many of the best ideas they saw in these zoos and tried to incorporate them all into the new elephant house back in Colchester. Dominique was determined that the elephant house should be sensible and economical but also of a complexity great enough to allow the keepers as many options as possible for moving their animals around, for doing training sessions with them and also for allowing visitors to see and meet them in a variety of ways.

Foremost among Dominique's priorities was that the indoor facilities should be large enough to keep the elephants comfortably indoors during bad weather. The cow side of the house was to be designed with a large central area for feeding and training. Around the edge of this area individual stalls were to be provided, along with separated sections as well as a heated pool with a waterfall for bathing. The bull's quarters in the north end of the building were to be separated from the cow's quarters by bars instead of a wall, to allow some contact with the females. Other details were important: many of the bars throughout the enclosure would be diagonally slanted in order to reduce the possibility of the animals whipping people with their heavy trunks.

Elephants are proportionately the most dangerous animals kept in zoos worldwide and the needs of staff at Colchester were carefully considered accordingly. Protected walkways and areas were incorporated into the plan for this new house, in order for the keepers to be able to move around the building in safety. A staffroom was even provided, along with CCTV facilities in order to be able to study the animals' activities.

The paddocks beyond the house, covering several acres, were to be far larger than any space given to the elephants previously at the zoo, and were provided with more pools and waterfalls. Again, Dominique and Peter were keen to give the keepers options in their work, and fences and gates were thus provided at opportune spots in order to allow the animals to be separated and contained when necessary.

These outdoor paddocks would be separated from the visitors' walkways by trenches, as at the old Colchester elephant enclosure, but would also be fronted with raised rocks to prevent the animals from falling in and hurting themselves. In contrast to the part-concrete paddock at the old elephant enclosure, these new paddocks would comprise open soil with which the elephants could cover themselves, as they do in the wild. Concrete still had its uses, however – an additional wide hard-standing area would be provided between the main paddocks and the house, so that the animals could still spend time outside if days of heavy rain made the paddock ground too treacherous.

In other words, this was not going to be just a larger version of Frank's shed and yard. Every last detail was considered, including indoor visitor viewing areas and educational displays. The only thing missing from the plan was any great degree of imaginative theming for the building. The planning rules for such a large building, just as for the entrance hall, demanded a plain black barn upon a brick plinth according to the old Essex vernacular. It is often tempting for a zoo to over-do its theming for large and prestigious enclosures and there are plenty of examples around the world of zoo animals housed in elaborate fake Hindu temples or ancient Egyptian palaces. The only real gesture in this direction at Colchester was the grand name given to the new enclosure – 'Elephant Kingdom'.

Looking back, Anthony sees it as curiously appropriate that the new elephant house maintained a certain austerity, given that its fundamental purpose was to make good the terrible mistakes of the past. Colchester Zoo was famous, for good and for ill, on account of its elephants. On the table at last was a plan for an elephant facility of which it could be proud.

It was an ambitious scheme and would not easily be put into action. Colchester Council had rebuffed the initial suggestion in 1993, and it was not until an agreement was reached for the planting of a thick row of trees all around the new development that the application had been given closer consideration. The plans passed their first obstacle at the beginning of April 1994, when councillors provisionally approved the development. Further assent was eventually given for the land to be turned over from farming use to zoological use and the new development was given the full go-ahead.

There was much embarrassment all round when it was later discovered that a public right of way existed across the land. No one had previously identified this footpath and as far as anyone was able to tell it was never used, running, as it had, through a cow field. Public complaints were nevertheless made. Eventually a government inspector came down to consider a diversion to the footpath. All this caused many delays and the issue would not conclusively resolve itself until the day Deputy Prime Minister John Prescott intervened on behalf of the zoo. Work was underway again on the elephant house by the summer of 1997. Fortunately the weather was good, and by the end of August that year the new elephant house was starting to appear, with public interest growing accordingly. Everything was going smoothly.

Then, one morning in February 1998, an unusually thick package arrived at Stanway Hall in the post, along with the usual slew of daily correspondence. Before anyone had got round to opening it, the office staff received a strange telephone call asking if they had liked

Elephant Kingdom under construction, 1997. (Peter Johnson)

what they had seen. Suspicions were immediately raised. Mail bombs were big news in those days as a result of deadly campaigns by people such as Unabomber Theodore Kaczynski and groups such as the Irish Republican Army. There was also ongoing concern about the continued militancy of animal rights organisations into the 1990s. Colchester's butcher shops had repeatedly had their windows smashed and had their walls daubed with the old Morrissey slogan, 'Meat is Murder'. Activists had even been known to target local shops that allowed circus advertisements in their windows.

It had been only a few years since the Animal Liberation Front had broken through the fence at Colchester Zoo one night and stolen two little Scottish wildcats, later claiming to have released them into the wild. Memories also remained of the time when a nearby farm had been attacked by the ALF, who had secretly cut the brakes in all the heavy vehicles there. Dominique was not at all happy about this chunky, unidentifiable parcel which now sat on his desk. And the cryptic, alarming phone calls persisted: *Do you like what you have seen?*

By the time a police bomb disposal team had reached the zoo, the mysterious package had been placed in a field beyond the car park. After some deliberation the decision was taken not to blow up the parcel but to try to open it, perhaps in order to be able to trace its source. Inside the envelope was found nothing more than a videotape. Watching the video back in the Hall, Dominique and the others found it was a film that had been shot covertly by an activist group called Animal Defenders between October 1997 and January 1998. It featured three abused African elephants: a male called Tembo and two females named Opal and Rosa.

These elephants were owned by the Chipperfields, the famous English circus family, and lived at a farm just north of Southampton in the village of Middle Wallop. Tembo was faring the worst of the three, suffering beatings with spades and suchlike. On one occasion he was thrashed so hard and so repeatedly with an iron bar that it broke. The others were almost as badly treated. Anyone may accept, for instance, that an elephant may be chained briefly if a medical procedure must be carried out. Tembo, Rosa and Opal were, however, being chained regularly and for long periods of time.

Animal Defenders were aware that Colchester Zoo was putting the finishing touches to a vast new elephant complex, yet had only two cows. Despite the weird and tentative anonymous phone calls they had initially made, they eventually opened frank discussions to find out if the zoo could do anything to help.

Dominique was therefore presented with a classic dilemma. He could foresee that any court case which might lead to the confiscation of the Chipperfields' elephants would drag on for a long time. (Mary Chipperfield and her husband Roger Cawley were eventually convicted on multiple separate counts of animal cruelty in 1999. Their elephant keeper, Stephen Gills, was sentenced to four months in jail.) In the meantime, Tembo, Rosa and Opal would continue to live in misery and pain while everyone wrangled in the courts. Could Dominique bring himself to put money in the hands of animal abusers, even if it meant instantaneous rescue for these suffering elephants?

He could have ignored the whole thing and acquired his own herd of elephants at no cost through the international breeding programme. Instead, he decided that the expense of purchasing the animals from the Chipperfields was immaterial if it meant that these elephants could be retrieved immediately from torture. Tembo, Rosa and Opal were bought for £53,000 (£80,000). A Colchester keeper was immediately dispatched to Southampton to ensure that no further abuse could occur before transportation.

Dominique was criticised for his decision to buy these three elephants. A programme broadcast by BBC2 showed that Colchester Zoo was in breach of Federation regulations, which stated that member zoos ought not to purchase animals from circuses. A newspaper said that the sale contravened the rules laid down by CITES. Dominique freely admitted that such criticisms were understandable, but he had no regrets. In his words at the time, he was 'saving Tembo, Rosa and Opal from hell'.

The dilemma was the kind of answerless and time-consuming moral question which delights planners of religious education and philosophy seminars everywhere. Yet while debates about true dilemmas tend to focus on the fact that there can be no right answer, it is often overlooked that there can also be no wrong answer. Whatever the case, it would be a brave person who could say that Dominique did not act on principle. It was his way of continuing to redress Colchester Zoo's past, both in his day and in previous times. His own inexperience had compounded Frank's errors when, in 1985, the world had seen that Colchester was not able to keep all its elephants alive. Things were different in 1998: Dominique's zoo now boasted a world-class breeding centre for rescued elephants.

When the public invitation to the grand opening of Elephant Kingdom was announced early in 1998, there was excitement such as had not been known for years. For the zoo itself, the new elephant house represented its true entrance, at long last, onto the national stage. And for the Tropeano family it marked their fifteenth anniversary at Colchester Zoo. The zoo was beginning to close the door on the bleak days of the past.

The local police service had often helped to organise traffic outside the zoo in earlier days. Now, for probably the first and only time, they were forced to help with crowd control inside the park itself: a huge crowd of 10,000 people turned out to see the official opening of the new elephant house.

Everyone then present now testifies to having felt a tremendous sense of joy on that sunlit April day as the elephants emerged into their new paddocks. Everyone knew that Tanya and Zola had lived for a long time in substandard accommodation. Most were aware of the wretchedness of Tembo, Rosa and Opal's previous life with the Chipperfields. Some admit to having shed a tear at the sight of Tembo, gouges still visible on his shoulders, tentatively exploring his new home.

A number of ghosts were laid to rest at Colchester Zoo that day. The relationship between the town and its zoo had been steadily improving year on year, but on that sunny day in 1998 there was rekindled a little of that true love which had died in the 1970s.

Greater things still were coming. The Elephant Kingdom enclosure, the park's bright and bouncing newborn, was destined to have a sister. A twin building and paddock, to be named Kingdom of the Wild, was planned next door to it. In symmetry across a wide path running between them, these two structures would, side-by-side, come to dominate the park.

Previously, this spot had been the furthest hinterland of Colchester Zoo. The western edge of the new elephant house lay – as would that of the Kingdom of the Wild house – directly along the original boundary line of Frank's zoo at its most distant end. With the new expansion, Elephant Kingdom and Kingdom of the Wild would come to sit at the heart of the new, enlarged zoo in the way that the site of Rajah's cage and (later) Chimp World had provided the zoo's axis in more modest years.

Although this new building was to appear, outwardly, almost identical to the elephant house, the scale of its ambition was of a yet higher order. In the early 1990s, Dominique and Anthony had visited Emmen Zoo in the Netherlands. There they had seen a large and innovative exhibit, which successfully mixed together a wide range of species of African mega-fauna in one paddock. Having been used for so long to zoos that kept species largely separate from each other, father and son were both dumbfounded with amazement. They decided that their zoo ought to have something similar to Emmen.

Not until almost ten years later would Colchester Zoo's own huge mixed-species exhibit begin to rise out of the ground. However, as Kingdom of the Wild neared completion beside Elephant Kingdom at the end of 2000, it was clear that it was going to have been worth the wait. It had been designed with the best arrangements in mind, for, as with Elephant Kingdom, Peter Johnson and Dominique had toured zoos all over Europe looking for advice and ideas.

As Kingdom of the Wild began to take shape, the level of its sophistication became breathtakingly apparent. There was, for a start, a bewildering mass of stalls variously suitable for rhinos, zebras, kudus and ostriches. This area was designed with sliding sections, like some vast Chinese puzzle, in order to give keepers plenty of opportunities to combine or separate animals for training, breeding, birthing, veterinary procedures and the like.

High across the top of these stalls would later span a wide indoor gallery, attractively finished in exposed timber, for visitors to walk among many large educational glass exhibits containing birds, reptiles, fish and insects.

The female paddock at Elephant Kingdom, seen from the north-west. The combined paddocks are many times the size of Colchester Zoo's old, now-demolished elephant enclosure. This picture was probably taken when these large new paddocks first came into use in 1998, for no sign is visible in the background of the Kingdom of the Wild complex which followed shortly. (Colchester Zoo)

A visitor would even be able to get themselves something to eat or drink at a little café placed halfway along, and then perhaps step out onto the large balcony overlooking the outdoor paddock. At the far end of this gallery, a wide ramp would lead down to a ground-floor section inside the southern end of the building. Here were to be placed more vivaria, as well as primate, meerkat and pygmy hippo enclosures.

Such a remarkable, spacious, handsome building had not come cheap. Many visitors had generously donated towards the cost of the building but the £1.5m (£2.1m) pricetag had bitten deeply into the zoo's own funds. Nevertheless, every penny had been wisely directed to deliver the message clearly to guests that Colchester Zoo was serious about providing opportunities for seeing and understanding its collection in new ways and about giving its animals and its keepers the best facilities available.

Colchester Zoo was setting itself up as a far-reaching zoo that catered for people from every place and background: so much was all good and well. Yet at the forefront of Dominique and Angela's minds for some time had been the desire to do something specifically for the people of Colchester: something that would show special gratitude to those locals who had

Kingdom of the Wild under construction in around 2000. (Peter Johnson)

believed in their vision for the park; to those who had stuck by them over the years; to those who had offered them help and support through the bad years as well as the good.

Ever since the day the Tropeanos had first set foot in their park in 1983 they had been pestered above all with questions pertaining to a single matter. When are you getting giraffes back? Have you got giraffes again yet? Where are the giraffes? Old Frank had all but burst the town's heart with joy when he had inducted Roz and David into the zoo in 1969. They had soon gone, however, but a new pair of giraffes had arrived directly on Colchester Zoo's eighth birthday in 1971. These two seem, likewise, to have vanished before very long, and 1975 saw the arrival of Frank's last pair, Toco and Gwendoline, from Bristol Zoo.

Toco and Gwendoline were probably gone well before the end of the 1970s. Despite the fact that Frank's zoo had kept this species for no more than eight years or so (and intermittently, for that matter), the public's memory of them remained strong. The endless giraffe-shaped questions which followed the Tropeanos everywhere perhaps seemed odd, since they had never really known what the zoo and this particular species had meant to the people of Colchester in the late 1960s and early 1970s. Yet even after all these years it was clear that Colcestrians still thought of their zoo

The giraffe stalls at Kingdom of the Wild, 2003. (Peter Johnson)

as a 'giraffe zoo' and felt it to be somehow denuded in that species' long absence.

Dominique and Angela let it be known in March 1998 that giraffes were to return to Colchester. It would nevertheless take more than two years to complete a search among the captive population in Britain and to arrange the transfers. Consideration was given to a number of candidates. Eventually, two young males were donated to Colchester; one by London Zoo and one by Whipsnade. On Thursday 15 February 2001, Edmund and Killian took up residence at Colchester Zoo's spectacular new Kingdom of the Wild building. Edmund was the elder of the pair, at two years and two days. Killian was still only one, but was shortly due his second birthday on 21 March.

According to some reports, Colchester Zoo had now become the most popular tourist destination in East Anglia. It did not much feel like it at the beginning of 2001, for there had been a very wet start to the year; one of the very wettest on record, in fact, with three and a half inches of rain in the fortnight leading up to the arrival of these new giraffes. Many empty weeks had therefore passed at the zoo since Christmas, but no one much minded this recent loss in income, for Edmund and Killian were sure to bring many thousands into the park during the run-up to Easter and beyond.

Aerial photograph of Colchester Zoo from the west, early 2000s. The Elephant Kingdom building (with pale roof) is seen at the centre, with its large diagonally bisected paddock extending into the foreground. The sister Kingdom of the Wild building and paddock sit to the right. These new developments came under the catch-all name of 'Spirit of Africa'. The striped area in the background is the zoo's main car park. (Newsquest)

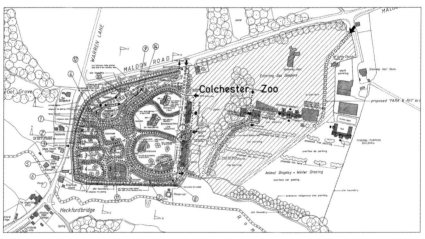

Architectural plan of ongoing developments within Colchester Zoo's western expansion zone, December 2000. (Peter Johnson)

The early signs were excellent – the first few visitors to see them, especially the children, were giddy with delight. Not only had giraffes returned at last after a quarter of a century, but the stunning Kingdom of the Wild facility promised long lives of happiness and contentment to these two youngsters. Or not.

Within days of Edmund and Killian's arrival it seemed as if bringing them to Colchester had, in truth, been a matter of signing their death warrants. And within mere weeks it would seem that the zoo as a whole was tumbling irretrievably towards darkest disaster.

6

A PALE HORSE

O N 19 FEBRUARY, the Monday following Edmund and Killian's arrival, a suspected case of foot and mouth disease was reported at an abattoir called Cheale Meats in a village south of Brentwood, just thirty miles down the A12 from Colchester Zoo. The contamination was confirmed the next day.

This was the first incident of foot and mouth disease in Britain for twenty years. It had been seen on the Isle of Wight in 1981 but the virus' chance to spread had therefore been limited and the problem had soon disappeared. This time things would be very different. It would produce this country's first modern media frenzy, instigate a political crisis for Tony Blair's government and eventually cost the national economy perhaps as much as £20bn.

By 2001, Britain found itself in the oily grasp of the petrol age. The mobility of individuals and industries was reaching levels unimaginable to prior generations. The whole country was now being permanently criss-crossed night and day by tens of millions of cars, vans, trucks and lorries ferrying people and materials the length and breadth of the island. The farming industry was no exception. In earlier times, farmers and their animals had been largely tied to one spot of land. Many old nursery rhymes and fairy stories suggest the sense of adventure pertaining even to the walking of a cow to a local market. Into the twentieth century, animals, animal feed and animal products were being moved all over Britain between farms and import and export stations by thousands of workers every day.

One of the unfortunate side-effects of the new freedoms which the petrol age afforded the farming industry was that contagious viruses with long incubation periods, such as foot and mouth (which can take up to two weeks to make itself known), could be spread on wheels, shoes and clothing far and wide before anyone suspected a thing. As soon as foot and mouth was confirmed at Cheale Meats, farmers began to impose their own restrictions around their land. It was, however, already much too late. The virus had quietly been spreading along Britain's motorway arteries for weeks. Nothing could stop the appearance of new cases as these previously silent infections started to make themselves known everywhere.

Tony Blair's government started to act with resolution and the countryside began to be shut down. Bans were placed on the movement of animals; livestock markets were cancelled; people were forbidden from walking on open land on pain of fines of £5,000 (£7,000); and shoes and vehicle wheels were being disinfected everywhere. Even hospital ambulances were forbidden to travel within the huge restriction zones except in cases of immediate life and death. Into March 2001, hundreds of cases of foot and mouth disease had appeared. It was an event of national proportions – there was no doubt about that – but the great majority of infections were occurring in one half of the country, to the west of an imaginary line running north to south from York to Portsmouth.

The area to the east of this line remained, by and large, free of infection. There was, however, one spot that was hit as hard as any other region in Britain – the Home Counties and the Thames Estuary area surrounding the country's first reported case. Almost as soon as the first viral outbreak at Brentwood had come to light, Colchester Zoo had taken matters into its own hands and voluntarily closed itself to visitors for the first time since the death of Moto sixteen years earlier. Hopefuls turning up to visit giraffes Edmund and Killian at the end of February were greeted by a sign on the gates: 'Due to the foot and mouth outbreak in the region, the zoo is closed to the public until further notice, for the protection of the animals.'

Everything was fine, really: there was no direct threat to the zoo, this was merely a wise precaution. Dominique and Angela considered that the loss of a few days' takings was a small price to pay for ensuring that their animals remained free of infection. In any case, Blair and his agriculture minister Nick Brown were becoming more combative in their attempts to contain the virus, which was reassuring. The case of swine fever in Essex during the previous August had passed over with comparatively little fuss, had it not? This problem would surely be under control soon too.

Yet instead of going away, it seemed to get a little more pressing with each day that ended. The zoo watched with growing unease as new cases of foot and mouth began to creep up the A12 towards Colchester. A new incident was confirmed at Blue House Farm on the other side of Maldon, just twenty miles away. The Ministry ordered the immediate slaughter and cremation of 600 sheep there. Another case of the virus would shortly be discovered at Marsh Farm in nearby South Woodham Ferrers. Its animals were likewise condemned immediately to the pyres.

With its gates shut to visitors, Colchester Zoo was eerily silent. At first it had been something of a relief for the staff when the park had closed. They had jumped on the chance of a couple of quiet days to catch up on the kinds of odd jobs that tend to get delayed under the distractions of receiving thousands of guests each week. Before long though, the novelty had worn off and many among the staff were beginning to ask themselves whether they would still be in work at all if the park remained closed for much longer. And still the virus crept its way towards the gates of Colchester. Unconfirmed reports of foot and mouth emerging at outlying villages, such as at Assington to the north and on Mersea Island to the east, made it feel almost as if the town was being surrounded.

Jez Smith, a young falconer who had joined Colchester Zoo in 1996, was exceptionally worried. He felt a strong attachment to his birds and was already concerned that they were now stuck indoors all day. As Jez followed the constant news bulletins, his apprehension steadily developed into anxiety. So strong did his fears become that they even followed him into his dreams. Going to bed one night, he dreamed that the disease had been discovered next to the zoo and that the area had been declared an infection zone.

When he arrived at the zoo early next morning he was sickened to find at the front gate one of the zoo's drivers, Bob, newly kitted out with a shoulder-mounted disinfectant gun. Bob was spraying all the cars, motorbikes and bicycles of staff members as they arrived for work. Foot and mouth had been found at Wick Farm in the village of Layer-de-la-Haye, not two miles to the south: its one pig, twenty-four cows and 1,300 sheep had all been marked for burning.

All the major British zoos except London and Jersey were already closed. Colchester would, however, now be officially closed by Nick Brown's Ministry, having fallen within a high-category biological hazard restriction area, and all kinds of emergency procedures were now put in place by Dominique and Angela. Foot and mouth is carried on the wind, so the decision was taken that all animals of every description were to be kept inside at all times. Certain species were to be kept in isolation from each other. Checks were also to be made on each susceptible animal every couple of hours to look for symptoms of lameness, excessive salivation or blisters around the mouth and hooves.

Many staff members feared the worst when Nick Brown's white-clad officials showed up to test the zoo. When it was found that the park had yet escaped infection, the zoo as a whole breathed a sigh of relief. Then a tenth case of foot and mouth in Essex was discovered at Rye Farm, again just south of Colchester Zoo, to which the Ministry instantly sent its slaughter-men to incinerate seventy-two cows and 450 sheep. Spring was coming and the winds were gently starting to come in from the south, bringing with them the promise of a dark summer as the clouds of fire-smoke drifted over the horizon. Many keepers were convinced that the game was up: the zoo could not fail to become contaminated now.

The timing could not have been worse. Recent years had seen the zoo put huge sums of money into Elephant Kingdom and Kingdom of the Wild. The continuing development of a further range of new enclosures along the western fringe of the zoo's new expansion area was proving costly too. Frank had left a small portion of his animal fortune to the Tropeanos at his death a few years earlier, but the bulk of his money, which ought to have been re-invested in the zoo, had gone elsewhere and money remained tight at Stanway Hall.

There was supposed to have been great pomp and circumstance accompanying the introduction of giraffes to the collection, just as there had been when Roz and David had made their debut. Adoring crowds should have been flocking to see Colchester's old rhinos enjoying their wonderful new accommodation. Instead, everyone was at home in front of television screens watching men in white biohazard suits burning mountains of dead animals across the nation.

This was not the first time Colchester Zoo had experienced a foot and mouth crisis. The national 1967 crisis had not seriously threatened the zoo directly but Frank and Helena had nevertheless closed their gates late in November that year, just to be on the safe side. The zoo gates had not opened again for eight weeks but this had simply not been a problem then. For one thing, they had been closed through the very depths of winter. For another, Frank and Helena had still been making most of their money out of television appearances and animal deals, and did not much miss December and January's minimal gate money.

By 2001 Colchester Zoo's revenue derived almost solely from visitors to the park. The end of March was now approaching and bringing with it the prospect of financial collapse. Dominique and Angela had already lost

£250,000 (£350,000). If they were to miss out on the Easter holiday too, and lose perhaps a full £1m (£1.4m), it was anyone's guess as to what the future might hold. If, like Frank and Helena in 1967-8, they were to remain closed for two months, it would certainly mean the end of the zoo. More depressing still was the fact that the Tropeanos had initially closed voluntarily and the park was therefore not even entitled to an insurance pay-out for this.

The very worst part of it all for Dominique and Angela's son Anthony, by this time thirty-one years of age, was the fact of simply not knowing what might happen. No one could seem to get straight answers from the Ministry. One of the reasons for this was that most of the officials who had worked through the 1967 crisis were now retired or deceased. Few people in 2001 had experience of dealing with this disease. Nobody could seem to agree on basic questions relating to zoos and, even when they did, there seemed to be no clear message on policy. Were animals such as elephants susceptible to the disease? And even if they were not, might they be destroyed as potential carriers? Would any animals escape a blanket cull if the order came? Or would everything, including the Madagascan cockroaches and Australian stick insects, legally have to be dispatched too? If any person knew what this epidemic meant for a place such as Colchester Zoo, they were keeping their answers to themselves.

Before the end of March, foot and mouth had been confirmed at 1,000 sites in Britain. Keeper Jez found himself standing in the zoo's empty car park looking south towards where Rye and Wick lay burning. Behind him stood the new entrance hall like some great soundless monument to misplaced optimism. For a falconer like Jez, whose great love was to get right in among the crowds to show off his birds' spectacular abilities, he strongly sensed the spooky emptiness in the zoo. For a month now the park had been in stasis and could not continue much longer in this way. The turning point would have to come soon, in one direction or the other.

A few days later, at the beginning of April, Anthony went to speak with Tony Blair at a conference held in Colchester, to beg for answers about the fate of the zoo and to ask whether some kind of special arrangement might be made for the more exotic or endangered species. Blair was sympathetic and listened intently, yet, as with Nick Brown's Ministry, no answers came forth.

Foot and mouth disease is highly contagious, true, just like the common cold. However, also like the common cold, it clears up after a time and is rarely fatal. It was an accepted part of country life all through the nineteenth century after it was first identified in Britain in 1839. Blair, by contrast, was determined to eradicate the disease by whatever means possible, for he and Nick Brown were fixated on the economic harm of facts such as the reduced milk yield which the disease can cause.

Blair had learned a stern lesson during the September 2000 national fuel blockade which surely would have felled his government, had he not put his foot down when he did. Though it would be delayed by the crisis, the 2001 general election was now only weeks away and he had to be seen to be acting decisively. Moreover, nothing was going to stand in Nick Brown's way once his Ministry had been publicly accused of indolence. At the orders of these two men, controversial mass executions of healthy animals were now being initiated across the nation, notionally in order to prevent the further spread of disease. Opposition MPs also began to call for pre-emptive culls, including in western Colchester. Anthony had already stated publicly that he would resist just such a move at Colchester Zoo, but what confidence could remain if, say, one of the zoo's goats should develop a tell-tale limp?

The British government was in no mood for compromise. Some small-holders elsewhere had already tried to resist the slaughter-men's bulldozers and had been threatened with High Court action. Before the end of the crisis more than ten million animals would burn. Perhaps no second thought would have been given to the execution of a few hundred cats and monkeys on the north-eastern border of Essex if it meant that another rural site could be declared clean. In the dying days of March it had already been announced that Colchester's 13th Air Assault Support Regiment was due to mobilise in order to help the Ministry purge East Anglia once and for all. That sunny April day which had drawn thousands to see the opening of the Elephant Kingdom enclosure just a few short years previously now seemed but a dim memory from another era entirely. Tembo, Opal, the pregnant Tanya and the other elephants; orangutans Rajang and Djambe; old Jemma the wolf; Sasha the white tiger; rhinos Simba and Flossy; Billy Joe, Pippin, young Tombe and all the other chimps; zedonks Sandy, Mary and Shadow; Buster and the mandrills; Lofty the cheetah; Baldy Man, Nautilus, Zippo and their penguin comrades; lion Subu and his sisters Ashanti and Massing; Edmund and Killian; and all the hundreds of creatures to whom so much affection had been devoted, would surely fall to pitchfork and fire.

This national crisis was a very public one, reaching into everyday life in a number of ways. Many people had nowhere to walk their dogs. Sporting fixtures and music festivals were being cancelled. There were milk and meat shortages in the shops. The 2001 foot and mouth crisis also happened to be sweeping through Britain in the early days of rolling news channels. Sky News had been up and running since 1989 but it had not been until 1997 that BBC News 24 had launched. Drawn-out disasters with dramatic images are fodder to such channels, and the foot and mouth epidemic gave them all the material they could possibly want.

When Colchester Zoo had first begun to be mentioned in the regional and national news during the crisis, many members of the public probably listened at first with nothing more than fleeting interest. As the days passed and the zoo began to be mentioned with increasing frequency, more and more local people began to realise that it was in trouble. Uniformed keepers found themselves being tapped on the shoulder in supermarket queues after work by people who had been growing concerned about the animals. Anthony, who had already been the face of Colchester Zoo for some time, was now becoming fairly well known as he appeared with increasing regularity on television, as well as in the press and on radio programmes as the days of closure turned into weeks.

The grim memories of Colchester Zoo from the early 1980s were still vivid and many people might have ignored it all. Fortunately, the Tropeanos had managed to do just enough to rebuild Colchester Zoo in their eighteen years at Stanway Hall. When the people of Colchester were, effectively, asked in 2001 whether or not they still wanted their zoo, their answer was, overwhelmingly, yes. And they gave their answer of their own volition, freely sending money to the park. Youngsters sent in their pocket money. Some asked their parents to drive them up to the zoo's gate to give their envelope to driver Bob. Cheques arrived from old-time visitors as well as animal-loving newcomers to the town. A local sub-postmaster named Neil Wolton was sponsored by his patrons to the tune of £500 (£700) to have his hair, moustache and beard shaved off to raise money for the zoo, and a group of Colchester United fans clubbed together to donate £1,000 (£1,400). The Colchester and East Essex Co-operative Society set up collection pots in forty-eight of its shops and supermarkets, raising over £7,000 (£10,000).

These and many other events in aid of the stricken zoo would be held in the borough's schools and businesses. Anthony said at the time that he, his family and the zoo as a whole were humbled by this spontaneous generosity.

Anthony Tropeano with Tanya during the national foot and mouth crisis, 2001. (Newsquest)

He was not talking about the money. Many thousands of pounds had been donated but it was a drop in the ocean: the zoo was now running a loss of £300,000 (£420,000). He was talking, in truth, about the sentiment and the boost to morale within the park.

The foot and mouth crisis would drag on for some time yet, with Colchester and Southend being the last areas in Essex to have their restrictions lifted; but eventually the threatening clouds of disaster over the zoo quietly receded. At long last, when it was announced that High Woods Country Park, Hilly Fields, Lexden Park, Lexden Springs, Lowe Lodge Farm, Welshwood Park and Wivenhoe Wood were all to be reopened, the Tropeano family decided that the risk must have reduced sufficiently to allow the reopening of the zoo.

With foot dips and disinfectant mats still in place everywhere, the farm section sealed off, and constant checks continuing to be carried out on the animals, Colchester Zoo opened its gates once again to its public on 7 April after forty days and nights in the wilderness. There was no huge influx on that Saturday, but people had evidently been watching closely for news of the reopening and numbers were moderately good. No one was counting heads. The staff and the family were simply overcome with relief that all their animals had come through unharmed and that things might start getting back to normal.

The cover of the guidebook of 2002. (Colchester Zoo)

On 27 April an open letter from the Tropeanos appeared in the local press, thanking the people of Colchester for the financial and emotional support they had proffered. The message of this letter was that the zoo felt it had emerged from the crisis more robust as a result of the public's backing. Yet this was only half the story, for behind its shut gates the zoo had also been growing subtly stronger despite the surface feelings of hopelessness.

The final years of the twentieth century had seen a sharp rise in the number of staff members working at Colchester Zoo, as the huge expansion work gathered pace and greater visitor numbers were anticipated. Some of the older keepers remember the mid-1990s, which preceded this explosion, as a time of great camaraderie, for the staff body had still been comparatively small and the keepers had all known each other well. They now look back on it wistfully as a time of cosy Christmas dinners together, of silly practical jokes on birthdays, and of entertainingly staggering up and down the earthworks of the zoo's building sites while trying to get back to their caravans after an evening together at the Heckford Angel pub on Saturday nights.

By 2000 this had all but disappeared. There were now 120 full-time staff members working at the zoo and the place seemed to have lost its old personality without yet developing a new one. It was during the 2001 crisis that Colchester Zoo's new, current disposition was born. The reopening in April 2001 effected a new unity among the staff who felt, as one, that they had shared an emotive (albeit horrible) experience with each other and had been left with the reminder that they all had a common goal.

Other changes had come over the zoo in that silent March of 2001. Given that there was less work to do, with the park empty of visitors and the animals shut away indoors all day, many members of staff had turned their attention to sharing their knowledge with each other by developing short training programmes. The youngsters on the team were invited to learn a little from the more experienced keepers about public speaking and presentation skills for the sake of their talks and displays, which had become such an important part of daily life at Colchester Zoo. Demonstrations and mini-seminars were also held, concerning things like animal training and how to carry out daily record-keeping more efficiently. The retail and kitchen staff members, too, were given new training in customer service and food hygiene. Much of the in-house training given today to incoming and existing staff members has its origins in the foot and mouth closure of spring 2001.

This was new territory for the zoo, which had, since 1963, broadly maintained a policy of learning on the job. Perhaps there would be less personal freedom among staff in the zoo after 2001, but it was this formalisation of training that would allow the zoo to make the most of its new facilities as it moved, tougher than ever, into the new millennium.

7

HAULED FROM THE WALLOW

THE FIRST DECADE of the twenty-first century would prove to be a remarkable time not only for the zoo, but also for Colchester at large. The developed world as a whole was about to live through a time of greater personal affluence than had ever been known in all human history. It would also prove to be a time in which the town of Colchester would demonstrate that it was — and is — anything but mediocre.

Early in 2001, plans were presented for a far-reaching overhaul of Colchester's garrison at a cost of more than half a billion pounds and, in the event, carried out to a high standard.

The decade would also see the University of Essex leave behind its troubled past and embark on a number of bold expansions, becoming one of the biggest employers in the area. By 2008 it would be regarded as a leading university, with its Politics and Sociology courses listed first in the country, and its Finance and History courses listed second. By 2012 the institution as a whole would be ranked twentieth in the entire world by *Times Higher Education*, among universities under the age of fifty.

In 2008, Colchester United would be re-homed at Cuckoo Farm to the north of the town in a brand-new £14m 10,000-seat stadium, not long after achieving their best-ever finish in the league.

In 2005 a planning application would be made for a huge £25m modern art gallery to the east of the town centre, eventually to open in the autumn of 2011. This decade of achievement and expansion in Colchester would be reflected just as keenly by its zoo, which would now begin to make its transition from its medium-term plan to its long-term.

This transition would come to be symbolised by the appearance of a bonny 200lb baby in the grounds of Stanway Hall. There had already been

An artificial insemination procedure is carried out on elephant Tanya in the 2000s. (Colchester Zoo)

joy when the announcement came in 1999 that elephant Tembo was due to become a father. A pioneering artificial insemination treatment had seen his seed taken to Austria, where a fourteen-year-old cow named Sabi had been impregnated with success at the world's oldest existing zoo. The healthy baby, Abu, was born at Vienna Zoo on 25 April 2001 after a 643-day pregnancy. He was the first elephant in Europe to be born as a result of artificial insemination and only the fourth in the world.

This was excellent news for Colchester Zoo. Everyone was delighted to have played an important role, by working closely with Berlin's Leibniz Institute of Zoo Biology and Wildlife Research, in the development of a new conservation technique. (In the year 1900, the wild population of African elephants numbered around 9,000,000. A century or so later that number stands perhaps at about 400,000 and continues to drop.)

The birth of Abu also showed that Colchester's bull was a good stud. And, sure enough, all the efforts to provide a good home for the elephants and to breed them carefully were rewarded when a fine male was born to Tanya in the grounds of Stanway Hall on Friday 6 December 2002, likewise as a result of artificial insemination. This was the first successful elephant AI treatment in Britain and the very first in the world to be successful on the initial attempt. The baby had been conceived just as the foot and mouth crisis had come down in 2001, and his eventual debut came to represent Colchester Zoo's instinct for survival and rebirth. Speaking in the *Essex County Standard*, Anthony declared it to be the pinnacle of the zoo's achievements to date.

Visitors to the zoo appropriately named the new arrival Kito: a Swahili name meaning 'gem' or 'precious one'. Tanya proved to be an excellent mother and people watched the progress of her confident little boy with

Dominique and Angela with baby elephant Kito at Colchester Zoo, in early 2003. (Newsquest)

fascination. Within days, Kito was learning to pick things up with his trunk. By Christmas Eve he had grown to the proud height of 3ft. New Year's Eve saw him beginning to cut his first tooth.

By the beginning of February, Kito had learned to use his trunk properly and was picking things up and putting them in his mouth. As the warmer weather arrived at the beginning of April 2003, he was allowed outdoors for the first time, and on the 11th of that month he had his first proper mud bath. Since birth, Kito had been in the habit of communicating in little howls: on 29 April he attempted to make his first proper trumpet call but managed no more than a squeak.

Kito's early life was not without its moments of high drama. On 20 May he got stuck in the mud wallow and had to be helped out by Tanya, Zola, Opal and his keepers. Similarly uncertain ordeals were emphatically over-mastered and, by the end of June, Kito was generally starting to take care of himself, learning how to hold water in his trunk, along with all the other important skills a good elephant needs.

The elation of watching Kito's development had been magnified by the announcement, when he was hardly a few weeks old, that his 'aunts' Rosa and Zola had both fallen pregnant. Unlike Tanya in 2001, Rosa and Zola had each been able to mate naturally with Tembo who, as a result of the ministrations of Colchester's keepers, had changed from the nervous and aggressive creature which the Chipperfields had created into a remarkably even-tempered and agreeable elephant.

Zola's baby was, unhappily, lost during the following winter. Her keepers had been on twenty-four-hour watch for a fortnight and their grief lasted for many weeks after the Berlin Institute confirmed by ultrasound that her calf was dead. Having retreated into a common process called calf retention, Zola's waters broke on 5 December 2003 but her baby did not appear. (Its body was not passed until more than two years later.) The sadness for staff began to ease only when Zola's stable-mate Rosa unexpectedly went into labour two weeks early on the morning of 15 March 2004, giving birth to Kito's half-brother Jambo at 8 a.m.

Like Kito, Jambo was a very healthy little boy. Within eighteen months he was cutting his tusks and becoming a strapping young lad. They themselves had no idea, of course, but these two juniors between them played a big part in providing some bumper years for Colchester Zoo at precisely the needful moment. The Tropeanos and their staff watched as visitor numbers began to reach record highs of up to 550,000, as visitors who came to see Jambo and Kito were added to those who had simply been reminded by the endless news reports during the foot and mouth crisis that Colchester Zoo had not, in fact, disappeared in the 1970s.

Kito the elephant in 2003. (Colchester Zoo)

It was a great relief to all concerned after the huge outlay of expanding the zoo between 1994 and 2000 had been directly followed by the painful financial injury of 2001. The years immediately following saw Colchester Zoo's annual turnover touch previously unknown heights of £7m, with pre-tax profits of more than £1m.

Dominique and his family continued, as they have always done, to live comparatively modest lives, working long hours every week on the transformation and maintenance of Colchester Zoo. No one under the Tropeanos has ever been paid grotesque directorial fees. There is no board of shareholders cutting away at the surplus. The money that Colchester Zoo received in each year of its fifth decade was, as before, ploughed straight back into the zoo and its related environmental projects.

With the zoo's expansion area essentially complete by 2001, Dominique and Angela's attention had already returned fully towards the 'old' zoo. What did they see? In contrast to the planned boulevards and zoning of the new half of Colchester Zoo, they saw at the top end of the zoo a jumble of new things piled on old: a miscellany of all the odd corners and strange appositions one sees in all villages which have stories to tell. Here there might have stood an old enclosure, unchanged from the day it was built in the 1960s. Further up, there might have been a brand-new modern enclosure, its paint almost still wet. And, sandwiched between them, perhaps another old enclosure, expanded and redeveloped, the better to accommodate its inhabitants, while still bearing in its foundations the archaeological imprint of Frank's obsolete vision.

There were now strange paths which led nowhere, having been cut off by new buildings put up almost with a sense of blind urgency in days of trauma. There were abandoned structures littered around the park, long out of use.

It seemed that the crises were over and the zoo's time had come at last to make its break with its past. The additional money which had been flowing into the zoo since the day Elephant Kingdom had opened would, in the new century, be directed into a systematic makeover of the medieval muddle around Stanway Hall. Throughout the new decade, Colchester Zoo finally emerged from its chrysalis. The grey cocoons of Frank's hulking old enclosures were shed as the park began to unfold its wings as each new construction went up.

A grand and jubilant statement was made when the old elephant house was torn down. An equally grand and jubilant statement was needed to

L-R: Sea lions Nia, Pat and Agola in the mid-1990s. This pool, on the northern edge of the zoo, is now known as Inca Trail and is today home to one of two groups of Humboldt penguins at the zoo. (Sarah Knuckey)

replace it. The zoo's sea lion family meant a lot to Dominique and Angela, and they already nurtured a desire to improve their lives. Ever since Pat, Ago and Nia had arrived in 1986, they had been a big part of the success of the park. Along with their trainer (the Tropeanos' daughter Sarah) they had pleased countless crowds over the years with entertaining educational displays.

The eldest sea lion, Ago, had died in 1992 but her place had been filled six months later by a female called Agola. Sarah had also disappeared from the zoo in the 1990s, having moved away to start her own family. A daughter cannot, alas, be replaced. Sarah still loved the zoo and visited when she could, but the sea lions were daily reminders to the Tropeanos of their absent daughter and the time had come to give them a better home. The animals' pool was not terribly large or deep. They had also frequently suffered from eye and skin complaints over the years as a result of living in chlorinated water (standard in many zoos).

Once Kingdom of the Wild was finished, Peter Johnson and Dominique set about drawing up plans for a new sea lion pool early in 2002. As with all the foregoing developments, the bar was set high. This pool was to be big; large enough, in fact, for up to half a dozen or more individuals, in order

Installation of the first section of the Playa Patagonia sea lion pool viewing tunnel, 2002. (Colchester Zoo)

that it might one day serve as a breeding centre. The new pool was under construction by the summer of 2002, directly on the site of Frank's elephant enclosure. Once the old building had been taken down, Dominique's construction team set to the gruelling work of digging out tons and tons of soil and shoring up the sides of the new hole, as well as planning for a separate birthing pool, a kitchen, a staffroom and a large facility for the gigantic new filtration systems.

Dominique had decided there was also to be an underwater viewing area inside the pool. An order was sent to a firm near Tokyo for a 24-metre transparent acrylic tunnel, which would be the longest of its kind in this country. The tunnel was shipped to Felixstowe in four sections, which were then brought to Colchester Zoo on a convoy of four lorries, with a fifth to carry the large secondary windows. (Separate vehicles were required because the tunnel sections were very fragile and could not be stacked: they were designed to become strong once locked in place and under the inward pressure of water.)

Once the tunnel's accompanying Japanese engineers had fixed each section in place and everything had been tested for water-tightness, Dominique and Peter had only to lay their hands on half a million gallons of water. This was a bit of a problem, for it was not going to be a case of leaving a tap running and hoping no one would notice. They had already been barred from filling the pool from the mains since it would drain everyone else's water supply all down Maldon Road.

The authorities suggested to Peter Johnson that he might ask the local fire brigade very nicely if one of their hydrants could be used. Upon the promise of a payment to the brigade's benevolent fund, a hose was let from a hydrant by the Leather Bottle pub, more than a mile away, all the way along the main road and up and over the zoo's fence. Even with this fire hose gushing at full pelt it took forty-eight solid hours to fill the new pool. Careful calculations were then made to turn these 500,000 gallons of freshwater into saltwater of the correct salinity. Three tankers were ordered from a salt-works in Cheshire (not far from old Southport Zoo, which was living out its final days by that time). Upon arrival at Stanway Hall, these trucks pitched up on Maldon Road, threw their hoses over the fence just as the fire brigade had done, and likewise emptied their cargo into the water.

Everyone was sure that this new pool (named Playa Patagonia), the largest saltwater sea lion pool in the country, would provide a great new home for these sea lions who had done so much for the zoo. It opened on 14 August 2003 to a warm public reception. Sadly, this glorious splash of colour on the zoo's new wings was to be framed with black bands, for all three sea lions would be gone within six months. Nia, one of the two females, was found dead on the morning of 19 August, after just a few days in the new pool. Pat, the large male, passed away exactly three months later on 19 November; the remaining female, Agola, alone in the pool, died just before Valentine's Day of the following year.

The story is a perfect demonstration of how few things in zoology are simple or assured. The decision had been taken to guarantee these three sea

A section of the Playa Patagonia sea lion pool filtration unit, 2011. (S.C. Kershaw)

lions a fabulous new life. No effort or expense had been spared in creating a pool as good as any in Europe. Yet, as so often when working with animals, people's hopes were crushed.

There was no doubt that the move itself had been stress-free. There had been no darts or cranes involved; the sea lions were superbly well-trained and had simply followed their keepers the 100 yards up to the new pool with no bother at all. Perhaps Pat, Agola and Nia had somehow grown used to chlorinated water and, for whatever reason, had reacted badly to being back in their natural saltwater. Perhaps they simply exhausted themselves: the new 4-metre-deep pool offered much more opportunity for play than had their old enclosure and the additional exercise may have been too much for them.

It may, of course, have all been a coincidence. Pat and Nia were both over twenty years old, which is not a bad age for sea lions. Then again, Agola was only about twelve – but sea lions are socially complex creatures and it is possible that she just pined away, being left behind. Whatever the reason for the rapid chain of deaths, it could not have been for want of preparation on the zoo's part, nor any flaw in the design of the new enclosure. A fresh cohort of female Patagonian sea lions, named Winnipeg, Milan, Paris, Sydney and Atlanta, have since thrived, year on year, at Playa Patagonia.

The Playa Patagonia pool is not the only modern enclosure at Colchester Zoo that has been touched with sadness and setbacks. The story of the new Orangutan Forest enclosure which opened in 2008 is another good example of how unpredictable life with animals truly is, and demonstrates some of the types of struggles and delays which the zoo has faced in its continued effort to reinvent itself.

By the middle of the first decade of the new century, orangutan Rajang was becoming one of the longest-serving residents at Colchester Zoo. He had been born on 14 June 1968 at Chester Zoo and had been purchased at the age of eleven by Frank, arriving at Colchester in the spring of 1980. Since then he had become a firm favourite with visitors and was well-known in the town, even among those people who did not necessarily know his name, partly on account of his life-long fascination with human beings, having been raised by hand after the death of his mother, Josephine, when he was less than four weeks old.

Rajang had outlived a number of mates through the years – most recently Annie, who had been born in Chicago in 1970 and who had come to Colchester Zoo at the age of seventeen. Annie had been born with a

The Playa Patagonia sea lion pool viewing gallery, 2012. (S.C. Kershaw)

digestive disorder and had died fairly young in September 1998. Five weeks after Annie's death, Rajang had been introduced to a younger female by the name of Djambe. He had always been an easy-going soul and the two of them soon became good friends. Rajang and Djambe were housed in a smallish glass enclosure just off the south-east corner of Stanway Hall. They were happy enough, but the area inside received little sunlight and was not really wide or tall enough for two adult orangutans. It was certainly not going to be big enough for three if ever the zoo was to decide to breed orangutans in the future.

In a letter to the *East Anglian Daily Times* in January 2004, Dominique drew attention to predictions by groups such as the World Wildlife Fund that orangutans would possibly be extinct in the wild within the next couple of decades. Yet it was not a mere complaint Dominique was making: he intended to try to do something about it. He, Angela and Peter Johnson were shortly to be hard at work planning a new breeding centre at Colchester Zoo.

Rajang and Djambe themselves were not planned as a breeding pair. Djambe was a purebred Sumatran orangutan, but Rajang was a hybrid of Sumatran and Bornean lines and therefore inadmissible to the modern

Orangutan Rajang at Colchester Zoo in 2011. Rajang is one of the best-known animals in East Anglia today and one of the last remaining links to Colchester Zoo's past. He celebrated his forty-fourth birthday on 14 June 2012. (S.C. Kershaw)

international breeding programme. The original plans for the new orangutan enclosure, therefore, intended to separate the building into two halves so that Rajang could still be luxuriously re-housed, while the other half could be given over to breeding pairs, but this plan underwent considerable revision.

The formal plans for the new £1.75m orangutan building were announced shortly afterwards, in October 2004. Rajang and Djambe would not, however, take up residence in their new home for another four years, on account of many hold-ups. For twenty years the Tropeanos had been frantically transforming their park into a workable modern zoo; meanwhile, the church of All Saints, which had previously been used as a major selling-point by Frank and Helena, and was accordingly looked after fairly well up to 1981, was now beginning to be reclaimed by the earth. Unfortunately for Rajang and Djambe, the church sat right next to the projected site of their new home.

Peter Johnson knew that because All Saints was one of the oldest religious sites in North Essex and a Grade II listed building, any planning officer looking at the new orangutan house scheme was bound to start asking awkward questions about the sorry condition into which the church had fallen. The rescue work on it was not going to be cheap. True, the zoo was making very good money in these days – the sunny Easter of 2004 had seen 30,000 holidaymakers come to the zoo – but it was hardly as if Dominique and Angela had infinite millions to throw at every problem which came their way.

Colchester Zoo had never in its history sought public money. For Dominique and Angela, just as for Frank and Helena, seeing the zoo earn all its own money through commerce and fundraising drives was a source of considerable satisfaction. An exception to this was mooted for the sake of All Saints. Since everyone wanted as much of the zoo's money as possible to be spent on improving the lives of Rajang and Djambe, and maybe one day even helping to sustain a captive breeding population of orangutans, Peter and Dominique turned to the public organisations which support such projects in pursuit of financial help with the church renovation.

Following a protracted struggle to get the church relisted as Grade II*, and after a number of delightful circumnavigations of the funding committee world (a voyage which saw many wonderfully decorative maps drawn and yet no Americas discovered) Dominique eventually decided, as ever he had done, to go it alone and pay for the church renovation himself. With the wild population of orangutans having already dropped to perhaps as few as 70,000, and disappearing at an increasing rate of thousands each year, he simply wanted the breeding centre built and to begin producing baby orangutans. The birth of a few orangutans at Colchester Zoo was not going to outweigh the frankly horrific population decline in the wild, but it would allow new opportunities for education and fundraising in the zoo, and offer further opportunities for vets and researchers to learn more about these animals in captivity in preparation for their work in the field.

Yet more delays came. No work could now be started even on All Saints until the Colchester Archaeological Trust had completed a dig at the church to study the buried human skeletons. Eventually, however, the restoration of the church got underway. Most of the arches were reconstructed and the walls were capped. The tower's top was re-finished; other sections of it were repaired, interestingly, with tiles that had previously been used for the original cellar of St Paul's Cathedral in London.

A huge old iron water tank was also removed at last, piece by piece, from inside the top of the church tower, which for years had been threatening to fall through and crush somebody. This was replaced by a new lead roof. In all, the church project cost nearly £200,000. No one, however, really

Archaeological dig at All Saints' Church in around 2006. (Peter Johnson)

begrudged the necessity of undertaking what had been the first real care shown to this building since the time of Shakespeare, even if (now that it was open to visitors again) the Tropeanos would occasionally be accused of bad taste for having built a fake church as a tourist attraction in their zoo.

With the future of All Saints guaranteed for at least another two centuries, the full focus could now turn to the new orangutan enclosure that was already beginning to appear against the north face of the church. Rajang and Djambe's enclosure was to be twenty times the size of their old one. Significantly, for a naturally tree-dwelling species, this enclosure was also to be considerably higher than the old one, with netting and climbing frames reaching high into the air.

The Orangutan Forest was, like Kingdom of the Wild, an ambitious project. Some ideas had to be abandoned for practical reasons. The public viewing stage, for example, was originally conceived as an area in which exotic butterflies would be in free flight, but the money and the continuing additional working hours required for such an arrangement would have been astronomical.

The result was nevertheless a remarkable building in which was mixed indoor, outdoor and holding facilities for the orangutans, two aquaria,

The Orangutan Forest enclosure under construction, 2007. (Colchester Zoo)

The Orangutan Forest's main viewing area in 2012. (S.C. Kershaw)

a number of large glass cases set into the walls for animals such as tortoises and invertebrates, and necessaries such as public toilets and benches, as well as high-tech staff quarters. Everything was finished off with a wealth of exotic plants, as well as carefully designed educational material to tie in with the new enclosure's vivid conservation message.

Rajang and Djambe moved into Orangutan Forest on 6 October 2008. Unfortunately, Djambe, rather like Pat, Agola and Nia, did not get to enjoy the space and comfort of her new enclosure for long: she died not three weeks after the move. The day of the transfer itself (as it had been for the sea lions at Playa Patagonia) was free of trouble. In this case, however, the animals were put under general anaesthetic. While handling the sleeping Djambe, keepers reported feeling a large swelling on her side. Blood samples were taken but nothing could be concluded. After a short time in the new Orangutan Forest, Djambe developed a lung infection and her veterinary consultant later prescribed antibiotics. On the morning of 25 October, Djambe was reported to be alert and feeding well. In the afternoon, Rajang was found carefully trying to move her dead body.

A post-mortem was carried out which showed that Djambe had been suffering from a severe ovarian swelling, which had possibly ruptured during a tumble she had taken while recovering from the anaesthetic after the move to the Orangutan Forest at the beginning of the month. It was an appalling episode for everyone: at thirty years old, Djambe had not been young but nor had she been very old. She had been in the collection for a decade, and keepers and regular visitors had become just as attached to her as to Rajang.

Rajang, ten years older than Djambe, had undergone the transfer between enclosures at the hands of his keepers with no ill effects whatsoever and has flourished in all the years since, in what is agreed to be an enclosure of exceptionally high quality. It seems unfair that Djambe did not get to enjoy the larger and lighter house as Rajang has done. Solace may yet be taken from the fact that a young Bornean male named Tiga, who arrived in June 2009, has since settled in well and may one day be paired with a new female. But memories of Djambe linger.

8

IMAGO

ZOO LIFE IS not for the faint of heart: setbacks and agonies lurk around every corner. Nevertheless, these early years of the twenty-first century saw the Tropeanos' zoo begin to stand firmly on its own terms as its past fell away into history. Fifty-one years after Sammy had taken up residence there, Southport Zoo was closed down in 2004 by its owners, Doug and Carole Petrie, who moved to the Yorkshire Dales Falconry Centre near the town of Settle. Shortly afterwards, back at Stanway Hall, Frank's dilapidated old giraffe house was taken down – it had been so dangerous that it could not even be demolished while other buildings around it remained in use. Gradually, most of the whole area to the west of the main car park where it stood was levelled and replaced by a state-of-the-art Komodo dragon enclosure which opened just before Easter 2006. This new enclosure worked well and Colchester Zoo was rewarded in 2012 with a large clutch of eggs, which were placed into incubation with great anticipation.

Many more new developments in this decade produced similar success as more and more of Frank's park vanished. The old aviaries, the old paddocks, the old rhino house – all were thoroughly modernised from the inside out or demolished and replaced by a wealth of new features, giving the strong impression of a zoo continually in the process of transforming itself and always offering something new to its visitors. A wide enclosure named Gelada Plateau appeared in September 2002 on the former site of the rhino pen, housing what was (at the time) this country's only group of Gelada baboons. The spring of 2003 saw the opening of a second tiger enclosure named Tiger Taiga, at what was then the southernmost tip of the zoo. At Easter 2004, Subu and Ashanti moved into their new £200,000 enclosure,

The old 1969 giraffe house: empty, sealed and shortly to be demolished at Colchester Zoo, 25 March 2004. Indications of long-term structural failure were visible from a distance, in the sagging roof and window lines. (Russell Tofts)

Lion Rock, on the northern edge of the zoo – the spot where Colchester's zebra had long been on show before moving to Kingdom of the Wild.

The old sea lion pool reopened late in 2006, refurbished as a second Humboldt penguin pool called Inca Trail. The old aquarium on the eastern side of Stanway Hall was redeveloped into a charming indoor mixed-species 'walkthrough' enclosure, containing South American creatures. It was opened in May 2008 and named Worlds Apart. In all sorts of different ways, these and other new enclosures were imaginative, attractive, constructed to the highest standards, and bound closely to the zoo's educational messages and ongoing charitable fundraising.

Despite the sadnesses along the way, or any wistfulness that might have attended the removal of many of the last reminders of Frank, positively no one was sentimental about the loss of the old zoo itself, including not only the older buildings but also many of those built by the Tropeanos in the mid-1980s. With its fiftieth anniversary steadily approaching, Dominique and Angela's zoo was finally beginning to extend into the long-term phase of development which had been envisaged more than twenty years previously.

The zoo today is very different to the one which was bought in 1983. The number of gardening staff alone is almost equal to the whole staff of the early 1980s. There are now more than seventy animal keepers, along with nearly twenty administrators, a building construction team of almost thirty, and a catering staff of more than eighty. Added to all the other cleaners, drivers, retail and facility assistants and education staff, Colchester Zoo, at its fiftieth anniversary, provides paid employment for more than 300 people, on top of a sixty-strong team of unpaid volunteer staff.

On average, about 500,000 people buy a day-ticket at Colchester Zoo each year – a number which compares favourably with long-established and esteemed institutions such as Bristol Zoo and Edinburgh Zoo. Of this number, 30,000 will be children on school visits, of which nearly 20,000 will take part in the formal classes and educational activities for which the Tropeanos have always refused to charge additional money, just as there are no charges for any of the dozens of talks and displays given in the zoo every day, nor for the supervised public feeding of the giraffes and elephants.

The real number of visitors to the park in any given year is, however, much higher when one includes the visits made by annual pass holders. The system of annual zoo passes (known as 'gold cards') has been chang-ing the way in which people experience Colchester Zoo. A gold card

A mixed South American species house named Worlds Apart, seen here under construction with Stanway Hall in the background. (Colchester Zoo)

permits a visitor to return to the zoo as many times as they like for the life of the card, allowing them to get to know the zoo far better than they would otherwise do. The days when one might visit a zoo to see a huge quantity of largely anonymous animals on display have been passing away over the last few decades. Today, we see a zoo such as Colchester inviting people to get to know members of the collection by name and to follow their lives as they grow up, have babies and go through all their various adventures, illnesses and recoveries before either transferring to another zoo or passing away.

The gold card system also allows visitors to get to know Colchester Zoo's staff, resulting in a far more rewarding and informative experience all round. And it works. In 1993, the number of gold card-holders numbered 3,000. Today, twenty years on, the standing figure is well over 50,000, with many card-holders returning every seven or eight weeks. Some people come every week; a few almost every day.

The twenty years that have seen this huge rise in the number of staff and visiting pass-holders at Colchester Zoo has also seen a rise in the number of endangered animals being kept and bred as part of European breeding programmes. Since the early 1990s, when the Tropeanos were first beginning to produce some high-quality animal facilities, the zoo has become steadily more focused on the captive breeding of species which stand at serious risk in the wild. The red-ruffed lemur, black-and-white ruffed lemur, cheetah, golden lion tamarin, pied tamarin, Goeldi's monkey, buffy-headed capuchin and waldrapp ibis are just a few of the many threatened species which have passed through as part of international breeding programmes and which have frequently produced healthy offspring at Colchester Zoo. Many have then gone on to other zoos around the world for further breeding.

The infrastructure built up over the last twenty years at the zoo has also allowed for external research to be carried out. As well as yearly supporting dozens of studies carried out by students of subjects like biology and conservation, Colchester Zoo has played host to groups such as the International Zoo Veterinary Group and the Royal Veterinary College. In 2006 Colchester's carefully trained elephants were able to take part in infrared motion research into problems such as arthritis in the species. More recently, over New Year 2012, the superb design of the Kingdom of the Wild building, combined with Colchester Zoo's sophisticated animal training programme, allowed the Royal Veterinary College to carry out important new research into the workings of the feet of rhinos.

Entrance to the Orangutan Forest in the summer of 2012. (S.C. Kershaw)

Indeed, Colchester's rhinos have always had an unusual talent for catching headlines, ever since Frank's first generation broke Britain's national dock strike of 1972. In 2007, a female called Lulu at Budapest Zoo was impregnated with semen taken from Colchester's male white rhino Simba. This was seen as a scientific breakthrough for it was the first time anywhere in the world that long-frozen rhino semen had resulted in a successful birth. Simba, one of Colchester Zoo's oldest residents, died on 9 April 2009 at the age of forty after developing digestive and joint problems. Sadly, he did not live to see the birth of his second son, Zamba, in October: the first rhino to be born at Colchester and the very first to be born in this country as a result of artificial insemination.

As with elephants, the development of such a technique may represent another step towards unseen future methods with which to combat the alarming drop in the world's population of rhinos, such as the Northern white rhino, the Western black rhino and the Javan rhino, all of whom in recent years have been reduced to a tiny handful of individuals or are now suspected to be extinct in the wild. Nevertheless, though the birth of Simba's baby rhino Zamba at Colchester Zoo was a cause for great celebration, the park was yet again forced to accept that its joys and sorrows are

Anthony Tropeano with a giant panda
at the Chengdu Research Base of
Giant Panda Breeding, China, 2005.
(Colchester Zoo)

often closely bound together, for the relentless destruction of the rhino was brought home with forbidding clarity at almost the self-same moment.

Upon his death, Simba's body had been sent for incineration at an abattoir, as the law requires. His head went missing from the abattoir soon afterwards – one Donald Allison was later found guilty by Manchester Crown Court of attempting to smuggle Simba's horns to China. Allison, who ran an antiques dealership and who had previously worked as a police aide in tracing stolen property, seems to have persuaded himself that the risks – which he knew better than many – were worthwhile, for his business had been struggling in recent years. Allison might have earned anything up to a quarter of a million pounds for Simba's horns in eastern Asia, where such things are wrongly thought by some people to cure various illnesses. Instead, he ended up sentenced to a year in jail after being caught by the UK Border Agency.

Britain's National Wildlife Crime Unit has since advised Colchester Zoo that, as with other rhino centres in this country, the living animals they are breeding may now be under threat. Anthony speaks of his anguish and fury that the trade in rhino horn has proliferated to such a degree, and that wild rhino numbers are decreasing so sharply that even captive rhinos like Cynthia, Emily, Otto and Flossy can no longer be considered safe even in the grounds of Stanway Hall. Long gone now are Frank's relaxed days when Simba and Flossy lived in a shed. Today's Kingdom of the Wild building is subject to patrols and has recently been fitted with new and expensive security systems.

This shows just what a miserable situation we have found ourselves in. One of the main reasons for keeping rhinos in a zoo such as Colchester is to allow breeding, research and fundraising to go on in order ultimately to help counteract the threat to the wild population. Now even the captive population is threatened with execution, meaning considerable work and money going into domestic protection, which organisations such as Colchester Zoo would rather see going into their wild conservation projects.

Such are the endless, evolving challenges facing Colchester Zoo, and it would seem almost to take all the running one can do simply to stay in the same place. The Tropeanos' zoo has not, however, stayed in the same place. Viewed from the longest perspective we see a place that has outlived its tough days with vigour and looks to the struggles yet to come with determination.

As the years have passed, this metamorphosis has not gone unnoticed by industry and society. Awards started to come in gradually in the 1990s; of late there has been a positive deluge. In 2005 Colchester Zoo won an EAZA award, for example, for the excellence of its education programme. The zoo has twice won the East of England Tourist Board's award for 'Large Visitor Attraction of the Year'. Many other awards and commendations have been forthcoming for the zoo's animal training scheme, for animal husbandry, and for its assistance with a local wild re-introduction programme for the Fisher's estuarine moth, which has come under threat of extinction.

Mandrill enclosure on the western edge of Colchester Zoo, 2012. (S.C. Kershaw)

On 18 July 2007, Dominique joined the likes of men and women such as Harold Wilson, Sir David Attenborough and Imogen Holst by accepting an honorary doctorate from the University of Essex. In his speech, Professor Graham Underwood spoke of Dominique's success as an entrepreneur and hailed him as an ecological 'visionary'. In 2009, Dominique went on to be presented with BIAZA's esteemed 'Award for Outstanding Achievement' and was inducted into the Order of the British Empire.

With such salutes to their life's work, the time had come, perhaps, for Dominique and Angela to step back. Colchester Zoo had become consistently profitable and regarded as one of the finest zoos in Europe.

Anthony was finding success as the park's Zoological Director and a strong management team stood in place around him. Both in their sixties, Dominique and Angela decided to make a definite effort to put some distance between themselves and the zoo at last. They resolved to enjoy the park more as visitors than as staff, to spend more days with their grandchildren, and to generally do all the things for which they had always struggled to find time.

After nearly thirty years surrounded by nothing but Colchester Zoo and all its excitement and its problems, the two found themselves a rural property in Suffolk. Both remained intimately connected with the zoo but, ironically, it was this new detachment that allowed Angela to indulge her love of animals once again. Dominique believes he is good with animals but points out that much of his skill was learned during his years working as a keeper on Colchester Zoo's front line in the 1980s. Angela was different: she was a natural with animals in the way that Frank had been (and now Anthony was); this was something which they had all somehow inherited from old great-grandfather Farrar, who had opened the original zoo on Southport's Scarisbrick New Road almost a century previously.

Angela had been central to Colchester Zoo's success since 1983, not least thanks to her painstaking rearing of animals in the tradition of Helena and Frank. Over time, Angela had hand-raised all sorts of sick or rejected animals who, so recalls the zoo's Communications Director Alex Downing, often made office life in Stanway Hall that little bit more interesting: Josie the wolf, a puma, a jaguar, a patas monkey, a cotton-top tamarin called Fidget, an Asian fishing cat called Columbo, a ring-tailed lemur called Maki and an endless parade of spider monkeys. There had even been a Rajah II in the early 1980s who lived with Angela and the family. Young Anthony had gained tremendous satisfaction from showing him off to his school mates.

Sad to say, Rajah II died at the age of nine months but Angela, like Frank and Helena, generally had uncanny success with animal rearing, helping in this manner to sustain Colchester Zoo in the days when this way of doing things was usual and necessary.

Once the practice of hand-raising had largely died out in zoos, Angela's work had become more decidedly focused on profit and loss, on retail strategies and on catering and facilities, for these had become the things which were to guarantee Colchester Zoo's viability and the continuity of its conservation work. Only once she had removed herself from the zoo had she been able to put herself once again with her animals. Angela had always reserved a special love for dogs and horses in particular. Having worked sixteen-hour days all through her young adult life in Southport, and having worked all but constantly for almost thirty years at Colchester Zoo, finally she now had time simply to enjoy life with her creatures in the retreats of Suffolk.

Though she remained closely connected to the never-ending projects at the zoo, within a few months Angela had started keeping a garden, was learning to cook new dishes, and was taking pleasure in all the things of which many women daydream for their retirement – when her doctor informed her that she had only six months to live. Her son was with her when she passed away in the summer of 2011. To the very end Angela had continued her work: coming into the zoo, checking up on attendance figures, the gift shop's takings and so forth. Even when she had been too weak to see for herself, she had still asked others to bring her all possible news of her zoo: of animal births and animal deaths and all the continuing life of the park.

Angela Tropeano was the one thread running quietly through the whole story of Colchester Zoo, from her childhood growing up next to the beautiful Sammy and the glorious Rajah, to her days with Frank at Southport Zoo, to her joint purchase of Colchester Zoo in the 1980s and her part in turning it from a failure into a successful centre for education and conservation. Dominique confesses to a sense of honour at having known such a strong and intelligent person as Angela. But though she had not lived to see Colchester Zoo reach its triumphant fiftieth anniversary, she had seen enough to know that their zoo was, at long last, unfurling its wings.

Yet Angela accepted the bad days with the good. She had learned in as hard a way as any other person that life, however wonderful, will always be bounded with pain; that it is a brave soul who goes among animals and men.

Angela Tropeano (1942-2011).
(Newsquest)

For all the tribulations, her days had been lively and there were no regrets, for the work of her life had been rewarded. Though Angela did not live to see the final victory over the grim times of the past in the zoo's fiftieth anniversary celebrations, her last years there had been a time of marvellous lightness as the park's wings had begun to fill and dry, ready for use in the zoo's approaching sixth decade.

9

THE OWL AND THE PUSSYCAT

A T THE TIME of Colchester Zoo's fiftieth anniversary in 2013, its newest major animal enclosure is Bears of the Rising Sun. Prior to the planning of this enclosure, it had been some time since the zoo had kept bears. Susie, Bruno and Mandy, who had been the focus of such heartache, had each lived to fairly advanced years but, one by one, had been recommended by their vet for euthanasia as they had aged and declined in health, and all were gone by the middle of 2002.

Susie had developed painful arthritis, common in older bears, and went in 1998. After struggling for a time with spinal arthritis, cataracts, heart murmurs and considerable weight loss, Bruno had been put to sleep in 2001. By the April of 2002 the elderly Mandy, with her bad teeth, painful eye problems and such creaky joints that she had begun to have trouble moving, was judged to be better off dead than alive and was also humanely destroyed.

Frank's old bears had all been well loved by Dominique's staff and there was no rejoicing in their passing. Yet there had been a sense of release when that particular chapter, with its persistent bad feeling and anxiety, finally closed. Anthony strongly recalls that everyone at the time agreed that they would never again keep bears until such time as they could be given all they needed. It is clear that they meant what they said – though bears are enduringly popular in zoos, there was no active search undertaken for such individuals to introduce to the Colchester collection.

Some years later, the Rare Species Conservation Centre in Kent started to undergo some big changes, and a number of its animals were offered to Colchester Zoo for re-housing. Colchester accepted some bearded saki monkeys, two species of hornbill and a group of otters. Also among the animals who needed a new home was a pair of young Malayan sun bears

Malayan sun bear Jo Jo at Colchester Zoo in 2011. (S.C. Kershaw)

named Jo Jo and Srey Ya. They were both rescue animals from Cambodia who had come to Britain in 2007. Srey Ya had been taken in by a governmental anti-poaching patrol after she was found as a 300-gramme cub wandering in a village called Ya Dow, dying of pneumonia. Jo Jo, growing up as a pet in a karaoke bar in Ratanakiri province, had been confiscated by the authorities at the age of six months.

The moment Anthony saw young Jo Jo and Srey Ya he was smitten and began to worry about what might happen to them if he turned them down. His colleagues expressed strong reservations about bringing these bears to Colchester: would it dredge up bad memories from the past and reignite public anger? More importantly, would the zoo be able to provide the bears with a good life?

Dominique and Angela were also unenthusiastic about the idea, much as they had been about the gift of axolotls which Anthony had eagerly accepted from Frank back in Southport. It was a tough choice for everyone but nobody could doubt Anthony's determination. For him, it was not only a chance to give a good home to a pair of animals who had been given the worst possible start in life. It also happened to be a chance to wipe the slate clean for good; to prove that Colchester Zoo could do anything as well as any zoo.

Anthony's persistence won through and Jo Jo and Srey Ya arrived at Colchester on 9 September 2010. The zoo had not planned on having bears and the only space available was Rajang and Djambe's old enclosure, off the south-east corner of Stanway Hall, which was not really adequate. It was, however, much better for the bears than the situation in which they had found themselves as cubs. In addition, an intensive daily routine of scatter feeds and various types of enrichment was embarked upon in order to keep the bears constantly occupied.

Plans and fundraising were initiated to build a large and expensive tailor-made enclosure for Jo Jo and Srey Ya on the opposite side of Stanway Hall. After many more of the usual unforeseen and unavoidable delays, which are all but inextricable from zoo life, work began in earnest on this development in the summer of 2012. The signs are promising that the new accommodation will serve as a fine enclosure for the bears, with exceptionally good indoor facilities. Bears of the Rising Sun is also expected to be good enough to permit breeding from Jo Jo and Srey Ya, something which has sensibly been prevented with hormone contraception as long as they have remained in Rajang's old house.

The Bears of the Rising Sun enclosure under construction, summer 2012. (S.C. Kershaw)

Syrian brown bear Susie before she died in 1998. (Colchester Zoo)

It has been brave of Colchester Zoo to choose to place its new Bears of the Rising Sun enclosure so close to where the last generation of bears lived, amidst the memories which still adhere to that area of the park. Yet the high standard of care that is forthcoming to Jo Jo and Srey Ya ought ultimately to serve as a mark of respect to Susie, Mandy and Bruno, for whom Dominique wishes he could have done more and whom he says will not be forgotten.

After decades of struggling to overcome the past with all its mistakes and misunderstandings, will the zoo finally shut the door for good on all sadness and misapprehension? Absolutely not – if the story of Colchester Zoo shows anything, it is that nothing is guaranteed in a world of change. Yet whatever will be the fate of Jo Jo and Srey Ya, they each, as with all the other inhabitants at the zoo, will live as contented and as protected a life as can possibly be afforded to them at Stanway.

It is fitting that Bears of the Rising Sun should be big news at Colchester Zoo's fiftieth anniversary. It sums up the past, present and future of the park; in its bricks and timbers the worst times are resolved with the best. This enclosure perhaps represents the final reconciliation of the zoo with the people of Colchester. People coming into the zoo between 2010 and 2013 have often expressed surprise upon seeing Jo Jo and Srey Ya, for they bring back memories of the ugly years and negative front-page news stories about Bruno. Bears of the Rising Sun should put to rest the old criticisms deriving from misunderstandings about how the zoo conducts its work.

The story of Sasha the white tiger is another typical example of misperception. Even Sasha's very name has been an issue. Almost every single visitor who mentions Sasha, even today, talks of 'she' when in fact Sasha was a 'he'. (Sasha is a unisex name in countries all over Asia and Europe.) An equally persistent but far more grievous misunderstanding started late in 1999 when he killed his mate, fellow white tiger Anna.

Both cats had come from ZooParc de Beauval in France on breeding loan in January 1998. Anna was already four years old but Sasha, having been born in March 1995, was only three and still sexually immature. It was not until November 1999 that the zoo attempted to put the two together. At the beginning of a seven-day breeding schedule, he and Anna were put together in Tiger Valley (by then called White Tiger Valley) for half an hour on the morning of 26 November. There were no problems and on the following morning the two were due to be put together for a further hour. Anna was put in with Sasha just before 9 a.m. All seemed well once again, but after about ten minutes Sasha suddenly jumped on Anna and bit into her throat. The assembled crowd of zookeepers tried in whatever ways they

White tiger Sasha at Colchester Zoo in the mid-2000s. (Colchester Zoo)

could to distract Sasha with brooms and cold water, to no avail. A dart-gun was also used but Sasha's bloodstream was evidently thick with adrenaline and he was determined to make his kill.

With poor Anna dead, the zoo released a statement to the press, describing the event in precise detail. In spite of this, within a very short time Sasha became famous as the tiger who had eaten his mate; that the keepers had come down in the morning and simply found that Anna was completely gone. As a white tiger, Sasha was already a fascinating animal, being often the only individual creature to stick fast in the mind of a chance visitor to Colchester Zoo. Once the daft hearsay had spread, people looked upon him as an Al Capone or Charles Manson figure, their sense of fright mixed with awe or irresistible morbid curiosity. As it happens, Sasha's notoriety was such that Anthony credits him, ironically, with single-handedly raising thousands upon thousands of pounds for conservation projects such as 21st Century Tiger, as well as providing a good portion of the gate takings up to his death on 15 December 2010.

When Sasha passed away, the zoo faced a new struggle with the public mind. The time had long since passed at Colchester Zoo when white tigers were thought to have been conservationally important. Colchester, seeing itself as a progressive zoo, considered that there was no longer a place for white tigers in its collection. Nevertheless, whenever visitors were asked what they would like to see in replacement of Sasha, time and again the answer came back: another white tiger.

For most of 2011, the White Tiger Valley enclosure lay empty and became overgrown. In part this was a form of respect for Sasha who had lived there for so many years, but it was also because the zoo was struggling to make the difficult choice between its commitment to the desires of its public and its self-image as a conservation-based park. In the end the courageous decision was taken potentially to forgo the extra visitor numbers and charitable donations: white tigers were consigned to the past along with zoo traffic and zedonks. (Shadow, the last of Frank's zedonks, had died on 3 April 2009, sparking similar public requests for more.)

White Tiger Valley has since been converted into a lemur enclosure named Lost Madagascar. Yet though this enclosure is spectacular, being the largest of all Colchester Zoo's 'walkthrough' exhibits to date and initially housing two troops of ring-tailed lemurs and red-ruffed lemurs, many people coming into the zoo still say they would rather have seen more white tigers.

African lion Bailey at the Lion Rock enclosure, 2011. (S.C. Kershaw)

If sentimentality or innocent ignorance can sometimes be said to hamper proceedings at modern zoos, it is certainly the case that reactions can occasionally border on ridiculousness and hysteria. When the story of the 'Essex lion' first hit Britain's headlines in the silly season of 2012 (it later turned out to be a pet cat named Teddy Bear), a leading national newspaper categorically stated that the beast had escaped from Colchester Zoo. This scoop was, unfortunately, rather spoiled by the fact that Stanway Hall's three lions, Bailey, Malika and Naja, were all still present and correct in their Lion Rock enclosure.

All this was reminiscent of another stir caused earlier in the same year, when one of Colchester Zoo's owls became disorientated during a falconry display and ended up as an impromptu meal in the lion enclosure. What was remarkable was not the fact that a bird was eaten by a cat, but that in a matter of mere decades we have gone from being a nation who would routinely pay money to watch live creatures being fed to zoo animals, to one which considers a mishap with a free-flying bird to be a news item of national importance. There is, in fact, a literal element of childishness in modern Britain's relationship with its zoos.

Until the 1950s, British zoos had largely been the preserve of monarchs, scientists and interested adults. Children had also long been a target market for zoos, but it was the post-war explosion in the number of young nuclear families, possessed of newly increased spare time and cash, which saw the beginning of the mid-to-late-twentieth-century idea of the zoo as being, above all, a place for children's outings – brilliantly capitalised upon by people such as Frank.

This perception of zoos as places for children has been changing in recent times, but for the last sixty years most Britons have tended to experience zoos only as small children, not returning until thirty years afterwards, as parents themselves, to have some of their infantile fantasies somewhat spoiled.

It is notable, for instance, how much time has been found in recent decades for hand-wringing when one in a thousand zoo animals starts to act oddly (a proportion one might reasonably expect anyway), yet how little time or money has ever been offered to groups such as the RSPCA who have been trying for decades to combat the far more serious long-term pandemic of the physical and psychological abuse of Britain's domestic pets. Other nations are more enlightened when it comes to zoos. A number of Continental European countries freely and openly accept, for example, that culling and hormone contraception in zoos can be a necessary part of conservation work.

It seems counter-intuitive, for instance, to destroy individuals of an endangered species that one wishes to conserve, or to prevent them from breeding. It is just as well to remember, as the philosopher Bryan Magee has said, that common sense is a form of metaphysics which says, wrongly, that the world must work as one's personal intuition says it does. If a litter of animals turns out to be all male, for example, it may be necessary to put down one or more of them in order to make room for a female. Sometimes an animal will have to be put on contraception if its genes are over-represented in the international captive population. Politically sensitive policies, such as breed-and-cull, may become increasingly common in British zoos in the future.

Colchester Zoo's deeply ingrained habit of talking to its visitors offers all the opportunities an interested person might require to learn more about how modern zoos work, by listening to the educational presentations at feeding times or by chatting with the keepers and education staff. Many zoos have been following the lead set by places such as Colchester in this regard over the past twenty or thirty years, and Britain's relationship with its zoos is, as a result, beginning to mature. Nevertheless, it is a slow process that will have to go much further in the future.

Amur tigers Anoushka and Igor at the Tiger Taiga enclosure, 2012. (S.C. Kershaw)

We are going to need good zoos more, not less, in the coming years, and these institutions will need to grow more efficient if they are to become (as people say they want them to become) even more focused on animal welfare and conservation. Some tough choices wait for us. We may have to wave goodbye to certain species. Dolphins were once an accepted part of the British zoo landscape but have gone and do not look set for an immediate return. Elephants may be phased out in like manner. Animals such as giant pandas may also have to go. It is difficult to foresee what may happen in zoos over the next fifty years but one can imagine a future in which even lions will vanish from Britain. If ever a decision has to be made about these latter animals, the English in particular may find it exceptionally hard to make a choice, for they are a nation of Helenas, for whom lions are a part of their identity.

It may yet be that we see only African lions depart our zoos, leaving behind Asian lions who are under greater threat in the wild. But Asian lions are smaller and less striking than their African cousins. The males have slighter manes and do not have quite so much of that spectacular aspect which so many zoo-goers look for in exhibited animals. (Old Rajah had been an

Anthony Tropeano and cheetah Katavi at Colchester Zoo. Katavi was an accidental birth and suffered numerous health problems and had to be hand-reared by Anthony. She is pictured here two weeks before her death on 6 November 2009 at the age of seventeen months. The zoo's cheetah breeding enclosure now bears her name. (Chris Reeve)

Asian lion, true, but he had been unusually big and, in any case, most of his fantastic appeal had derived from the fact that one could pet him and that his mane was always finely coiffured by Helena.) The difference between African and Asian lions is not great but it could be enough to ensure that the place of Nyoka's Simba in the Guinness Book of World Records remains unchallenged, which in turn would ask quite a number of questions of the British public's willingness to temper its desire for superlatives.

Things may of course not turn out this way: we now learn that the lion may yet be following the steady pace of the rhino, the orangutan and the tiger into oblivion. A study led by North Carolina's Duke University concluded in 2012 that the wild African lion population has dropped by about two-thirds in the last fifty years, partly as a result of the damage done to up to 75 per cent of African savannah land by deforestation, new human settlements and agriculture since the 1960s. With a mere 33,000 lions now estimated to be left in the African wild, the U.S. Fish and Wildlife Service has even announced that it is considering petitioning for the official status of these creatures to be upgraded to Endangered – something which most people would have thought inconceivable just ten or twenty years ago.

Endangered or not, however, the lion may still leave the zoo. Biodiversity is of far greater importance to the health of ecosystems than the preservation of a single remarkable species. If in the future it finally comes down to an ugly choice between saving one large, costly and time-consuming species or a multitude of smaller, lower-maintenance species, the latter may win.

One strong counter-argument is that animals such as lions and elephants are immensely beautiful and striking animals, who raise a lot of money for the conservation work undertaken by places such as Colchester Zoo. Then again, we could have the best of both worlds if we could teach ourselves to love animals such as the waldrapp ibis and the pygmy hippo as strongly, and continue to visit zoos in order to see and support greater numbers of such species which are in immediate mortal danger in the wild.

It is improbable that we will ever see pygmy hippos replace lions on British coins, crests, pub signs and sporting badges, but whatever should happen in the future it is highly likely that zoos will have to become more streamlined by removing lesser-threatened species from their collections and specialising in greater numbers of less-demanding creatures. This will

Education staff member Nikki Acton-Brown and zoo volunteer Sarah Berry present the paddock feed at Kingdom of the Wild, 2012. (S.C. Kershaw)

Anthony Tropeano greets a pair of one-year-old new arrivals, reticulated giraffes Lili and Isha, September 2009. (Colchester Zoo)

not please the casual visitor who looks above all for instant wonder in a day out at the zoo. Regardless, as expensive and difficult disciplines around the new science of genetics begin to develop in the twenty-first century, it may become necessary for needier species to be given more of the time, room and resources which would otherwise be given to animals with few qualifications for being part of a zoo collection besides being impressive or cute or interesting.

The coming changes that await British zoos may be as dramatic as those we have seen in the last fifty or sixty years. With species even such as the African lion apparently now on the slope towards extinction, perhaps all bets are off. But though no one can truly say what will happen, some predictions are easier to make than others. We will likely continue to see the remaining species in good zoos given ever-larger and more elaborate enclosures. This will impose new demands on zoo-goers, making the animals harder to see and leaving some people feeling cheated and perhaps less inclined to continue backing their local zoo. Zoos may also have to become more utilitarian and less attractive to the human eye as greater proportions

Dominique Tropeano at
Colchester Zoo in the
2000s. (Colchester Zoo)

of funds are directed into conservation work, as wild habitats vanish at an
accelerating pace.

If the last fifty years have been a time of great upheaval for the British zoo
world, Dominique Tropeano foresees that the next fifty will be even more
challenging. Good zoos weathered the problems posed by activist groups
in the 1980s and 1990s mainly as a result of the support of zoo-goers. Yet
those latter people, who have guaranteed the continued existence of zoos to
date, are going to be presented with some tricky situations as the next few
decades roll by. Our animal institutions, for their part, are going to have to
become ever more inventive in their efforts to continue to stimulate interest
in endangered species.

The British zoo world is buoyant today, but we may yet see a decline in
tandem with the long-term decline of our country. Already we lag behind
many European countries. Some commentators are suggesting that we may
wake up in fifty years' time and find academics in China, India or Brazil
looking down on Britain as a 'developing nation'. Should this come to pass
it will be a test, among many other things, of Britain's supposedly special
love of animals. The next half-century may yet show that we, as a nation,

have, in truth, allowed some attractive exotic animals merely to eat the crumbs from our table while we prospered, and claimed it as a great moral act of beneficence towards our world's collapsing ecosystems.

The long economic crash which began in 2008 has seen environmentalism slip far down the political agenda as nations struggle with monetary paralysis, food and fuel shortages, civil unrest, war and the resurgence of fascist ideology in democratic states. Time alone will show whether we will honour the pledges we made to Gaia during the years of unprecedented plenty – but the signs look bad. When Sgt Farrar opened his diverting menagerie in Southport in 1953, Britain was indeed slowly moving forward into the broad, sunlit uplands which Prime Minister Churchill had promised the nation if only Hitler could be stopped. In contrast, the conservation and education centre in Colchester over which Dr Tropeano presides today, sixty years later, exists in a world that shows every sign of sinking towards the abyss of a new dark age.

10

THE LATENESS OF THE HOUR

EXTINCTION IS NATURAL and normal. Some studies suggest that between one and ten species of plant or animal goes extinct every year at the hands of nature. This has long been a necessary part of life on Earth. As a direct result of man's activity, however, the rate of animal and plant extinction is now approaching perhaps as many as 100,000 species every year.

Mass extinctions have happened before on Earth. In fact, they happen regularly: about once every twenty-six million years. There have been twenty or so of these events in our planet's history. Many have been only moderately lethal. Five have been exceptionally deadly.

Perhaps the most extreme extinction event of all, nicknamed the Great Dying, happened about 250 million years ago and extinguished nearly all of the Earth's species. The most famous, however, is of course the so-called 'K-Pg catastrophe', which seems to have been triggered when an asteroid came down in what is now the Gulf of Mexico and destroyed most of the world's dinosaurs along with a great deal else.

Earth is now firmly in the grip of a new mass-extinction event. This extinction, the sixth major one, has been going on for at least twelve thousand years, roughly since the end of the last ice age. Twelve thousand years sounds like a long time, but it is similar in duration to that of other extinction events and, from the perspective of evolution, is a mere blink of an eye – about 0.0004 per cent of the history of life.

This new moment of death has a name: it is called the Holocene Extinction. It is happening right now. It would, however, be wrong to think we humans are living through the Holocene Extinction – we *are* the Holocene Extinction. These last twelve-thousand years, which have seen the acceleration of the Holocene Extinction, matches the growth of advanced human civilisation that, since the last ice age, has girdled the globe. This extinction event is now approaching its climax.

What does this mean for zoos? Zoos have shown themselves capable of rescuing species from extinction and sometimes even reintroducing them to the wild. The Arabian oryx is one example of a successful rescue story. Among others, one could point also to the Przewalski's horse, the red wolf and the Californian condor: all species that have been brought back from the edge of oblivion by zoos. Yet in the time in which these few have been bred with care and painstakingly protected at great financial cost, thousands upon thousands of other species around the world have perished, never to return.

One organisation that has not given up but has instead been growing progressively more radical in its reaction to the Holocene Extinction is Colchester Zoo. Frank Farrar, in his heyday in the 1960s, did more than many of his peers to inform the general public about the challenges facing the natural world, the seriousness of which was only then coming to light. He also genuinely believed in the captive breeding of endangered species as being valuable for its own sake. Frank, sadly, was much too old-fashioned for his fervour to have great effect, educationally or ecologically.

It fell to his niece, Angela, who learned much from her uncle, and to her husband Dominique to transform Colchester Zoo into a conservation centre of real substance. Wednesday 30 March 1994, almost a year after Frank's death, saw the formal launch of a scheme called Action for the Wild (AFTW). This name had already been floating around Colchester Zoo for some time, but it had been nothing much more than a general slogan by which the park had referred to its habit of supporting external conservation projects.

From the spring of 1994 onward, Colchester Zoo, through AFTW, became more tightly focused in its fundraising for organisations around the world which strive to protect wild animals from the harm of human beings. By the end of its first year, AFTW had raised £4,000 by staging children's events and celebrity appearances. In May 1995 Johnny Morris returned to Colchester Zoo after thirty years, at the age of seventy-eight, to help AFTW raise money for tiger poaching patrols in Russia.

By the end of 1995, AFTW had donated money to, and raised awareness of, conservation groups like Tusk Force, Rainforest Action Costa Rica and Save the Rhino. By the end of the 1990s and into the new century, it had gone on to help the Cheetah Conservation Fund, the Dian Fossey

Johnny Morris with cotton-top tamarin Fidget at Colchester Zoo, 21 May 1995. (Newsquest)

Gorilla Fund, the Orangutan Foundation, the International Snow Leopard Programme, the Madagascar Fauna Group and the World Land Trust. By 2004, Colchester Zoo had, under AFTW's flag, raised more than £40,000 for big cat charities like 21st Century Tiger.

In 2004, eleven years after it was named, AFTW achieved charitable status in its own right. This was not easy. Even after all its efforts to support conservation, the proposal was scrutinised long and hard by the authorities, who were suspicious that it might be some elaborate tax evasion scheme. They were, however, eventually satisfied, and AFTW changed from an agreeable idea into Colchester Zoo's official fundraising arm.

In the years since 2004, AFTW has raised over £700,000 for animal protection ventures around the world, through simple things like selling stickers and badges during animal displays at Colchester Zoo, and through initiatives often involving local schools and businesses. The money raised is carefully portioned out, often a little at a time, in order to allow its benefi-ciaries to have some stability in their work and to plan for the long term. One of many examples is the Gyps Vulture Restoration Project in Pakistan, which has received £1,000 annually from AFTW since 2009.

In more recent years, AFTW has worked with rescue and rehabilita-tion groups like the Borneo Orangutan Survival Foundation and also the Elephant Orphanage Project in Zambia, a country which had previously seen almost all its elephants destroyed. AFTW has also supported other groups such as CERCOPAN, which works to save primates in Nigeria, a country which has lost most of its rich forests in the last forty years.

AFTW has donated money to human charities, too. After the savage Cyclone Indlala hit Madagascar in 2007, AFTW joined the international aid programme by sending £3,500 to people left without shelter, food and clean water. AFTW has also combined its force into other, wider fundraising drives. In 2004-5, for example, it contributed £20,000 to the total amount raised by EAZA's international charity project 'Shellshock', in aid of turtle and tortoise conservation projects. In 2008, broadcaster Chris Packham became a patron of AFTW in recognition and support of the considerable work it has undertaken, and continues to undertake, to help independent researchers and conservationists pursue their work in the wild.

However, Dominique and Angela from the very start wanted a conserva-tion project that AFTW could call its own. Supporting education, research and captive breeding within the walls of Colchester Zoo and donating money to external groups was all very well, but they wanted to provide their own direct benefit to the outside world. As early as 1990, some years before AFTW was dreamed up, Dominique and Angela declared their intent to buy a piece of land in Africa, Asia or the Americas in order to protect plants and animals. The preferred site was in the Central American country of Belize, where perhaps as many as 20,000 acres of irreplaceable ancient forest (about the size of thirty Glastonbury Festivals) was, and is, being destroyed every year. These Belize plans were forgotten as soon as Tarmac offered Colchester Zoo the land into which it expanded during the 1990s. It was only after the 2001 foot and mouth crisis had subsided and the final sections of the Kingdom of the Wild building had been fully completed that the idea resurfaced of a grand exterior project for AFTW to embark upon.

Late in 2003, Colchester Zoo chanced to be in talks over a pair of young white rhinos, Emily and Cynthia, who would eventually come to Britain to

Chris Packham and keeper Clive Barwick open a new enclosure for cheetahs McEwan and Sean in 1995. (Colchester Zoo)

breed with Colchester's male. During the discussions, Anthony and others went out to meet Emily and Cynthia on a South African game reserve. In conversation with the gamekeepers there, Anthony and the others learned that a group of three large cattle farms nearby in KwaZulu-Natal were coming up for sale shortly. Anthony returned to Natal a couple of years later to inspect these properties, having wondered whether the purchase might be a good substitute for the reserve in Belize which had never materialised.

Anthony and his parents made the decision to buy these farms and turn them into a semi-wild game reserve, and, as planning went ahead, more and more ideas appeared. Might they build lodges on the reserve and let them out to tourists? Could they build a set of luxury residences on the site and sell them as second homes to wealthy business people? The family knew that the park would have to make money somehow in order to support itself. They were being pushed quite hard by their associates in South Africa to turn it into a hotel site or a hunting ground. Eventually, the family decided that the commercial side of the project was taking over everything and that the principle behind AFTW was not being given enough consideration.

Blesbok at UmPhafa Private Nature Reserve, South Africa, 2011. (Amy Sutcliffe)

The overtly commercial plans were scrubbed and the Tropeanos resolved instead to experiment with a different model. People might pay to come to work on the reserve, whether they were affluent individuals interested in ecology or students being funded by their colleges to get some hands-on training. With this plan in mind, work began on what has since come to be known as 'UmPhafa Private Nature Reserve', or simply 'UmPhafa' (a word deriving from the Zulu name for the buffalo thorn tree which grows in the area).

At over 4,000 hectares, the reserve was about 150 times the size of Colchester Zoo today. Accordingly, there were many considerations to be taken into account and great obstacles to overcome. The parks authority in South Africa enforces strict rules about what species may be kept within certain perimeters. The legal hurdles concerning the purchase were formidable, especially at a distance of 6,000 miles from Colchester. The land itself was also a mess after years of cattle farming. It had been partially deforested and over-grazed: as a result, the soil was badly eroded in many areas. There was, furthermore, a fair amount of junk left behind which had to be cleared: there were old fences and masses of rusting barbed wire everywhere.

Further matters needed attention. One cannot simply buy a piece of land and plonk a load of wild animals down in it. Detailed vegetation studies must be completed in order to work out which kinds of animals may be stocked immediately and which kinds of animals may thereafter be supported once the biology of the reserve has begun to alter as a result.

Nature, however, was already making decisions on the Tropeanos' behalf. Before the first loop of anti-poaching electric fencing had been completed around the first part of the reserve in the spring of 2006, the rangers were already seeing wild impala, greater kudu, warthog and duiker, which had all been attracted to the area in the absence of man and his domestic animals once farming had ceased. There had even been a caracal spotted. Life continued to show its contempt for organised procedure: if there was any great ceremony planned for the first official release of animals onto the reserve, it was not to be: the first formal release of an animal into UmPhafa was a single serval, who had been caught by a local farmer in about March 2006 and who needed somewhere to go.

In the summer of 2006 (winter in South Africa), Dominique and Angela went to UmPhafa to oversee what had been intended as the first release. For the first time in a century and a half the land again saw giraffe on it, when ten individuals who had been roaming agricultural land elsewhere, and were thus under threat of being killed by farmers, were let onto UmPhafa. The year 2006 also saw the release of red hartebeest, blesbok and zebra. Other species, such as common reedbuck and rock python, were also set free.

Ten waterbuck and fourteen more zebra were released in 2007, and, around the time of the reserve's first anniversary, wild red-billed oxpeckers were seen flying into the reserve, having been absent from the area since the 1950s. The following years saw many more releases and a great deal of successful wild breeding going on within the reserve. A census in 2011 estimated that, among other species, UmPhafa had become home to two eland, five white rhino, seventeen giraffe, twenty blue wildebeest, twenty common reedbuck, twenty mountain reedbuck, thirty grey duiker, thirty waterbuck, forty nyala, forty red hartebeest, seventy warthog, ninety blesbok, 140 zebra, 150 kudu and 175 impala.

Suspicions in that same year that a wild leopard was also at large on UmPhafa were joyously confirmed when his photograph was taken by a camera trap set up by staff. Animals continue to be incorporated into the UmPhafa population, including, recently, a further twenty-two blue wildebeest. Anthony has said he would one day, if the reserve grows large enough, like to see the release of cheetah and possibly even black rhino if such creatures are then still in existence.

Game guards Deon Kubeka (left) and Vukani Mkhwanazi (right) with head game guard Michael Mabaso (centre) at UmPhafa Private Nature Reserve, South Africa, 2012. (Liam Westall)

Zebra at UmPhafa Private Nature Reserve, South Africa, 2011. (Amy Sutcliffe)

Dominique and Angela Tropeano with children from Colenso, near UmPhafa Private Nature Reserve in South Africa, in around 2008. (Colchester Zoo)

Sunday 2 May 2010 saw another species released onto UmPhafa for the first time, when the reserve's first trio of volunteers reported for work. In the three years since then, the park has welcomed over forty volunteers and has many more booked for the future.

UmPhafa is an extraordinary project for a British zoo to have undertaken, to say nothing of a private zoo. It is hoped that as it develops it will become a good training ground for zoologists, being a controlled halfway-house between the artificial zoo environment which imposes certain limitations on research and the truly wild environment which can be difficult and dangerous for young or inexperienced conservationists.

The reserve cannot yet support itself and has absorbed huge quantities of money from the takings at Colchester Zoo back in Essex, in order to become established. UmPhafa may eventually become self-sufficient as the number of volunteers rises, but for now remains dependent on the willingness of people to support projects such as these by continuing to visit the creatures of Stanway Hall.

EPILOGUE

I T IS A sunny spring day at Stanway Hall. Dr Tropeano sits across the table from me against a window, which shows the renovated All Saints' Church tower in the distance. His telephone rings without cease. He says, with a wry smile, that he still believes the worst decision he ever made was to buy Colchester Zoo.

He has just returned from UmPhafa. It was his first visit for four years; Anthony has lately assumed control of the reserve, along with certain members of Colchester Zoo's current generation of staff, such as Rebecca Moore and Liam Westall.

Tropeano is quick to point out that he had travelled to South Africa on business: the main purpose of the trip had been to meet a lawyer who is assisting with the work at UmPhafa. He talks in a matter-of-fact way about employment regulations and animal welfare rules. He also mentions management practices and financial issues. Yet, beyond all the clutter of daily business, it is evident that it was also an emotional journey. He talks of his sorrow that Angela had not been at his side. He also speaks of his renewed fears for the fate of the natural world at large.

In a way that could never have been imagined in 1963, Colchester Zoo has, with the foundation of UmPhafa, effectively become the 'Whipsnade-type zoo' of which Frank Farrar had spoken through the receding frosts during that first spring at Stanway Hall. Tropeano is not, however, one for looking too deeply into the past, nor has he become complacent – he is concerned with new prospects, new ideas and new paths.

The debt to Moto and Bruno has been paid at Colchester Zoo, perhaps this much is true. Tropeano now hopes, as UmPhafa expands, to repay the debt owing to all the animals which he has kept in captivity over the years in order ultimately to protect them from the depredations of man.

UmPhafa is small in contrast to established African reserves like Kenya's famous Amboseli, but it is still young and is growing fast. UmPhafa now employs nineteen people and is currently on the verge of adding another 1,200 hectares to its area. Like old Frank Farrar at his desk at Knights National in the early 1950s, dreaming of what might be possible with his zoo, Dominique Tropeano seated at his table in Stanway Hall in 2012 is imagining what might one day be possible with his reserve.

He admits he could almost have a tear in his eye when he thinks of what UmPhafa means for the future. He foresees rising numbers of animals and workers on the reserve. He talks of the nearby school, which he has equipped with new computers and a kitchen. He talks of the children there who sing and dance. He talks of sun, long grass and high trees, of giraffe, antelope and leopard.

He ponders cautiously whether UmPhafa might one day grow large enough even for elephants to be released there. What might be possible in the future cannot be known. Dr Tropeano is talking of beauty and freedom when his telephone rings again. As he reaches to answer it he speaks, unblinking, of the edge of the endless and infernal struggle from where he has seen into paradise.

FURTHER READING

I T WOULD NOT have been appropriate in a book such as this to have burdened the text with a mass of footnotes and reference material. Instead, here follows a list of the books which formed the background of my research and which helped thereby to frame this history of Colchester Zoo, followed by a list of specific references to additional material.

Adamson, Joy, *Born Free* (Fontana Books, 1962)

Alldis, James, *Animals as Friends: A Headkeeper Remembers London Zoo* (David & Charles, 1973)

Badham, Molly, *Chimps with Everything: The Story of Twycross Zoo* (W.H. Allen, 1979)

Badham, Molly, Nathalie Evans & Maureen Lawless, *Molly's Zoo: Monkey Mischief at Twycross* (Pocket Books, 2002)

Baratay, Eric, & Elisabeth Hardouin-Fugier, *Zoo: A History of Zoological Gardens in the West* (Reaktion Books, 2002)

Barrington Johnson, J., *The Zoo: The Story of London Zoo*, (Robert Hale, 2005)

Benham, Harvey, *Two Cheers for the Town Hall* (Hutchinson & Co., 1964)

Blunt, Wilfrid, *The Ark in the Park: The Zoo in the Nineteenth Century* (Book Club Associates, 1976)

Boulter, Michael, *Extinction: Evolution and the End of Man* (Fourth Estate, 2002)

Cherfas, Jeremy, *Zoo 2000: A Look Beyond the Bars* (BBC, 1984)

Cooper, Janet, (ed), *A History of the County of Essex: Volume 10 – Lexden Hundred* (Victoria County History, 2001)

Denney, Patrick, *Colchester: History and Guide* (Tempus, 2004)

Diamond, Jared, *Collapse: How Societies Choose to Fail or Survive* (Penguin, 2006)

Döring, Martin and Brigitte Nerlich (eds), *The Social and Cultural Impact of Foot-and-Mouth Disease in the UK in 2001* (Manchester University Press, 2009)

Edwards, Christina, *The Parish of Stanway: People and Places c1700-c1840* (Belhus Books, 2001)

__, *Stanway c1900-c1920:A Community and its Fallen Soldiers* (Belhus Books, 2010)

Foster, Harry, *Southport:A History* (Phillimore & Co., 2008)

Graham-Jones, Oliver, *Zoo Tails* (Transworld, 2001)

Hahn, Daniel, *The Tower Menagerie* (Pocket Books, 2004)

Hediger, Heini, *Wild Animals in Captivity* (Dover, 1964)

Jacob, Naomi, *Me – Again* (Hutchinson, 1937)

Keeling, Jeremy, *Jeremy and Amy:The Extraordinary True Story of One Man and his Orangutan* (Short Books, 2010)

Knowles, John, *My Marvellous Life* (Book Guild Publishing, 2010)

Leakey, Richard, & Roger Lewin, *The Sixth Extinction: Biodiversity and its Survival* (Phoenix, 1999)

Lloyd, John, *Wonders Never Cease: Edinburgh Zoo into the 21st Century* (ABR Company, 2006)

Lovelock, James, *Homage to Gaia* (Oxford University Press, 2000)

__, *The Revenge of Gaia* (Penguin, 2007)

__, *The Vanishing Face of Gaia:A Final Warning* (Allen Lane, 2009)

Madden, Janice, *Reared in Chester Zoo:The Story of June Mottershead* (Ark Books, 2008)

Masters, Brian, *The Passion of John Aspinall* (Coronet Books, 1989)

McKenna,Virginia,Will Travers & Jonathan Wray (eds), *Beyond the Bars – The Zoo Dilemma* (Thorsons, 1987)

Morris, Desmond, *The Naked Ape* (Corgi, 1969)

Mullan, Bob & Garry Marvin, *Zoo Culture* (University of Illinois Press, 1999)

Rees, Martin, *Our Final Century* (Arrow Books, 2004)

Rowell, Andrew, *Don't Worry It's Safe to Eat – The True Story of GM Food, BSE & Foot and Mouth* (Earthscan, 2003)

Smith, Anthony, *Animals on View* (Book Club Associates, 1977)

Tofts, Russell, 'Colchester Zoo: Bucking a Trend' in *Zoo!*, Issue Number 18; Winter 2001

Tudge, Colin, *Last Animals at the Zoo: How Mass Extinction Can Be Stopped* (Oxford University Press, 1992)

Walker, Ian W., *Harold: The Last Anglo-Saxon King* (The History Press, 2010)

Warin, Robert & Anne, *Portrait of a Zoo: Bristol Zoological Gardens 1835-1985* (Redcliffe, 1985)

REFERENCES

Part One

Chapter One: The Kings and Queens of Birkdale
'Helena was no more in the habit of remembering to warn people about Rajah … a young orangutan called Porky who came and put his arm round his shoulders.' (*Southport Visiter*, 10 September 2004)

Chapter Two: Days at the Beach
'When this film came to town, Ken Lloyd, the manager of Southport's Gaumont cinema theatre … to lock himself in the ladies' powder room.' (*The Star*, 9 November 1989)

Chapter Five: From Caroline to Callas
'Frank's grandiose ambition for his park and its desperate need for large amounts of money … the triumphant revival production to reprise their roles.' (*Daily Mail*, 3/29 June 1965; *Daily Telegraph*, 3 June 1965; *Evening Standard*, 21/26 June 1965; *The Illustrated London News*, 12 June 1965; *The Sunday Times*, 20/27 June 1965; *Tatler*, 23 June 1965; *The Times*, 3/29 June 1965)

Chapter Eight: Breeze Blocks and Chicken Wire
'It seems that Frank did not learn his lesson, for a black leopard was stolen … reassuring a disdainful lion that he would be safe from now on.' (*Colchester Express*, 16 January, 6/28 March and 16 April 1975)

Chapter Nine: The Zoo of the Past
'… such as "POWER CUT AT FETE:TEAS AT STANDSTILL". (*Essex County Standard*, 23 August 1963)

Part Two

Chapter One: The To-and-Fro Conflicting Wind and Rain
' … with the worst local harvest since 1900. (As the *Essex County Standard* weatherman, Terry Mayes, later put it: "All in all it was a summer most people would like to forget.")' (*Essex County Standard*, 27 September 1985, 3 January 1986)

'… a young elephant called Diksie had even died at London Zoo in 1967 after her forelegs were crushed when she fell into her moat.' (*Colchester Express*, 12 October 1967)

Chapter Three: Resurfacing
'Just before the Diana monkey enclosure opened … Dominique and Angela seemed to be trying to improve things.' (*Essex County Standard*, 26 February 1988)

Chapter Four: Orange Squash and Popcorn
'Sarajevo's giraffes, eagles and wolves would be among the first … Tahirovic (an unpaid volunteer, like all the keepers at Sarajevo's zoo) had died on the way to hospital.' (*Chicago Tribune News*, 5 November 1992 (http://articles. chicagotribune.com/1992-11-05/news/9204100195_1_zoo-employee-animals-bear); *Los Angeles Times*, 19 April 1998 (http://articles.latimes. com/1998/apr/19/news/mn-40785); *The New York Times*, 4 November 1992 (http://www.nytimes.com/1992/11/04/world/at-sarajevo-zoo-the- last-survivor-dies.html))

Chapter Five: Behold Now Behemoth
'Watching the video back in the Hall … at the time, he was "saving Tembo, Rosa and Opal from hell".' (Animal Defenders International web-site, 27 January 2009 (http://www.ad-international.org/media_centre/ go.php?id=1446&si=12); BBC News website, 19 January 1999 (http:// news.bbc.co.uk/1/hi/uk/258191.stm) and 2 September 2002 (http://

news.bbc.co.uk/1/hi/uk_politics/2230913.stm); *Essex County Standard*, 29 January/12 February/1 October 1999/7 January 2000)

Chapter Six: A Pale Horse
'… disease was reported at an abattoir called Cheale … contamination was confirmed the next day.' (*Essex County Standard*, 23 February 2001)

'Tony Blair's government … turning point would have to come soon, in one direction or the other.' (*Essex County Standard*, 16/23/30 March and 6 April 2001)

'Before the end of the crisis … ten million animals would burn.' (Andrew Rowell, *Don't Worry It's Safe to Eat – The True Story of GM Food, BSE & Foot and Mouth*, Earthscan, 2003, p.58)

Chapter Seven: Hauled from the Wallow
'… the institution as a whole would be ranked twentieth in the entire world by *Times Higher Education*, among universities under the age of fifty.' (*Times Higher Education*, 31 May 2012 (http://www.timeshighereducation. co.uk/ story.asp?storycode=419908))

'… Abu, was born at Vienna Zoo on 25 April 2001 after a 643-day pregnancy. He was the first elephant in Europe to be born as a result of artificial insemination and only the fourth in the world.' *Essex County Standard*, 4 May 2001)

'… the first successful elephant AI treatment in Britain and the very first in the world … Anthony declared it to be the pinnacle of the zoo's achievements to date.' (*Essex County Standard*, 13 December 2002)

Chapter Nine: The Owl and the Pussycat
'… U.S. Fish and Wildlife Service has even announced that it is considering petitioning for the official status of these creatures to be upgraded … inconceivable just ten or twenty years ago.' ('Africa's Savannahs – and Their Lions – Declining at Alarming Rates': article on Duke University's website, 4 December 2012 (http://www.nicholas.duke.edu/news/ africas-savannahs-and-their-lions-declining-at-alarming rates?utm_ source=click&utm_medium=web&utm_campaign=hpbanners);

U.S. Fish and Wildlife Service website, November 27 2012 (http://us.vocuspr.com/Newsroom/Query.aspx?SiteName=FWS&Entity=PRAsset&SF_PRAsset_PRAssetID_EQ=131415&XSL=PressRelease&Cache=True); *The Guardian*, 5 December 2012)

Chapter Ten: The Lateness of the Hour
'Extinction is natural and normal … now approaching its climax.' (Michael Boulter, *Extinction: Evolution and the End of Man*, Fourth Estate, 2002, pp.185-193; Richard Leakey & Roger Lewin, *The Sixth Extinction: Biodiversity and its Survival*, Phoenix, 1999, p.6; James Lovelock, *The Revenge of Gaia*, Penguin, 2007, p.156; Colin Tudge, *Last Animals at the Zoo: How Mass Extinction Can Be Stopped*, Oxford University Press, 1992, pp.30-40)

INDEX